Second Edition WORLD OF

STUDY GUIDE

BUSINESS

Lawrence J. Gitman
and Carl McDaniel

Prepared by
Jerry Kinskey and Scott King
Sinclair Community College
Dayton, Ohio

SOUTH-WESTERN College Publishing

An International Thomson Publishing Company

Acquisitions Editor: Randy Haubner
Sponsoring Editor: Alice Denny
Developmental Editor: Ann Torbert
Production Editor: Eric Carlson
Production House: Tom Howard

GB60BD

ISBN: 0-538-83626-1

1 2 3 4 5 6 7 PN 0 9 8 7 6 5 4

Printed in the United States of America

International Thomson Publishing

South-Western College Publishing is an ITP Company. The ITP trademark is used under license.

CONTENTS

INTRODUCTION

The chapters in this Study Guide follow the order and content of *The World of Business*, Second Edition, by Lawrence Gitman and Carl McDaniel. Each chapter provides an overview of the structure and relevance of the chapter in the text. Each starts with a topical outline of first- and second-level headings, with page numbers for the first-level headings that refer back to the textbook. The outline is followed by the chapter's learning goals, which are identical to the goals listed in the text. These serve as a reminder of the chapter's essential purpose.

The outline and goals are followed by a section titled "TESTING YOUR KNOWLEDGE," which consists of:

* True/false questions keyed to the learning goals of the chapter.

* Multiple-choice questions covering important concepts and terms from the chapter as a whole.

* Matching questions (in two or more sets) to associate key terms with definitions.

* A chapter review in the form of essay-type (open-ended) questions. These questions address key points from each major chapter subsection. In general, they can be a useful test of your knowledge because they ask you to consider the chapter material and express your understanding of it in your own words.

The last major section in each chapter is "Experiencing Business." It consists of two different activities or exercises. Many incorporate basic concepts of the chapter with open-ended questions to encourage thought. Others provide opportunity to expand your skills and knowledge of business. Many include specific tasks that call on you to go beyond the basic chapter material. Many associate material from other chapters to help tie together your learning experience.

USE OF THE STUDY GUIDE

The Study Guide can be a helpful adjunct to the textbook. It offers opportunities to review the text material and to consolidate your learning. The best way to use the Study Guide will depend on you and your study habits, as well as on whether your instructor makes assignments from the Study Guide. In general, after you have read and studied each chapter, you may want to test your knowledge of it by answering the various sets of questions. If you find you need further work on a particular topic, go back to the text and review that topic. Don't be content just to find the answer to one or two questions you're not sure of—your goal should be mastery of general concepts as well as of particular pieces of information.

COMMENT ON THE EXPERIENCING BUSINESS EXERCISES:

Application:

Students and instructors will find considerable variety in the Experiencing Business exercises provided with each chapter—variety in format, activity involved, level of difficulty, and potential learning outcome.

Many of the exercises are fairly straightforward and self-contained in the sense they can be worked with the source material of the text. Many go beyond a basic introduction-to-business course; the intent is to provide opportunity for a broader learning experience and to generate interest in areas for future study of business.

Some examples of the possible applications:

Exercises that involve library or outside research:

2-1	The U.S. Economy	20-1	Disappearing Local Banks
4-2	Joint Ventures	21-1	Managing Finances
10-1	Productivity and Quality	23-1	Court Systems and Jurisdiction
17-1	Differential Advantage	23-2	Administrative Law

Exercises for an out-of-class project such as an interview:

3-2	Managing a Diverse Workforce	18-1, 18-2	System Applications
7-2, 7-2	Starting Your Business	24-2	Health Insurance
13-1	Union Values		

Exercises that could be the basis for a group discussion/debate:

3-1	Cultural Misunderstandings	5-2	Business Purpose and Social Responsibility
4-1	Exports	10-2	What Is Quality?
5-1	Social Responsibility		

FORMAT

Some of the exercises are very specific and include solutions. Examples include crossword puzzles (6-2, 14-1, 17-2); an organizational chart (9-1); a matching exercise (11-2); and accounting problems (19-1, 19-2).

Some of the exercises go beyond the scope of an introductory course. The intent is to provide a "bridge" to other courses. In these exercises, the answers will be readily available from material such as an introductory text in management, marketing, economics, or international business.

Open-ended questions are used extensively throughout the exercises. These exercises, in whole or in part, are a rich source for classroom discussion material. Examples of such open-ended questions are: 3-1 Cultural Misunderstandings; 8-1 Leadership Style; 9-2 Delegation; 10-2 What is Quality; 16-1 and 16-2 Distribution Strategy.

Good luck in the course. We hope you find it an enjoyable and useful introduction to the world of business.

ACKNOWLEDGMENTS

We would like to express our appreciation to the many people who have contributed to this project.

To my wife, Janet, for her invaluable advice and assistance. (JMK)

To Virgil and Chester, for helping to sort it all out. (GSK)

Jerome Kinskey

Sinclair Community College

G. Scott King

Sinclair Community College

PART ONE

THE ECONOMICS OF BUSINESS

Part One examines the inputs and outputs of the business system, basic economic systems (capitalism, socialism, and communism), and the U.S. business economy.

BUSINESS SYSTEMS

OUTLINE

LEARNING GOALS

After studying this chapter, you should be able to:

1. Gain an appreciation for the study of business.

2. Understand the term *business*.

3. Recognize how the four basic inputs and the two basic outputs of the business system are related.

4. Discuss the differences among basic economic systems.

5. Understand how gross domestic product, productivity, and standard of living measure the performance of economic systems.

6. Trace the historical development of U.S. business.

TESTING YOUR KNOWLEDGE

TRUE-FALSE

Directions: *Test your knowledge of each learning goal by answering the true-false questions following each goal.*

1.   Gain an appreciation for the study of business.

             a.   The study of business is a lifelong opportunity.

             b.   A social worker, government employee, or a manager does not need to understand fundamental business practices.

             c.   Most jobs are found in private business.

2.   Understand the term *business.*

             a.   The term *business* means different things to different people.

             b.   Business is not a part of the economic system of Russia.

             c.   Regardless of a nation's political structure, goods and services must be produced and distributed.

3.   Recognize how the four basic inputs and the two basic outputs of the business system are related.

             a.   Money is one of the basic inputs.

             b.   Capital includes money.

             c.   Firms use the basic inputs to produce the basic outputs desired by customers.

             d.   Services are tangible items provided by organizations for their customers.

             e.   Profit is one measure of the success of the firm.

             f.   The circular flow of inputs, outputs, and money constitutes the lifeblood of the business system.

4.   Discuss the differences among basic economic systems.

             a.   Profit is the major incentive in the capitalistic system.

             b.   Competition is good for both business and consumers.

             c.   Farming is a good example of monopolistic competition.

             d.   Burger King and McDonald's are oligopolistic industries.

             e.   Socialism operates differently from country to country.

             f.   Karl Marx is known as the "Father of Capitalism."

             g.   A mixed economy is typically a mixture of capitalism and socialism.

             h.   The United States is considered a mixed economy.

5.   Understand how gross domestic product, productivity, and standard of living measure performance of economic systems.

             a.   Gross domestic product is not a very good indicator of economic health.

             b.   In recent years productivity in the U.S. has not increased.

             c.   The standard of living in Eastern European countries is twice that of the U.S.

6. Trace the historical development of U.S. business.

_____ a. In colonial times, businesses were mostly family enterprises.

_____ b. The Industrial Revolution started in the U.S. in the mid-1800s.

_____ c. Labor specialization became the hallmark of the mass production era.

_____ d. Very few laws affecting businesses were enacted through the early 1970s.

_____ e. The next wave of mergers by U.S. firms will be overseas.

_____ f. The 1990s have seen a great decline in entrepreneurship.

MULTIPLE-CHOICE

Directions: *Put the letter of the response that best completes each of the following statements in the blank at the left.*

_____ 1. In order to understand one's rights as a consumer, it helps to first understand

    a. the economy.
    b. law.
    c. profit.
    d. business.

_____ 2. By understanding the impact of business on society, we can

    a. make intelligent decisions about the roles of business and find solutions to society's problems.
    b. make government see the importance of more regulations.
    c. cure all the social ills of the economy.
    d. decide how all businesses should be operated.

_____ 3. Adam Smith

    a. was known as the Father of Capitalism.
    b. wrote *Wealth of Nations.*
    c. referred to competition as the "invisible hand."
    d. all are correct

_____ 4. Business is

    a. an economic process.
    b. a transformation process (inputs to outputs).
    c. a creator of goods and services.
    d. a social process.

_____ 5. A factor of production required for economic activity is

    a. the electronic computer.
    b. capital.
    c. transportation.
    d. iron ore.

_____ 6. Productive resources used in business are called

    a. basic inputs.
    b. basic outputs.
    c. factors of production.
    d. capital.

_____ 7. Profit is

    a. a motivator of entrepreneurship.
    b. a measure of the success of a firm.
    c. the amount of money remaining from revenues after all costs and taxes are deducted.
    d. all of the above

_____ 8. When individuals rather than government determine what goods and services to produce and who gets the rewards from their production, the system is called

    a. an opportunity system.
    b. a socialistic system.
    c. a private enterprise system.
    d. a mixed economic system.

_____ 9. The factory system utilized the idea of

    a. work specialization.
    b. family enterprise.
    c. agribusiness.
    d. concentrated financial resources.

_____ 10. The Industrial Revolution produced the concept of

    a. mass production.
    b. tougher standards and regulation.
    c. mergers.
    d. specialization of labor.

_____ 11. Henry Ford introduced the concept of

    a. assembly lines.
    b. interchangeable parts.
    c. mass production.
    d. mass marketing.

_____ 12. The collapse of the economy in 1929 and the inability to recover led to

    a. a social welfare economy.
    b. stagflation.
    c. monopolies.
    d. government regulation of business.

_____ 13. The merger of the AFL and CIO took place in the year

    a. 1970.
    b. 1955.
    c. 1933.
    d. 1929.

_____ 14. Today, service industries are the fastest-growing segment of the U.S. economy because of

   a. consumer preferences.
   b. government regulations.
   c. labor unions.
   d. worker protection.

_____ 15. Basic inputs do *not* include:

   a. profit.
   b. wages.
   c. goods and services.
   d. inputs.
   e. interest.

_____ 16. The major economic systems are

   a. capitalism.
   b. socialism.
   c. communism.
   d. all of the above

_____ 17. Standard Oil was built by

   a. Andrew Carnegie.
   b. Henry Ford.
   c. J.P. Morgan.
   d. John D. Rockefeller.

_____ 18. The period of U.S. business history known for the refinement of mass production, great increases in productivity, and an emphasis on work specialization was

   a. 1790–1865.
   b. 1865–1900.
   c. 1900–1930.
   d. 1930–present.

_____ 19. Which of the following is *not* a reason for studying business?

   a. to make an intelligent decision about entering business
   b. to select a career
   c. to make intelligent consumer decisions
   d. to learn how to become wealthy without risk

_____ 20. From 1930 to present,

   a. consumer buying habits have changed.
   b. government regulation of business has increased.
   c. labor unions have grown and declined.
   d. all of the above

MATCHING QUESTIONS: SECTION A

a.	oligopoly	g.	entrepreneurs
b.	goods	h.	monopolistic competition
c.	barriers to entry	i.	capitalism
d.	mixed economies	j.	communism
e.	business	k.	capital
f.	socialism	l.	automation

MATCHING DEFINITIONS.   *Directions: Match the terms above with the definitions below.*

_____   1.   The replacement of workers with machines.

_____   2.   The economic process that involves the assembly and use of productive resources to create goods and services.

_____   3.   Market in which a few firms produce most of the output and in which large capital requirements limit the number of firms.

_____   4.   Risk takers who seek to profit by combining the factors of production.

_____   5.   Tangible items manufactured by businesses.

_____   6.   Tools, machinery, equipment, and buildings.

_____   7.   Factors that prevent new firms from competing equally with the existing firm in a monopoly.

_____   8.   Economies that use more than one economic system.

_____   9.   Economic system under which the basic industries are owned and operated by the government or by the private sector under strong government control.

_____   10.   Economic system under which the factors of production are owned collectively and the people receive economic benefits according to their needs and contribute according to their abilities.

_____   11.   Market in which large number of firms offer products that are similar.

_____   12.   Economic system based on competition and private ownership.

MATCHING QUESTIONS: SECTION B

a.	profit	g.	services
b.	perfect competition	h.	circular flow
c.	factors of production	i.	pure monopoly
d.	natural resources	j.	standard of living
e.	gross domestic product (GDP)	k.	Industrial Revolution
f.	productivity	l.	knowledge workers
		m.	labor

MATCHING DEFINITIONS.   *Directions: Match the terms above with the definitions below.*

_____   1.   Intangible items provided by organizations for their customers.

_____   2.   The reward to businesses for providing what consumers are willing to pay.

_____ 3. The flow of inputs and outputs and of money.

_____ 4. A form of capitalism in which there are a large number of small firms selling similar products, in which buyers and sellers are informed about the market, and which is easy to enter or exit.

_____ 5. Market in which a single firm accounts for all of an industry's sales.

_____ 6. Natural resources, labor, capital, and entrepreneurship.

_____ 7. Commodities that are useful as productive inputs in their natural state.

_____ 8. The economic contributions of people working with their minds and muscle.

_____ 9. The monetary value of all final goods and services produced within a nation annually.

_____ 10. The level of material well-being of a country.

_____ 11. The shift from cottage industries to the factory system.

_____ 12. The output of goods and services per unit of labor.

_____ 13. Highly educated workers who use new technologies.

CHAPTER REVIEW

1. Why should you study business?

2. a. List the four factors of production.

   (1)

   (2)

   (3)

   (4)

    b.   Identify the basic outputs of business.

       (1)

       (2)

    c.   _____ is the reward to business for providing what consumers are willing to buy.

    d.   Explain the circular flow of inputs, outputs, and money.

3.   a.   List and contrast the different economic systems.

    b.   How can we measure the performance of an economic system?

4.   Trace the development of U.S. business.

EXPERIENCING BUSINESS 1-1

PUBLIC GOODS AND SERVICES

Public goods (and services) have certain characteristics which distinguish them from private goods (and services):

a. Private goods are divisible into small enough units that individual buyers can afford them.

b. Private goods involve what the economists call the "exclusion" principle, the idea that individuals willing and able to pay the market price get the good, others do not.

A market system such as capitalism allocates "private" goods. Market systems take different approaches ranging from perfect competition to pure monopoly, but that is not the issue here. Even before your study of business, you were aware that some goods (and services) are not produced by a market system.

For example, the state and federal governments could "stay out" of the business of regulating food safety-processing, handling, preparation, etc.—but it was impossible for individuals to accomplish inspection and oversight on their own. As examples of abuses and neglect were exposed, individuals decided to have the governments take over. As the state or federal government took on the responsibility, it became a public good/service.

As another example, a city government could "stay out" of the business of trash collection and disposal—leaving it to one or more private businesses, but that caused conflicts in large cities and failed to ensure some basic level of service, sanitation, etc. Here, the motive was to correct underallocation of resources by the private sector, but the end result was the same: it became a public good/service. *Note:* Although the city may choose to contract out the work to a business, actually granting a monopoly right to one firm to provide the service, the governmental unit is still responsible for the service.

To do this exercise:

Identify whether the following should be produced through the market system or provided by government:

a. bread	g. medical care
b. street lighting	h. mail delivery
c. bridges	i. housing
d. parks	j. air traffic control
e. public safety (police)	k. libraries
f. water supply (household)	l. education (K-12)

(The solution is provided at the end of the chapter.)

EXPERIENCING BUSINESS 1-2   THE NATURE OF BUSINESS

The nature of business, an economic or value-added process that transforms basic inputs into basic outputs, is a straightforward concept. As an outside observer (such as a business student or customer), the input-to-output process may appear simple; however, the transformation is often quite complex and involves many factors not at first apparent. Understanding the range and variety of inputs and outputs can help us appreciate the real nature of business.

To do this exercise:

1. Select examples of an enterprise/organization in your local area from at least three of the following categories:

    a. A large, for-profit organization, primarily involved with "goods" (typically manufacturing or assembly)

    b. A large, for-profit organization, primarily involved with providing "services"

    c. A small, for-profit business involved primarily with "goods"

    d. A small, for-profit business involved primarily with "services"

    e. A large, not-for-profit organization (typically involved with providing a service)

    f. A small, not-for-profit organization (typically involved with providing a service)

2. Identify the types of inputs and outputs for each. You may wish to contact the organizations or someone who works for them.

Specifically:

    a. What inputs are important to the "business" that may not be obvious at first?

    b. Are their outputs simply goods or services, or some combination?

ANSWER KEY (CHAPTER 1)

TRUE-FALSE

1.	a.	T	3.	a.	F	4.	a.	T
	b.	F		b.	F		b.	T
	c.	T		c.	T		c.	F
2.	a.	T		d.	F		d.	F
	b.	F		e.	T		e.	T
	c.	T		f.	T		f.	F

g. T

h. T

5. a. F

b. F

c. F

6. a. T ~~WRONG ANSWER~~

b. F →T

c. T

d. F

e. T

f. F

MULTIPLE-CHOICE

1. d
2. a
3. d
4. d
5. b
6. c
7. d
8. c
9. a
10. a
11. a
12. d
13. b
14. a
15. c
16. d
17. d
18. c
19. d
20. d

MATCHING QUESTIONS: SECTION A

1. l
2. e
3. a
4. g
5. b
6. k
7. c
8. d
9. f
10. j
11. h
12. i

MATCHING QUESTIONS: SECTION B

1. g
2. a
3. h
4. b
5. i
6. c
7. d
8. m
9. e
10. j
11. k
12. f
13. l

CHAPTER REVIEW

1. The first reason for studying business is that it will help you appreciate career opportunities. A second reason is to understand the role of the worker. Studying business also can provide a solid foundation for success if you decide to start your own business. As citizens, we need to know what responsibility business has to society. Lastly, the study of business can increase our standard of living through intelligent consumer decisions.

2. a. (1) land

(2) labor

(3) capital

(4) entrepreneurship

    b. (1)   goods

        (2)   services

    c. profit

    d. Households provide the inputs. Businesses pay for the inputs in the form of profit, wages, rents and interest. The households use the money they receive from businesses to buy outputs in the marketplace.

3.   a. *Capitalism*—based on competition in the marketplace and private ownership of the factors of production.

        Socialism—Basic industries are owned and operated by the government or by the private sector under strong government control.

        Communism—Factors of production are owned collectively, and the people receive economic benefits according to their needs and contribute according to their abilities.

        Mixed economies—use more than one economic system.

    b. Measures include gross domestic product, productivity, and the standard of living.

4.   In colonial times, businesses were primarily family enterprises. Families began to trade or sell their surpluses, creating a market system. Eventually, the Industrial Revolution shifted production from cottage industries to the factory system. The captains of industry, who emerged in the second half of the nineteenth century, perfected the system of mass production and labor specialization. From 1930 to the present, consumer buying habits have changed, government regulations have increased, and labor unions have grown and then declined. The 1980s were characterized as the merger era. The 1990s promise a resurgence of entrepreneurship.

EXPERIENCING BUSINESS 1-1

a.	bread	market system
b.	street lighting	government
c.	bridges	government
d.	parks	government
e.	public safety (police)	government
f.	water supply (household)	government; can be market system (natural monopoly) with government agency to ensure provider sets a fair price
g.	medical care	government, if believed some cannot afford it; market system, if run for profit
h.	mail delivery	social/political choice: government, if believed all people should be served at a uniform rate; or market system (natural monopoly), with government agency to ensure provider sets a fair price
i.	housing	market system; government intervenes a lot here, but still works mostly through the market system
j.	air traffic control	government
k.	libraries	government because of "spillover" benefits to other parties
l.	education (K-12)	government because of "spillover" benefits to other parties

THE BUSINESS ECONOMY

OUTLINE

LEARNING GOALS

After studying this chapter, you should be able to:

1. Understand the importance of economics and circular flow.

2. Discuss how economic growth, gross domestic product, and business cycles are related.

3. Explain the economic goals of full employment and price stability.

4. Describe inflation, the two indexes used to measure it, and its two main causes.

5. Discuss how and why the government uses monetary and fiscal policy to achieve its macroeconomic goals.

6. Understand the basic microeconomic concepts of demand and supply and how they establish prices.

7. Describe the four key economic issues of the 1990s: national debt, globalization, service sector productivity, and dislocation of the work force.

TESTING YOUR KNOWLEDGE

TRUE-FALSE

Directions: *Test your knowledge of each learning goal by answering the true-false questions following each goal.*

1.   Understand the importance of economics and the circular flow.

_____   a.   Households provide production outputs.

_____   b.   Microeconomics is the study of the economy as a whole.

_____   c.   The resources of an individual, a firm, or a nation are limited.

2.   Discuss how economic growth, gross domestic product, and business cycles are related.

_____   a.   The most basic measure of economic growth is GDP.

_____   b.   The real GDP in the U.S. has steadily decreased.

_____   c.   A decline in real GDP that lasts for two consecutive quarters is called a recession.

_____   d.   Business cycles vary in length.

3.   Explain the economic goals of full employment and price stability.

_____   a.   Full employment doesn't actually mean 100 percent employment.

_____   b.   To determine how close we are to full employment, the government measures the rate of unemployment.

_____   c.   Structural unemployment is voluntary and unrelated to the business cycle.

_____   d.   If prices go up but income doesn't rise, a given amount of income buys less.

4.   Describe inflation, the two indexes used to measure it, and its two main causes.

_____   a.   Wage increases have historically been a major contributor to cost-push inflation.

_____   b.   Like GDP, there is little fluctuation in the CPI.

_____   c.   The PPI is an index of the prices of a "market basket" of goods and services.

5.   Discuss how and why the government uses monetary and fiscal policy to achieve its macroeconomic goals.

_____   a.   The money supply is controlled simply by putting more coins and currency into circulation.

_____   b.   The Fed can use monetary policy to contract or expand the economy.

_____   c.   Monetary policy is the way that the government guides the economy by increasing spending or cutting taxes.

_____   d.   Some economists believe that deficit spending is the route to economic growth.

_____   e.   The method used by supply-siders to allocate capital is tax policy.

6.   Understand the basic microeconomic concepts of demand and supply and how they establish prices.

_____   a.   The lower the price for a product, the higher the quantity demanded.

_____   b.   Market equilibrium is achieved through a series of quantity and price adjustments that automatically change in the marketplace.

_____   c.   Supply is affected by changes in costs of production inputs such as materials and labor.

7.   Describe the four key economic issues of the 1990s: national debt, globalization, service
     sector productivity, and dislocation of the work force.

     _____   a.   Deficit spending is one form of fiscal policy.
     _____   b.   Our improved productivity in the U.S. has come at a great cost in human terms.
     _____   c.   The shift from manufacturing to a service-based economy is a new phenomenon.
     _____   d.   About 80 percent of American workers are employed in service jobs.
     _____   e.   Growth in U.S. service sector productivity is far greater than manufacturing
                     productivity growth.
     _____   f.   Downsizing is affecting most industries, both in services and in manufacturing.

MULTIPLE-CHOICE

Directions: *Put the letter of the response that best completes each of the following statements in the*
                blank at the left.

     _____   1.   The science that is concerned with the way scarce resources are allocated to
                   satisfy human wants is known as

                   a.   forecasting.
                   b.   economics.
                   c.   business.
                   d.   profit maximization.

     _____   2.   "The higher the price, the lower the quantity demanded" is the basic concept behind
                   a.   the law of supply.
                   b.   the law of demand.
                   c.   economics.
                   d.   consumer psychology.

     _____   3.   The demand curve
                   a.   slopes upward and to the right.
                   b.   slopes downward and to the right.
                   c.   does not slope significantly for most products.
                   d.   is fixed and stable over the long run.

     _____   4.   The quantity of a good or service that is available at a given time is termed the

                   a.   quantity.
                   b.   surplus.
                   c.   supply.
                   d.   demand.

     _____   5.   According to the theory of supply and demand, the quantity of a product
                   supplied will

                   a.   be higher at higher prices.
                   b.   be lower at higher prices.
                   c.   be lower at lower prices.
                   d.   both a and c

_____ 6. The monetary value of all goods and services produced annually is known as the

    a. yearly index.
    b. national income.
    c. gross domestic product.
    d. consumer price index.

_____ 7. By U.S. government standards, full employment is considered to be _____ percent of those available to work.

    a. 100
    b. 94 to 96
    c. 90 to 93
    d. 86 to 89

_____ 8. If the federal government raises taxes to affect the economy, it is using

    a. fiscal policy.
    b. monetary policy.
    c. deficit spending.
    d. supply-side economics.

_____ 9. The macroeconomic goal of the U.S. and most other countries includes

    a. economic growth.
    b. full employment.
    c. price stability.
    d. all of the above

_____ 10. _____ may be the result of a mismatch between available jobs and the skills of available workers.

    a. Frictional unemployment
    b. Structural unemployment
    c. Seasonal unemployment
    d. Cyclical unemployment

_____ 11. Which of the following is *not* an example of frictional unemployment?

    a. a college graduate looking for a first job
    b. a new parent who has decided to stay home with baby for a year or two
    c. an unemployed aerospace engineer
    d. the unemployed spouse of a freshman Senator

_____ 12. The producer price index includes the prices paid for

    a. raw goods.
    b. partially-finished goods.
    c. finished products.
    d. all of the above

_____ 13. A surplus of goods

    a. places a downward pressure on price.
    b. places an upward pressure on price.
    c. has no effect on price but encourages production.
    d. will not affect the equilibrium in the short run.

_____ 14. Demand for a product or service is affected by

    a. the size of the market.
    b. prices of similar goods.
    c. consumer tastes and preferences.
    d. all of the above

_____ 15. The service economy now accounts for ___ out of 10 jobs in the U.S.

    a. 8
    b. 6
    c. 4
    d. 2

_____ 16. Which of the following statements concerning the U.S. is false?

    a. The U.S. is gaining in manufacturing output.
    b. The U.S. dominates all other countries in innovation.
    c. Business education has shifted in the U.S. toward finance and away from manufacturing.
    d. American manufacturers must adopt more flexible team-oriented systems.

_____ 17. _____ refers to a government program that controls the amount of money in the economy.

    a. Expansion policy
    b. Monetary policy
    c. Fiscal policy
    d. Contractionary policy

Questions 18-20 refer to the diagram below. The demand curve refers to specialty T-shirts sold monthly through a large college bookstore.

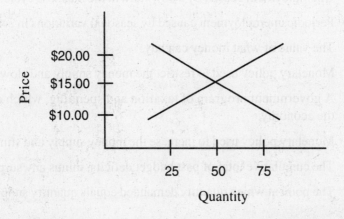

_____ 18. The line that slopes downward and to the right is known as the

    a. price/quality line.
    b. supply curve.
    c. demand curve.
    d. none of the above

_____ 19. The equilibrium, or market price, would appear to be about $_____ per T-shirt.

    a. $24.00
    b. $20.00
    c. $15.00
    d. $12.00

_____ 20. At this equilibrium price, we would expect to sell about _____ shirts a month.

    a. 5
    b. 25
    c. 50
    d. 70

Matching Questions: Section A

a.	business cycle	g.	nominal GNP
b.	microeconomics	h.	seasonal unemployment
c.	cyclical unemployment	i.	contractionary policy
d.	fiscal policy	j.	expansionary policy
e.	national debt	k.	equilibrium
f.	macroeconomics	l.	purchasing power

Matching Definitions. *Directions: Match the terms above with the definitions below.*

_____ 1. The study of the economy as a whole.

_____ 2. The changes upward or downward in a business activity.

_____ 3. A measure of GDP that uses current market prices.

_____ 4. The study of particular markets.

_____ 5. Unemployment caused by a downturn in the business cycle.

_____ 6. Periodic unemployment caused by seasonal variations in certain industries.

_____ 7. The value of what money can buy.

_____ 8. Monetary policy used to restrict the money supply and slow economic growth.

_____ 9. A government program of taxation and spending, which can be used to stimulate the economy.

_____ 10. Monetary policy used to increase the money supply and stimulate economic growth.

_____ 11. The cumulative total of past budget deficits, minus any surpluses.

_____ 12. The point at which quantity demanded equals quantity supplied.

MATCHING QUESTIONS: SECTION B

a.	supply	g.	demand
b.	producer price index (PPI)	h.	frictional unemployment
c.	recession	i.	full employment
d.	inflation	j.	unemployment rate
e.	economic growth	k.	supply curve
f.	demand curve	l.	monetary policy

MATCHING DEFINITIONS. *Directions: Match the terms above with the definitions below.*

_____ 1. The quantity of a good or service that businesses will make at various prices.

_____ 2. The quantity of a good or service people are willing to buy at various prices.

_____ 3. Graph of the relationship between quantity demanded and price.

_____ 4. An index that measures prices paid by producers and wholesalers of commodities.

_____ 5. Government programs for controlling the amount of money in circulation in a nation's economy.

_____ 6. A period of decline in GDP that lasts six months or longer.

_____ 7. Short-duration, voluntary unemployment, unrelated to the business cycle.

_____ 8. The general upward movement of prices.

_____ 9. Graph of the relationship between quantity supplied and price.

_____ 10. A situation where jobs are available for all who are willing and able to work.

_____ 11. The percentage of the total labor force that is not working but is actively looking for work.

_____ 12. An increase in a nation's output of goods and services.

CHAPTER REVIEW

1. Identify and describe the major areas of economic study and why economics is so important.

2. What are the three major macroeconomic objectives of the United States? Elaborate.

   a.

   b.

   c.

3.   Identify and describe the four categories of unemployment.

      a.

      b.

      c.

      d.

4.   How is inflation measured? What are the two major types of inflation?

5.   It has been said that the two principal tools used by the government to guide the economy to a sound balance of growth, employment, and price stability are monetary and fiscal policy. Explain how these instruments are used by government.

6.   What are some of the economic issues facing the U.S. in the 1990s?

EXPERIENCING BUSINESS 2-1

THE U.S. ECONOMY

We hear a lot about the "decline of manufacturing" and a shift to a service-based economy. However, if we define a service-based economy as one with more than half of all jobs in the service sector, the United States has been a service economy since 1950. Moreover, the idea of a "shift" can ignore the real growth in services for a variety of reasons.

What is the outlook for some of the United States' key industries?

To do this project:

This project involves some library research to look at one or more industries. There are many possible sources for this project. A suggested one is "Industry Outlook," published each January by *Business Week* magazine, which reviews 24 key industries. Use that or other sources to answer the following.

1. Select one industry from the manufacturing sector.

    What is the outlook for the industry?

    How much is the outlook affected by international aspects (exports, trade agreements, etc.)?

    How much is the outlook affected by the public policy (government regulation, etc.)?

2. Select one industry from the service sector.

    What is the outlook for the industry?

    How much is the outlook affected by international aspects (exports, trade agreements, etc.)?

    How much is the outlook affected by the public policy (government regulation, etc.)?

EXPERIENCING BUSINESS 2-2

MACRO- VERSUS MICRO-ECONOMICS

To do this exercise:

To help understand the different emphases of macroeconomics and microeconomics, relate the following items to one area of economics. Some items/topics may overlap based on an application, but select the one "best" or most general category.

	Macro	**Micro**
aggregate data	_____	_____
individual firms	_____	_____
individual consumers	_____	_____
unemployment rate	_____	_____
nterest rate	_____	_____
demand for a product	_____	_____
labor and material cost	_____	_____
gross domestic product	_____	_____
business cycles	_____	_____
recession	_____	_____
inflation	_____	_____
monetary policy	_____	_____
fiscal policy	_____	_____
supply and demand	_____	_____
equilibrium price	_____	_____

(Answers are provided at the end of the chapter.)

ANSWER KEY (CHAPTER 2)

TRUE-FALSE

1.	a.	F		c.	F	6.	a.	T
	b.	F		d.	T		b.	T
	c.	T	4.	a.	T		c.	T
2.	a.	T		b.	F	7.	a.	T
	b.	F		c.	F		b.	T
	c.	T	5.	a.	F		c.	F
	d.	T		b.	T		d.	T
3.	a.	T		c.	F		e.	F
	b.	T		d.	T		f.	T
				e.	T			

MULTIPLE-CHOICE

1.	b	11.	c
2.	b	12.	d
3.	b	13.	a
4.	c	14.	d
5.	d	15.	a
6.	c	16.	a
7.	b	17.	b
8.	a	18.	c
9.	d	19.	c
10.	b	20.	c

MATCHING QUESTIONS: SECTION A

1.	f	7.	l
2.	a	8.	i
3.	g	9.	d
4.	b	10.	j
5.	c	11.	e
6.	h	12.	k

MATCHING QUESTIONS: SECTION B

1.	a	7.	h
2.	g	8.	d
3.	f	9.	k
4.	b	10.	i
5.	l	11.	j
6.	c	12.	e

CHAPTER REVIEW

1. The study of economics is divided into two major areas. *Macroeconomics* is the study of the economy as a whole. It looks at data for large groups of persons, companies, or products. *Microeconomics* focuses on individual components of the economy, such as households and businesses.

   The study of economics is important because it affects both the personal and business aspects of our lives. Businesses have to make decisions as to what to buy or produce and how much to charge for items. You, as an individual, must decide how much and where to spend as well as how much to save and invest.

2. The U.S. has three major macroeconomic objectives:

   a. *Economic growth*, which is measured by the gross domestic product. The GDP is the total monetary value of all goods and services produced by the nation annually.

   b. *Full employment*, having jobs available for all willing and able to work.

   c. *Price stability,* maintaining overall price levels of goods and services.

3. Unemployment is usually divided into four categories:

   a. *Frictional unemployment* is usually of short duration. It includes persons temporarily unemployed while changing jobs, as well as those entering or reentering the job market.

   b. *Structural unemployment* is involuntary unemployment caused by a mismatch between available jobs and the skills of available workers in an industry or a region.

   c. *Cyclical unemployment* occurs when a downturn in the business cycle reduces the demand for labor throughout the economy.

   d. *Seasonal unemployment* occurs periodically due to seasonal variations in certain industries.

4. The rate of inflation is most commonly measured by looking at changes in the consumer price index. The CPI is an index of a market basket of goods and services purchased by typical urban consumers. *Demand-pull inflation* occurs when the demand for goods and services is greater than the available supply of goods and services. *Cost-push inflation* is triggered by increases in production costs, such as materials and wages.

5. The Federal Reserve may increase or decrease the amount of money in circulation (monetary policy). When it changes the money supply, the Fed affects interest rates which in turn affect consumer and business decisions to spend or invest. Tightening the money supply slows economic growth. Loosening the money supply stimulates economic growth.

   The government can also increase or decrease its spending as well as taxation (fiscal policy). Increasing spending or cutting taxes can stimulate the economy.

6. Some of the issues facing the U.S. in the 1990s include:

   a. The narrowing gap between economies of other industrialized countries and the U.S.

   b. The Federal budget deficit and the national debt.

   c. The ability of U.S. companies to compete globally.

   d. Improving service sector productivity and service exports.

   e. The dislocation of the workforce, including a growing number of unemployed white-collar workers.

   f. Education that prepares workers with the necessary technical skills for the future.

EXPERIENCING BUSINESS 2-2

	Macro	Micro
aggregate data	x	
individual firms		x
individual consumers		x
unemployment rate	x	
interest rate	x	
demand for a product		x
labor or material cost		x
gross domestic product	x	
business cycles	x	
recession	x	
inflation	x	
monetary policy	x	
fiscal policy	x	
supply and demand		x
equilibrium price		x

PART TWO

THE BUSINESS ENVIRONMENT

Part Two examines our multicultural society and its implications for business. It explores the ever-shrinking world of international business as well as the responsibilities and ethics of business.

OUR MULTICULTURAL SOCIETY AND ITS IMPLICATIONS FOR BUSINESS

OUTLINE

LEARNING GOALS

After studying this chapter, you should be able to:

1. Appreciate and understand the increasing cultural diversity of the United States.
2. Identify key characteristics and trends among African-Americans and opportunities to serve this market.
3. Identify key characteristics and trends among Hispanic-Americans and opportunities to serve this market.
4. Identify key characteristics and trends among Asian-Americans and opportunities to serve this market.
5. Understand how companies are managing cultural diversity in the workplace.

TESTING YOUR KNOWLEDGE

TRUE-FALSE

Directions: *Test your knowledge of each learning goal by answering the true-false questions following each goal.*

1. Appreciate and understand the increasing cultural diversity of the United States.

    _____ a. In the future, African-Americans will be the fastest growing segment of the population.

    _____ b. Most Americans believe that immigration is good for this country.

    _____ c. Ethnic groups are equally dispersed across the United States.

    _____ d. All of us are members of at least one minority group.

2. Identify key characteristics and trends among African-Americans and opportunities to serve this market.

    _____ a. African-Americans are the largest minority group in the United States.

    _____ b. It is a myth that African-Americans have very little discretionary income.

    _____ c. African-American spending patterns are somewhat different from those of other groups.

3. Identify key characteristics and trends among Hispanic-Americans and opportunities to serve this market.

    _____ a. The concept of multiculturalism is nowhere more evident than in the Hispanic culture.

    _____ b. Mexican-Americans are the oldest Hispanic subgroup.

    _____ c. The greatest concentration of Hispanic-Americans is in Miami.

    _____ d. Incomes are fairly equally distributed among Hispanic subcultures.

4. Identify key characteristics and trends among Asian-Americans and opportunities to serve this market.

    _____ a. The high level of Asian immigration to the United States has created a youthful population.

    _____ b. Asian-Americans have similar product preferences.

    _____ c. The main promotion medium for reaching Asian-Americans is television.

    _____ d. Asian-Americans are more comfortable with technology than is the general population.

5. Understand how companies are managing cultural diversity in the workplace.

    _____ a. Multiculturalism creates diversity in the workplace.

    _____ b. Successful diversity programs are good for businesses.

    _____ c. Almost all of the Fortune 500 firms have diversity managers.

MULTIPLE-CHOICE

Directions: Put the letter of the response that best completes each of the following statements in the blank at the left.

_____ 1. About _____ percent of the 200 researchers in the communications science
research wing at AT&T Bell Laboratories were born outside the U.S.

    a. 40
    b. 30
    c. 20
    d. 10

_____ 2. Which of the following cities is the most ethnically and culturally diverse?

    a. New York
    b. Chicago
    c. San Francisco
    d. Seattle

_____ 3. Today, minorities own about _____ percent of the nation's 14 million firms.

    a. 10
    b. 20
    c. 30
    d. 40

_____ 4. The highest rate of business ownership is among

    a. African-Americans.
    b. Asian-Americans.
    c. Hispanic Americans.
    d. Native Americans.

_____ 5. The largest concentration of African-Americans in a metropolitan area is in

    a. New York City
    b. Detroit
    c. Atlanta
    d. Boston

_____ 6. _____ now includes the nation's largest African-American-owned fast food
franchise company.

    a. Pizza Hut
    b. McDonald's
    c. Burger King
    d. Wendy's

7. Families of immigrants coming from which of the following countries would *not* be considered Latinos or Hispanic-Americans?

    a. Central America
    b. West Indies
    c. South America
    d. All of the above can be classified as Latinos.

8. Within the next twenty years, _____-Americans should become the nation's largest minority group.

    a. African
    b. Asian
    c. Hispanic
    d. Native

9. Mexican-Americans are _____ percent of Hispanic-Americans.

    a. 60
    b. 50
    c. 40
    d. 30

10. The largest metropolitan concentration of Hispanics is in

    a. Miami.
    b. Chicago.
    c. San Francisco.
    d. Los Angeles.

11. _____ has the second largest total of Hispanic-owned businesses.

    a. Miami
    b. Los Angeles
    c. San Diego
    d. San Francisco

12. The growth rate of Asian-Americans during the past decade was

    a. twice that of African-Americans.
    b. six times that of Hispanic-Americans.
    c. twenty times that of whites.
    d. 80 percent.

13. The largest Asian-American population submarket is made up of

    a. Chinese.
    b. Japanese.
    c. Koreans.
    d. Filipinos.

_____ 14. Immigration has accounted for nearly _____ of the Asian-American population increase.

    a.   two-thirds
    b.   three-fourths
    c.   one-half
    d.   one-fourth

_____ 15. The average age of Asian-Americans is just over _____ years old, compared with 36 for whites.

    a.   24
    b.   26
    c.   30
    d.   40

_____ 16. Asian-Americans households are more affluent than any other racial or ethnic group, including whites, for which of the following reasons?

    a.   They live in low cost of living areas.
    b.   Ninety percent of all Asian-Americans live in families.
    c.   They have a high level of education.
    d.   The low rate of business ownership among Asian-Americans.

_____ 17. In which of the following businesses will you generally *not* find Chinese-Americans?

    a.   retail
    b.   wholesale
    c.   financial
    d.   transportation

_____ 18. Which one of the following statements is *not* correct?

    a.   Asian immigrants have a tradition of self-employment.
    b.   Business cooperatives, or *kehs,* are an important source of interest-free venture capital for Asian-American entrepreneurs.
    c.   Asian concepts of honor insist on the business owner paying each family member for his or her work in the family business.
    d.   Business owners tend to employ people from their own subculture.

_____ 19. One recent study of 645 firms found that _____ of the respondents were concerned about increased cultural diversity.

    a.   three-quarters
    b.   one-third
    c.   one-half
    d.   one-fourth

_____ 20. In the same study that was mentioned in question 19, _____ felt that diversity affected their corporate strategy.

    a.   three-fourths
    b.   one-half
    c.   two-thirds
    d.   one-third

MATCHING QUESTIONS

a.	multiculturalism	d.	Hispanic-Americans
b.	African-Americans	e.	Native Americans
c.	acculturation	f.	Asian-Americans

MATCHING DEFINITIONS.   *Directions: Match the terms above with the definitions below.*

_____ 1. The process of adapting to the local culture.

_____ 2. The recognition and acceptance of a variety of cultures that are roughly equally represented in a particular region.

_____ 3. Those people whose families come from the area of the Western Hemisphere south of the United States.

_____ 4. This group has grown at a rate of twenty times that of the whites.

_____ 5. The largest minority group in the United States.

_____ 6. Sovereignty granted this group gives it some competitive market advantages.

CHAPTER REVIEW

1. The United States is undergoing a major transition as it becomes ethnically diverse. Explain.

2. How has recent immigration into the United States been different from the past and yet like the existing workforce?

3. What has been the impact of the Immigration Act of 1990?

4. Some minority groups have much higher rates of business ownership than others. Elaborate.

5. Why is there such a high rate of business ownership among Asians?

6. How do spending patterns of African-Americans differ from spending patterns of other groups?

7. The concept of multiculturalism is nowhere more evident than in the Hispanic culture. Comment.

8. What are some efforts that companies can make to develop a multicultural workforce?

EXPERIENCING BUSINESS 3-1
CULTURAL MISUNDERSTANDINGS

Culture is a population's taken-for-granted assumptions, values, and beliefs that have a powerful impact on behavior. The text chapter is about a fundamental transition in the United States to a multicultural society--from a society dominated by whites and rooted in Western values to a society less dominated by whites, more inclusive, and more diverse.

Developing awareness of cultural differences requires one to acknowledge common stereotypes and generalizations about groups. The text suggests a couple: (1) the value of building relationships, in the context of Hispanic culture/groups, and (2) deference to authority, in the context of Asian culture/groups. Stereotypes and generalizations can be risky; moreover, to associate a generalization with a group so mixed, so different, as "American managers" is surely risky. Nonetheless, this "white-dominated, Western-values" society has created some commonly held stereotypes about managers and business. Examples:

(continued)

Positive	Negative
individualistic	short-term focus
entrepreneurial	parochial
open-minded	technical, not well-rounded
trustworthy	materialistic
get-things-done	impatient
punctual, schedule-driven	
hard-working	
flexible	

To do this exercise:

1. What do you think about these generalizations? Would you "fit in" if these are accurate and typical for American managers?

2. What are some comparable stereotypes we hold about other groups?

    For example, consider qualities such as those listed below.

    Do you typically associate these with any group(s)?

loyalty	sexist
obedience	secretive
hard-working	untrustworthy
communicate nonverbally	
team players	

EXPERIENCING BUSINESS 3-2 MANAGING A DIVERSE WORKFORCE

To do this exercise:

Look into what some organization(s) in your area are doing about building awareness, valuing differences, managing diversity, etc.

You may contact the organization or talk to employees of the organization. For this exercise, consider more than businesses in the private sector; government organizations are often "ahead" of the private sector in social programs and issues.

ANSWER KEY (CHAPTER 3)

TRUE-FALSE

1.	a.	F	3.	a.	T		c.	F
	b.	F		b.	F		d.	T
	c.	F		c.	F	5.	a.	T
	d.	T		d.	F		b.	T
2.	a.	T	4.	a.	T		c.	F
	b.	T		b.	F			
	c.	T						

MULTIPLE-CHOICE

1.	a	11.	a
2.	c	12.	c
3.	a	13.	a
4.	b	14.	b
5.	a	15.	c
6.	a	16.	c
7.	d	17.	d
8.	c	18.	c
9.	a	19.	a
10.	d	20.	d

MATCHING QUESTIONS

1. c
2. a
3. d
4. f
5. b
6. e

CHAPTER REVIEW

1. The United States will change from a society dominated by whites and rooted in Western ways to a society that includes three large racial and ethnic minorities: African-Americans, Hispanic-Americans, and Asian-Americans. All three minorities will grow while whites will decline in share and size of the population.

2. Unlike past waves of immigration, the new immigrants have been mainly from Asia and Latin America. Like the existing workforce, these immigrants have been split between the highly skilled and well-educated and those with minimal skills and little education.

3. The Immigration Act of 1990 has increased the diversity among immigrants—especially at the upper end of the socioeconomic scale. The law allows people who have no family in the United States to immigrate if they have highly prized work skills or are ready to make a significant business investment.

4. The number of firms owned by Asians grew by 89 percent during the past decade, not far behind the rate of Asian population growth. The number of firms owned by Hispanics grew by 81 percent. Business growth was 38 percent among businesses owned by African-Americans.

5. First is the high level of education among Asian-Americans. Asian-Americans also have rather high incomes, so they have more capital with which to launch small businesses. Finally, a large share of Asian-Americans are recent immigrants, many of whom came to the United States specifically to go into business.

6. The average African-American spends about 35 percent less than the average non-African-American household ($20,000) on consumer goods. But African-Americans spend more than other consumers on rental appliances, boys' shoes and clothing, home repair and maintenance supplies and services, and taxi fares. They also buy different brands.

7. Mexican-Americans are 60 percent of Hispanic-Americans and are highly concentrated in the Southwest. Puerto Rican-Americans are the second-largest Hispanic subgroup, at 12 percent; they dominate the Hispanic population of New York City. Cuban-Americans are the majority of Hispanics in South Florida, although they are only 5 percent of all Hispanic-Americans. The remaining 23 percent of Hispanics trace their lineage to South America, Central America, or Spain.

8. To promote multiculturalism, companies can do one or more of the following: develop diversity programs that promote awareness of cultural differences; promote positive attitudes toward group differences; use a variety of communication channels; involve minority-group members in decision making; challenge stereotypes; include minority-group members in social organizations and activities.

GLOBAL BUSINESS

OUTLINE

(continued)

LEARNING GOALS

After studying this chapter, you should be able to:

1. Understand the importance of international trade and discuss the position of the United States in the world economy.

2. Understand some of the measures of international trade.

3. Explain why nations trade.

4. Understand the barriers to international trade, and list the major arguments for and against tariffs.

5. Explain economic integration and trade pacts.

6. Specify ways for businesses to enter into foreign trade.

7. Describe the impact of culture and political climate on international trade.

8. Explain the trade role of multinational corporations.

TESTING YOUR KNOWLEDGE

TRUE-FALSE

Directions: Test your knowledge of each goal by answering the true-false questions following each goal.

1. Understand the importance of international trade and discuss the position of the United States in the world economy.

   _____ a. International trade improves relationships of friends and allies.

   _____ b. The value of international trade is over $8 trillion a year and growing.

   _____ c. International trade helps bolster economies

   _____ d. Tensions among nations are eased through international trade.

   _____ e. The U.S. plays a major role in the international market.

   _____ f. The U.S. exports more than it imports.

   _____ g. Since 1970 the balance of payments and the balance of trade in the U.S. has been favorable

2. Understand some of the measures of international trade.

   _____ a. Exports are goods and services that are purchased from other countries.

   _____ b. A country that imports more goods than it exports is said to have a favorable balance of trade.

   _____ c. The exchange rate is set at a certain level by the federal government.

3. Explain why nations trade.

   _____ a. The U.S. has an absolute advantage in reusable spacecraft.

   _____ b. The principle of comparative advantage says that countries should be as self-sufficient as possible.

   _____ c. Even if a country has an absolute advantage in some areas, it should still engage in trade.

4. Understand the barriers to international trade, and list the major arguments for and against tariffs.

_____ a. Distance is one of the natural barriers to international trade.

_____ b. Congress has been debating the wisdom and necessity of tariffs since 1789.

_____ c. Very rarely are embargoes used for military purposes.

_____ d. Sometimes embargoes are established for health reasons.

5. Explain economic integration and trade pacts.

_____ a. Nations may agree on a preferential tariff, which offers advantages to one nation over others.

_____ b. The result of government meetings and agreements on a common economic policy is called economic integration.

_____ c. The European Community (EC) is separate from the European Common Market.

_____ d. The EC will probably never be a "United States of Europe."

_____ e. NAFTA is a bilateral treaty that will phase out trade barriers between Mexico and the United States.

6. Specify ways for businesses to enter into foreign trade.

_____ a. If a firm decides to take the international plunge, it will probably begin with exporting.

_____ b. EMCs are U.S.-based firms that are specialized by product group or country.

_____ c. An unusual type of countertrade is barter.

_____ d. International franchising has grown rapidly in recent years.

_____ e. Private-label manufacturing by a foreign company is called a nonexclusive license.

7. Describe the impact of foreign culture and political climate on international trade.

_____ a. Nationalism is rarely a concern in international business.

_____ b. Confiscation means that the government seizes ownership of a company's assets and agrees to provide compensation.

_____ c. Color has different meanings in different countries and is therefore a cultural consideration in international trade.

8. Explain the trade role of multinational corporations.

_____ a. Multinational corporations can often overcome trade barriers.

_____ b. Multinationals may be able to sidestep regulatory problems.

_____ c. Few countries welcome investment by multinational corporations.

MULTIPLE-CHOICE

Directions: Put the letter of the response that best completes each of the following statements in the blank at the left.

_____ 1. Which of the following is *not* an advantage of contract manufacturing?

a. enables company to build market position without a large investment in equipment
b. enables company to develop brand loyalty
c. enables company to develop name recognition of both multinational firms
d. good starting point for direct foreign investment or a joint venture

_____ 2. A control imposed over a period of time on the amount of material imported into a country is called a(n)

a. tariff.
b. dumping.
c. embargo.
d. import quota.

_____ 3. Government loans to and from other countries, gifts and foreign aid to and from other countries, and military expenditures made in other countries are

a. an area covered under exchange controls.
b. components of the balance of trade.
c. components of the balance of payments.
d. protective trade procedures.

_____ 4. Each year, the United States exports more _____ than it did in the preceding year.

a. food
b. raw materials
c. industrial supplies
d. apparel

_____ 5. A tariff that is set high enough to make imports less attractive to potential buyers than domestic products is a(n)

a. revenue tariff.
b. protective tariff.
c. import quota.
d. embargo.

_____ 6. Which of the following is *not* an argument for having tariffs?

a. protection of new domestic industries from established foreign competitors
b. protection of domestic jobs
c. protection of comparative advantage
d. defense preparedness

_____ 7. Embargoes may be used to

    a. raise money for the government.
    b. protect infant industries.
    c. protect public health.
    d. balance trade.

_____ 8. The principle that each country should specialize in goods that it can produce most readily and cheaply and trade those goods for the goods that foreign countries can produce most readily and cheaply is known as

    a. the law of favorable balance.
    b. competitive cooperation.
    c. specialization of labor.
    d. comparative advantage.

_____ 9. When imports exceed exports there is a(n)

    a. unfavorable balance of trade.
    b. favorable balance of trade.
    c. unfavorable balance of payments.
    d. favorable balance of payments.

_____ 10. The strongest trade barrier the United States can impose against a country to bring pressure on its political decisions is a(n)

    a. import quota.
    b. embargo.
    c. protective tariff.
    d. revenue tariff.

_____ 11. Which of the following is the approach to international marketing that a small, inexperienced company would most likely take first?

    a. joint venture
    b. contract manufacturing
    c. licensing
    d. exporting

_____ 12. When no single firm is willing to assume the financial risk for an international enterprise, the most likely answer to the problem is

    a. a joint venture.
    b. contract manufacturing.
    c. licensing.
    d. exporting.

_____ 13. A tariff is a tax levied by

    a. GATT.
    b. a nation.
    c. a multinational corporation.
    d. United Europe.

14. Which of the following would *not* be a cultural consideration in international business?

    a. language translations
    b. social norms
    c. eating habits
    d. the existence of other multinational companies

15. The U.S. tariffs on poultry, shoes, and some types of steel are

    a. unlawful.
    b. quotas.
    c. protective.
    d. revenue.

16. A form of international price discrimination in which a company charges, without justification, lower prices in foreign markets than it does for the same merchandise in its home market is

    a. prohibited by the Robinson-Patman Act.
    b. regulated by antidumping laws in most industrialized countries.
    c. an invisible trade barrier.
    d. known as economic integration.

17. To justify an antidumping duty, there must be a(n)

    a. developing nation involved.
    b. violation of the Trade Expansion Act.
    c. injury to a local industry.
    d. violation of the General Agreement on Tariffs and Trade.

18. In terms of barriers to international trade, language is a

    a. natural barrier.
    b. tariff barrier.
    c. nontariff barrier.
    d. economic sanction.

19. Preferential tariffs

    a. offer advantages to one nation (or several) over others.
    b. offer advantages to one exporter over another within a country.
    c. specify from whom a country will import certain goods.
    d. are illegal.

20. Of all the ways of entering the international market, the one which offers the greatest potential reward and the greatest potential risk is

    a. exporting.
    b. licensing.
    c. direct foreign investment.
    d. contract manufacturing.

MATCHING QUESTIONS

a. imports
b. Group of Seven (G7)
c. balance of trade
d. principle of absolute advantage
e. balance of payments
f. tariff

g. import quotas
h. GATT
i. NAFTA
j. direct foreign investment
k. principle of comparative advantage
l. preferential tariff
m. exports

MATCHING DEFINITIONS.   *Directions: Match the terms above with the definitions below.*

_____ 1. Domestically produced goods and services that are sold to other countries.

_____ 2. A tax levied by a nation on imported goods.

_____ 3. Goods and services that are purchased from other countries.

_____ 4. Limitations on the quantity of certain goods that can be imported over a period of time.

_____ 5. A multi-nation agreement to reduce tariffs and other barriers to international trade.

_____ 6. A tariff that offers advantages to one nation over other nations.

_____ 7. The seven economic superpowers, who meet regularly to set broad economic policies.

_____ 8. The difference in value between a country's exports and imports over a period of time.

_____ 9. Active ownership in a foreign company or foreign-based manufacturing or marketing facilities.

_____ 10. The idea that each country should specialize in producing goods that it can sell at a lower cost that any other supplier.

_____ 11. The idea that all countries will benefit from producing and trading those goods that each can produce best.

_____ 12. The difference between a country's total payments to other countries and its total receipts from other countries.

_____ 13. Treaty that is expected to produce an open market across North America.

CHAPTER REVIEW

1. Why is international trade important in the world economy?

2. Is it possible for a country to have a favorable balance of trade and yet have an unfavorable balance of payments? Explain.

3. Identify some barriers to international trade.

4. List at least six ways of entering the international market.

    a.

    b.

    c.

    d.

    e.

    f.

5. "Politics are an important ingredient to international trade." Elaborate.

6. What makes up a country's culture?

7. What advantages do multinational corporations (MNCs) possess?

EXPERIENCING BUSINESS 4-1 — EXPORTS

U. S. companies are significant producers and exporters of products such as:

autos and auto parts	aircraft and engines
information systems	chemicals
food and agricultural products	computers, telecommunications equipment
industrial equipment	construction equipment

Merchandise exports—goods sent out of a country—are the major source of international revenue for most countries, and merchandise exports tend to draw our attention and interest—for example, Japan (until recently) refusing to allow rice from the United States into the country, and IAMs dog food now exported to several countries.

International business takes many forms; some do not involve export of goods. Service exports are international earnings other than from goods. Examples include fees for management services, royalty payments for licensing, and franchising arrangements. Examples:

- Tokyo Disneyland is a replica of the parks in the United States. The Disney Corp. provided master planning, design, manufacturing, and training services during construction and consulting after completion. Disney received fees during construction and receives royalties from on-going operations.

- There are worldwide subscribers to Nexis, Mead Data Corporation's database.

- American Express (or VISA) financial services are available worldwide.

Are these exports? Absolutely, but not in the form we typically think of—as goods being shipped from U.S. ports.

To do this project:

Identify some service exports. You will find some "pure" services such as engineering design, information services, etc. You may wish also to consider exports involving goods, but look beyond "simple" merchandise exporting. In this category, consider companies that sell equipment but then continue with maintenance and technical services.

EXPERIENCING BUSINESS 4-2

JOINT VENTURES

To establish a presence in some markets, companies choose to enter into a "joint venture." Essentially when organizations share in the ownership of a direct investment, the operation is a joint venture. (This arrangement is appropriate for domestic business also.)

To do this project:

Answer the following questions. Suggested sources: a basic text on international business and current business periodicals.

1. Is a joint venture necessarily a sharing between two companies?

2. Is a joint venture necessarily a 50–50 sharing?

3. Is the joint venture formed for limited or for broad purposes?

4. A special type of joint venture wherein a government is in partnership with a private company is referred to as a _____.

5. What are some advantages of joint ventures?

(Answers are provided at the end of the chapter.)

ANSWER KEY (CHAPTER 4)

TRUE-FALSE

1.	a. T	3.	a. T	6.	a. T		
	b. F		b. F		b. T		
	c. T		c. T		c. F		
	d. T	4.	a. T		d. T		
	e. T		b. T		e. F		
	f. F		c. F	7.	a. F		
	g. F		d. T		b. F		
2.	a. F	5.	a. T		c. T		
	b. F		b. T	8.	a. T		
	c. F		c. F		b. T		
			d. T		c. F		
			e. F				

MULTIPLE-CHOICE

1.	c	11.	d
2.	d	12.	a
3.	c	13.	b
4.	a	14.	d
5.	b	15.	c
6.	c	16.	b
7.	c	17.	c
8.	d	18.	a
9.	a	19.	a
10.	b	20.	c

MATCHING QUESTIONS

1.	m	7.	b
2.	f	8.	c
3.	a	9.	j
4.	g	10.	d
5.	h	11.	k
6.	l	12.	e
		13.	i

CHAPTER REVIEW

1. International trade improves the relationships of friends and allies, helps ease tension among nations, helps bolster economies, raise people's standards of living, and improves the quality of life.

2. Yes. A country could have a favorable balance of trade but an unfavorable balance of payments if foreign aid and military spending abroad total more than the amounts collected from trade.

3. Barriers to international trade include tariffs, distance, language, import quotas, and embargoes.

4. a. Licensing

   b. Use of an export-management company

   c. Contract manufacturing

   d. Joint ventures

   e. Direct investment

   f. Exporting

5. In addition to the basic political structure of a country, nationalism is also a concern in international business. Rapid political changes can also cause major upheavals in a country's economic system. A government may decide to expropriate a foreign country's assets.

6. Culture is the set of beliefs, values, and social norms shared by members of a society that determines what is socially acceptable.

7.   a.   MNCs can often overcome trade problems.

      b.   They can also avoid political problems

      c.   Regulatory problems may be sidestepped by a multinational.

      d.   MNCs can often gain significant savings in labor costs.

      e.   MNCs also have the ability to shift costs from one plant to another.

      f.   Finally, they have the ability to tap new technology from around the world.

EXPERIENCING BUSINESS 4-2

1.   No. Two or more. When more than two participate, it may be called a consortium.

2.   No.

3.   Typically formed for limited objectives. May continue to operate indefinately as objectives are redefined.

4.   mixed venture

5.   To exchange complementary strengths.

      To gain economies of scale and marketing clout.

SOCIAL RESPONSIBILITY AND BUSINESS ETHICS

OUTLINE

(continued)

LEARNING GOALS

After studying this chapter, you should be able to:

1. Explain the concept of social responsibility.
2. Present arguments for social responsibility.
3. Describe the aspects of social responsibility.
4. Discuss the effects that environmental, consumer, employee relations, and financial responsibility issues have had on business.
5. Understand the relationship between ethics and social responsibility.
6. Explain the role of ethics in business decision making.

TESTING YOUR KNOWLEDGE

TRUE-FALSE

Directions: Test your knowledge of each learning goal by answering the true-false questions following each goal.

1. Explain the concept of social responsibility.

   _____ a.   Social responsibility is a voluntary obligation.
   _____ b.   Obligations of social responsibility are very narrow.
   _____ c.   Social responsibility consists of obligations that go beyond those provided for by law.

2. Present arguments for social responsibility.

   _____ a.   Social responsibility creates a better environment for business.
   _____ b.   Government regulations are increased with social responsibility.
   _____ c.   Businesses that become socially responsible improve their public image.

3. Describe the aspects of social responsibility.

   _____ a.   Temptations for illegal or irresponsible behavior exist in businesses when consequences are minimal and risk is low.
   _____ b.   Sometimes companies act irresponsibly, yet their actions are legal.
   _____ c.   Merck (pharmaceuticals) ranks near the bottom of America's most admired corporations.

4. Discuss the effects that environmental, consumer, employee relations, and financial responsibility issues have had on business.

   _____ a.   Many pollutants have no ill effect on humans but can kill plant and fish life.
   _____ b.   Ozone at ground levels is beneficial rather than harmful.
   _____ c.   Scientists predict that during the next century the earth's average temperature will rise between 3.6 and 5.8 degrees Fahrenheit.
   _____ d.   A number of companies have become active environmentalists.
   _____ e.   Our neighbor Canada has yet to become environmentally sensitive.

_____ f. The first consumer-protection law was passed in 1972.

_____ g. Consumerism reached its peak of influence in the late 1960s through the mid-1970s.

_____ h. Only a small portion of firms have been found guilty of consumer abuse.

_____ i. Many major companies have developed programs of consumer education.

_____ j. In recent years little effort has been made to overcome discrimination against racial minorities.

_____ k. Sexual harassment is a violation of the Civil Rights Act.

_____ l. The elderly have been especially affected by discrimination.

_____ m. Little progress is being made in reducing the physical barriers to employing handicapped people.

_____ n. The disadvantaged and unemployable does not include high school dropouts and ex-convicts.

5. Understand the relationship between ethics and social responsibility.

_____ a. Society does not expect business people to act ethically.

_____ b. A business person must consider various ethical implications in the decision-making process.

_____ c. Three guides to ethical conduct are: (1) consideration of consequences such as who is helped or hurt; (2) development of moral character; and (3) fear of punishment.

_____ d. Most businesspeople have a morality that is childlike in nature.

6. Explain the role of ethics in business decision making.

_____ a. Few businesses have moved beyond self-centered morality.

_____ b. Most business executives believe that ethics and social responsibility are intertwined.

_____ c. Many large firms have turned to outside social auditors.

MULTIPLE-CHOICE

Directions: *Put the letter of the response that best completes each of the following statements in the blank at the left.*

_____ 1. Social responsibility is

    a. businesses desiring to meet the needs of consumers.
    b. businesses contributing to their favorite charities.
    c. business concern for the welfare of society as a whole.
    d. limited to a specific group and its needs.

_____ 2. An argument for business acceptance of social responsibility is that social responsibility

    a. creates a better environment for business.
    b. minimizes profit.
    c. causes purchasing power to decrease.
    d. increases the need for government regulations.

_____ 3. A socially responsible business will most likely

    a. increase the possibility of labor strife.
    b. antagonize its customers.
    c. improve its public image.
    d. neglect production to serve society.

_____ 4. If your state passes a law that requires installation of air bags in all cars, but you decide not to comply because the fine is so much less than the cost of installation, you have chosen

    a. illegal and irresponsible behavior.
    b. illegal but responsible behavior.
    c. irresponsible but legal behavior.
    d. legal and responsible behavior.

_____ 5. The interrelationships of living things and their environments is called

    a. responsible consumption.
    b. pollution.
    c. sociology.
    d. ecology.

_____ 6. Responsible consumption is

    a. consuming as much as possible to aid the economy.
    b. a major water shortage.
    c. rational and efficient use of resources by consumers.
    d. overall reduction in world population.

_____ 7. The belief that males and females should perform the same job for different levels of pay or should be segregated by type of activity is known as

    a. job segregation.
    b. the battle of the sexes.
    c. racism.
    d. sexism.

_____ 8. Contamination of the environment with the by-product of human activity is called

    a. ecology.
    b. irresponsible consumption.
    c. pollution.
    d. evolution.

_____ 9. The organized effort, by independent groups and groups within government and business, to protect the consumer from undesirable effects resulting from the manufacture and sale of goods and services is

    a. manufacturing.
    b. consumerism.
    c. business.
    d. the EPA.

_____ 10. In 1962, President Kennedy outlined four rights of consumers, including

    a. the right to food, clothing, shelter, and protection.
    b. the right to vote, to speak out, to practice any religion, and to be free.
    c. the right to safety, to be informed, to choose, and to be heard.
    d. the right to employment, education, safe food and drugs, and health care.

_____ 11. The 1964 Civil Rights Act makes it illegal to discriminate on the basis of

    a. race and color.
    b. sex and age.
    c. religion and national origin.
    d. all of the above

_____ 12. Industry has taken steps to protect the environment from damage, primarily because of

    a. stockholder pressure.
    b. the profit motive.
    c. managerial pressure.
    d. government regulation.

_____ 13. The first U.S. consumer-protection law, passed in 1872, dealt with the issue of

    a. defrauding consumers through the mails.
    b. truth in advertising.
    c. conditions in Chicago's meat-packing houses.
    d. freedom from excessive taxation.

_____ 14. Pollution is

    a. creating a better environment for business.
    b. a necessary result of the rational and efficient use of resources.
    c. the contamination of the environment with by-products and the effects of human activity.
    d. not a serious problem in the 1980s.

_____ 15. A major area where society has called on corporations to assume social responsibility is

    a. marketing.
    b. consumerism.
    c. insurance.
    d. the securities market.

_____ 16. To be protected against goods that may be hazardous to health or life is the right to

    a. safety.
    b. be heard.
    c. be informed.
    d. choose.

_____ 17. If a national company does not hire anyone over 35 for entry-level management
            positions, this is referred to as

            a.   the aging of America.
            b.   ageism.
            c.   the youth syndrome.
            d.   35+ entry-level cut-off.

_____ 18. Management's obligation to social responsibility should be

            a.   regulated by government.
            b.   forced by demonstrators.
            c.   adopted voluntarily.
            d.   mandatory.

_____ 19. The concept of social responsibility obliges the business manager to consider

            a.   only his or her company.
            b.   his or her acts in terms of society as a whole.
            c.   minimizing its profits.
            d.   pollution a "public" problem only.

_____ 20. Which of the following topics would *not* be included in a firm's social audit?

            a.   employment and training programs for the disadvantaged
            b.   company programs to dispose of manufacturing waste
            c.   the per-share value of the firm's stock
            d.   financial support to cultural institutions

MATCHING QUESTIONS

a.	social audit	g.	affirmative action
b.	discrimination	h.	responsible consumption
c.	ecology	i.	social responsibility
d.	pollution	j.	global warming
e.	glass ceiling	k.	design for disassembly
f.	business ethics	l.	consumerism

MATCHING DEFINITIONS.   *Directions: Match the terms above with the definitions below.*

_____ 1.   The concern of businesses for the welfare of society as a whole.

_____ 2.   The efficient use of resources by consumers.

_____ 3.   A systematic assessment of company activities that have social impact.

_____ 4.   Standards for judging the rightness or wrongness of conduct in business practices.

_____ 5.   The unfair and unequal treatment of certain classes of people.

_____ 6.   Laws that require firms to make special efforts to hire minority groups.

_____ 7.   The set of interrelationships of living things and their environments.

_____ 8. The contamination of the environment with by-products of human activity.

_____ 9. A barrier of subtle discrimination that impedes upward mobility.

_____ 10. The predicted gradual increase in the earth's average temperature.

_____ 11. Technology that makes it easy to take apart and recycle parts and materials.

_____ 12. The organized effort by citizens, businesses, and government to protect consumers.

CHAPTER REVIEW

1. What is social responsibility and why is it so important?

2. Give an example of a firm that exhibits the following types of behavior:

   a. illegal and irresponsible behavior

   b. irresponsible but legal behavior

   c. legal and responsible behavior

3. What are some of the social issues that businesses must consider in their efforts to act in socially responsible ways?

4.   Identify some of the many pollutants facing the world today.

5.   What are companies doing to alleviate pollution and many other environmental problems?

6.   In 1962, President Kennedy outlined what he saw as the rights of the consumers. They include the right to

     a.

     b.

     c.

     d.

7.   What are the various forms of discrimination?

8.   Identify the financial responsibility issues affecting business.

9.   Businesspeople should have a personal set of ethics. How does one develop a set of ethics?

10. A businessperson with a mature set of ethical values accepts personal responsibility for decisions that affect the full community, including responsibility for:

   a.

   b.

   c.

EXPERIENCING BUSINESS 5-1

SOCIAL RESPONSIBILITY

Social responsibility is the concern of businesses for the welfare of society as a whole. Some would go farther than "concern"—they would express it as an "obligation" to set policies, make decisions, and act beyond the minimum requirements of the law to follow the values and objectives of society. Managers may willingly accept the obligation, but they must still balance the responsibility with the need to maximize profit for the owners.

To do this exercise:

Look beyond areas such as environmental protection and consumerism. Consider the "obligation" as it involves areas such as:

a. *public and community service:* Some companies contribute very directly in money or time of their employees to work in support of United Way, Red Cross, scouting, neighborhood groups, urban renewal, etc.

b. *cultural and recreational activities:* Some companies directly support activities nationally (Texaco's sponsorship since 1939 of the Metropolitan Opera) or locally (fine and performing arts, youth athletic groups, etc.).

   1. What are some examples in your community?

   2. As a member of the community, how do you feel about the contribution(s)?

   3. If you were a shareholder of the company and concerned about your income, how would you feel? Are you in effect donating, possibly to an organization that you personally do not support?

EXPERIENCING BUSINESS 5-2

BUSINESS PURPOSE, SOCIAL RESPONSIBILITY, AND ETHICS

Affirmative action involves special efforts to recruit, hire, and promote women and members of minority groups. Individual managers at the operating level can have a real impact here. Their decisions present challenges that bring together what is necessary for the enterprise, what is legal, what is socially responsible, and the ethics of the individual making the decision.

A term used frequently is "reverse discrimination." Without getting into the legal standing of such situations, the term is typically applied to a situation wherein a "majority" individual has been disadvantaged, denied, etc., in favor of a "minority" individual. The substantive issue for the purpose of this exercise will not be the legality (remember what is legal may not be ethical) but rather your determination of what would be good business—balancing social responsiveness and broader business goals. Moreover, in the situation below you must also balance your personal ethics with the business aspects.

Situation:

You are the hiring manager with the authority to make the decision. After interviewing many applicants for a position, you have narrowed the choice down to two. Both applicants, a male and a female, well exceed the minimum requirements. The male applicant is clearly more qualified than the female applicant in terms of education and experience.

This position is highly visible and is considered a critical career-building opportunity. Success in this position typically leads to promotion to a managerial position within the company. Throughout the company as well as in your department, there are virtually no women in this position. Moreover, your company has virtually no women in management. The company president and upper managers talk about the "under-representation" and the need to get more women into management. Here is your opportunity to contribute toward that goal.

You are convinced that the male candidate can take the job with considerably less training and work much more independently. You really are busy and are not enthused about taking on what would be an active training/mentoring role if you hire the female.

To do this exercise:

1. Make your selection based on the above.

2. Now consider this added information: the male is "white" or Caucasian; the female is a racial/ethnic minority (e.g., African American or Hispanic). Would the additional information change your decision?

ANSWER KEY (CHAPTER 5)

TRUE-FALSE

1. a. T	2. a. T	3. a. T
b. F	b. F	b. T
c. T	c. T	c. F

4. a. T		h. T		5. a. F	
b. F		i. T		b. T	
c. F		j. F		c. F	
d. T		k. T		d. F	
e. F		l. T		6. a. F	
f. F		m. F		b. T	
g. T		n. F		c. T	

MULTIPLE-CHOICE

1.	c	8.	c	15.	b
2.	a	9.	b	16.	a
3.	c	10.	c	17.	b
4.	a	11.	d	18.	c
5.	d	12.	d	19.	b
6.	c	13.	a	20.	c
7.	d	14.	c		

MATCHING QUESTIONS

1.	i	5.	b	9.	e
2.	h	6.	g	10.	j
3.	a	7.	c	11.	k
4.	f	8.	d	12.	l

CHAPTER REVIEW

1. Social responsibility is the concern of business for the welfare of society as a whole. It is important because it creates a better environment for business. Social responsibility also helps prevent further government regulation. Businesses have the resources that can be applied to social problems. Lastly, businesses that become socially responsible improve their public image.

2. a. A company that sells spoiled baby food.

    b. A hotel that offers a low rental rate but only one room out of 200 at that rate.

    c. A food manufacturer that gives food to the poor.

3. Currently, among the most important issues facing business are environmental problems, consumerism, and employee relations.

4. Among the many pollutants are liquid and solid waste, discharge of gas and particles into the air, noise, heat, poison, and radiation.

5. As a first step, many companies are making recycling efforts. A number of companies have become active environmentalists. Other companies have manufactured parts and materials that are easy and inexpensive to snap apart, sort, and recycle.

6. a. safety

    b. be informed

    c. choose

    d. be heard

7. Discrimination by race, national origin, religion, gender, and age, along with discrimination against the disadvantaged and handicapped. Also, sexual harassment is a violation of the Civil Rights Act.

8. Abuses in the area of financial responsibility include excessive executive compensation and insider trading.

9. One approach for developing a personal set of ethics is to examine the consequences of a particular act. A second approach to ethical behavior stresses the importance of rules. The last approach for developing a personal set of ethics emphasizes the development of moral character.

10. a. Employees' needs and desires and what is in the long-range best interests of the corporation.

    b. People directly affected by company activities and their long-range goodwill and interests.

    c. Social values and conditions for society at large.

PART THREE

BUSINESS STRUCTURE

Part Three examines the forms of business organization—sole proprietorships, partnerships, and corporations. It also provides an overview of doing business as an entrepreneur, small business owner, or franchise operator. These topics provide a framework for understanding business structure and the significance of small business in the U.S. business system.

FORMS OF BUSINESS ORGANIZATION

OUTLINE

LEARNING GOALS

After studying this chapter, you should be able to:

1. Define the three main forms of business organization.

2. Understand the factors to consider in choosing a form of business organization.

3. Discuss the advantages and disadvantages of sole proprietorships.

(continued)

4. Define the different types of partnerships, and discuss the advantages and disadvantages of partnerships.

5. Describe the organizational structure, advantages, and disadvantages of corporations.

6. Discuss cooperatives, joint ventures, quasi-public corporations, and limited liability companies.

7. Understand the basics of mergers and acquisitions and recent merger trends.

TESTING YOUR KNOWLEDGE

TRUE-FALSE

Directions: Test your knowledge of each learning goal by answering the true-false questions following each goal.

1. Define the three main forms of business organization.

_____ a. Most businesses start as sole proprietorships.
_____ b. Corporations are the most popular form of business ownership.
_____ c. Partnerships are the least popular form of business ownership.

2. Understand the factors to consider in choosing a form of business ownership.

_____ a. When you first start a business, you must do so as a sole proprietor and change to a partnership or corporation later if the business grows.
_____ b. The first decision to make when starting a business is the form of ownership best suited to your needs.

3. Discuss the advantages and disadvantages of sole proprietorships.

_____ a. The sole proprietorship is the easiest of all business forms to establish.
_____ b. Proprietorships are subject to special franchise taxes.
_____ c. Sole proprietorships are more heavily regulated than other forms of business ownerships.
_____ d. The success of a sole proprietorship is tied directly to the owner's talents.
_____ e. The sole proprietorship is a legal taxable entity.

4. Define the different types of partnerships and discuss the advantages and disadvantages.

_____ a. Limited partners are active in the running of the business but are limited in their liability.
_____ b. A master partnership is taxed like a partnership but operates like a corporation.
_____ c. Partnerships are difficult to form.
_____ d. General partners are not active in the management of their firms.
_____ e. Partnerships must be terminated or reorganized upon the death of one of the partners.

5. Describe the organizational structure, advantages, and disadvantages of corporations.

    _____   a.   Corporations are the most numerous business form in the United States and
                   also account for the largest share of sales and income.

    _____   b.   A corporation must incorporate in the state in which its headquarters are
                   located.

    _____   c.   Stockholders elect the officers of the corporation.

    _____   d.   Typically, small corporations are privately or closely owned.

    _____   e.   Limited liability is one of the principal advantages of a corporation.

    _____   f.   The life of a corporation is unlimited.

6. Discuss cooperatives, joint ventures, quasi-public corporations, and limited liabilities companies.

    _____   a.   Unlike a corporation, a cooperative does not retain profits.

    _____   b.   When firms undertake joint ventures they form a new company and lose
                   their own corporate identities.

    _____   c.   Quasi-public corporations are operated strictly with a profit motive.

    _____   d.   A limited liability company offers liability protection and taxation at per-
                   sonal rates.

7. Understand the basics of mergers and acquisitions and merger trends.

    _____   a.   As a result of a merger, a new corporate entity is formed.

    _____   b.   Mergers can be friendly and unfriendly.

    _____   c.   A vertical merger results when companies in the same industry merge to
                   reduce costs.

MULTIPLE-CHOICE

Directions: *Put the letter of the response that best completes each of the following statements
                in the blank at the left.*

    _____   1.   Sole proprietorships account for approximately _____ percent of the total of all
                   forms of business ownership.

                   a.   70
                   b.   50
                   c.   30
                   d.   10

    _____   2.   Which of the following is an advantage of a sole proprietorship?

                   a.   no special taxation
                   b.   unlimited liability
                   c.   difficulty in raising capital
                   d.   limited management

_____ 3. Which of the following is a disadvantage to both the sole proprietorship and partnership forms of business ownership?

    a. limited life
    b. ease of formation
    c. unlimited liability
    d. both a and c

_____ 4. Unlimited liability means that any damages or debts attributable to the business can be attached to the

    a. owners.
    b. stockholders.
    c. managers.
    d. creditors.

_____ 5. When some level of government—state, local, or federal—has an active role in the operations of a business, the business is referred to as

    a. institutional.
    b. quasi-public.
    c. a corporation.
    d. a joint venture.

_____ 6. Which of the following have relative freedom from government controls?

    a. sole proprietorships
    b. partnerships
    c. corporations
    d. both a and b

_____ 7. Most states require that the corporate name end in which of the following words?

    a. company
    b. limited
    c. corporation
    d. any of the above

_____ 8. Which of the following is automatically dissolved by the death or withdrawal of a principal?

    a. corporation
    b. franchise
    c. sole proprietorship
    d. partnership

_____ 9. The board of directors is responsible for

    a. appointing stockholders.
    b. naming the corporation.
    c. electing the officers in the corporation.
    d. making daily corporate decisions.

_____ 10. Which of the following is not an officer in the corporation?

    a. treasurer
    b. secretary
    c. vice president
    d. general manager

_____ 11. Which of the following is an advantage of a corporation?

    a. ease of formation
    b. limited liability
    c. freedom from government regulation
    d. ease of dissolution

_____ 12. Corporations account for _____ percent of all firms in the United States.

    a. 70
    b. 50
    c. 20
    d. 10

_____ 13. A corporation is organized

    a. by the shareholders at the annual meeting.
    b. under the laws of a particular state.
    c. by the Internal Revenue Service.
    d. under the laws of the federal government.

_____ 14. If merging companies perform essentially the same function in the same industry, the merger is called a

    a. vertical merger.
    b. horizontal merger.
    c. conglomerate.
    d. diversification.

_____ 15. In which of the following are profits distributed on the basis of the amount of business done?

    a. partnerships
    b. joint ventures
    c. cooperatives
    d. corporations

_____ 16. The charter of the corporation is issued on the basis of the information supplied in the

    a. classes of stock and number of shares to be issued.
    b. articles of the incorporation.
    c. bylaws.
    d. Internal Revenue Code.

_____ 17. Which of the following is *not* a strategy for fighting a hostile takeover?

    a. tender offer
    b. white knight strategy
    c. leveraged buyout
    d. poison pill strategy

_____ 18. Apex Tool Company buys all of the assets and liabilities of Dependable Tool. The transaction is called a(n)

    a. cooperative.
    b. merger.
    c. acquisition.
    d. divestiture.

_____ 19. Corporations account for what percentage of all business sales in the United States?

    a. 90 percent.
    b. 70 percent.
    c. 40 percent.
    d. 20 percent.

_____ 20. When mergers are financed by large amounts of borrowed money, they are

    a. leveraged buyouts.
    b. divestitures.
    c. horizontal mergers.
    d. vertical mergers.

MATCHING QUESTIONS: SECTION A

a. holding company	h.	board of directors
b. acquisition	i.	leveraged buyouts (LBOs)
c. joint venture	j.	subsidiary
d. parent company	k.	horizontal merger
e. bylaws	l.	tender offer
f. golden parachute strategy	m.	vertical merger
g. conglomerate merger	n.	quasi-public corporation

MATCHING DEFINITIONS. *Directions: Match the terms above with the definitions below.*

_____ 1. Firm that has part ownership in various companies and may give support but not be involved in day-to-day operations.

_____ 2. Expensive compensation packages promised to managers if they lose their jobs in a takeover.

_____ 3. Direct offer to buy some or all of a target.

_____ 4. The governing authority of a corporation, elected by the stockholders.

_____ 5. Legal and managerial guidelines of a corporation.

_____ 6. Purchase of a firm by a corporation or investor groups.

_____ 7. Mergers financed by large amounts of borrowed money.

_____ 8. An entity formed by two or more companies to undertake a specific product.

_____ 9. A corporation whose stock is largely or totally controlled by another firm.

_____ 10. The firm that controls most or all of another corporation's stock.

_____ 11. Combining of firms in the same industry to improve operations or reduce competition.

_____ 12. Purchase of a firm involved in an earlier or later stage of the production or sales process.

_____ 13. Combining firms in unrelated industries, to reduce risk through diversification.

_____ 14. Business operated and often subsidized by a unit of government.

MATCHING QUESTION: SECTION B

a.	divestiture	h.	sole proprietorship
b.	limited partnership	i.	partnership agreement
c.	merger	j.	articles of incorporation
d.	corporate restructuring	k.	S corporation
e.	general partnership	l.	general partners
f.	privately owned firm	m.	closely owned firm
g.	holding company	n.	partnership

MATCHING DEFINITIONS. _Directions: Match the terms above with the statements below._

_____ 1. An association of two or more persons as co-owners of a business.

_____ 2. A firm whose common stock is not available to the general public.

_____ 3. Selling selected operating units for either strategic or financial reasons.

_____ 4. A partnership that has two types of partners—general and limited.

_____ 5. A business established, owned, and operated by a single individual.

_____ 6. Written statement of the terms and conditions of a partnership.

_____ 7. The combination of two or more firms to form a new one.

_____ 8. The legal description of a corporation filed with the state in which it is incorporated.

_____ 9. Expanding or contracting a firm's operations.

_____ 10. A partnership in which all partners share in the management and profits.

_____ 11. Those partners in a limited partnership who have unlimited liability.

_____ 12. A firm whose common stock is owned by a small group of investors.

_____ 13. Business entity that provides limited liability to stockholders and taxation at personal rates and is limited in terms of number or type of owners.

_____ 14. Firm that owns stock of other companies and may contribute financial support, but is not involved in operations.

CHAPTER REVIEW

1. One of the major decisions that an entrepreneur must make is the form of business that is best suited for him or her. What are the three major forms of business ownership and how are they ranked in terms of number of firms?

2. What are the advantages and disadvantages of a sole proprietorship?

   Advantages:

   a.

   b.

   c.

   d.

   e.

   f.

   Disadvantages:

   a.

   b.

   c.

   d.

   e.

   f.

   g.

3. Identify and define the three major types of partnerships.

4. What are the advantages and disadvantages of a partnership?

    Advantages:
        a.

        b.

        c.

        d.

        e.

    Disadvantages:
        a.

        b.

        c.

        d.

        e.

5. What are the major steps involved in incorporating a business?

6.   What are the advantages and disadvantages of a corporation?

   Advantages:

   a.

   b.

   c.

   d.

   Disadvantages:

   a.

   b.

   c.

EXPERIENCING BUSINESS 6-1   FORMS OF BUSINESS OWNERSHIP

To do this exercise:

Talk to the owner(s) of a small business—perhaps an owner of a sole proprietorship or a partner in a partnership. Discuss what the owner(s) consider the advantages and disadvantages of their form of ownership.

EXPERIENCING BUSINESS 6-2   TERMS OF BUSINESS ORGANIZATION

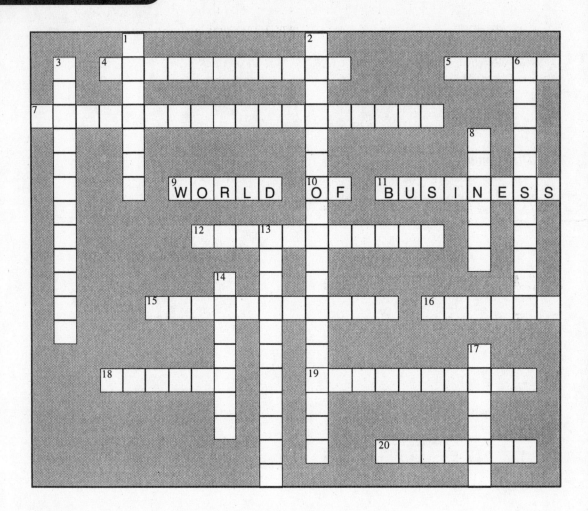

ACROSS

4 A legal business entity with a life separate from its owners, thereby limiting the owners' liability.

5 Legal and managerial guideline of the company.

7 (two words) A partnership that has two types of partners: general and limited.

9 WORLD

10 OF

11 BUSINESS

12 Organization formed by individuals or businesses with similar interests to reduce costs and gain economic power through collective ownership.

15 Selling selected operating units for either strategic or financial reasons.

16 _____ company: The firm that controls most or all of another corporation's stock.

18 The combination of two or more firms to form one new company.

19 Corporation whose stock is largely or totally controlled by another firm.

20 _____-owned: Firm whose common stock is owned by a small group of investors.

(continued)

DOWN
1   _____ takeover: A combining of firms in which the target company does not welcome the proposal of the acquiring company and attempts to block the transaction.
2   (two words) A business established, owned, operated, and often financed by a single individual.
3   (two words) An entity formed by two or more companies to undertake a specific project.
6   The purchase of a firm by a corporation or investor group.
8   _____ offer: Direct offer to buy some or all of a target company's stock at a price above the market price.
13   An association of two or more persons to carry on as co-owners of a business.
14   A partnership in which all partners share in the management and profits.
17   _____ company: A firm that is pursued by an acquiring company.

(Solution is provided at the end of the chapter.)

ANSWER KEY (CHAPTER 6)

TRUE-FALSE

1.	a.	T	4.	a.	F		e.	T
	b.	F		b.	T		f.	T
	c.	T		c.	F	6.	a.	T
2.	a.	F		d.	F		b.	F
	b.	T		e.	T		c.	F
3.	a.	T	5.	a.	F		d.	T
	b.	F		b.	F	7.	a.	T
	c.	F		c.	F		b.	T
	d.	T		d.	T		c.	F
	e.	F						

MULTIPLE-CHOICE

1.	a	11.	b
2.	a	12.	c
3.	d	13.	b
4.	a	14.	b
5.	b	15.	c
6.	d	16.	b
7.	d	17.	c
8.	d	18.	c
9.	c	19.	a
10.	d	20.	a

MATCHING QUESTIONS: SECTION A

1.	a	8.	c
2.	f	9.	j
3.	l	10.	d
4.	h	11.	k
5.	e	12.	m
6.	b	13.	g
7.	i	14.	n

MATCHING QUESTIONS: SECTION B

1.	~~i~~ n	8.	j
2.	f	9.	d
3.	a	10.	e
4.	b	11.	l
5.	~~g~~ h	12.	m
6.	~~h~~ i	13.	k
7.	c	14.	g

CHAPTER REVIEW

1. *Sole proprietorships* are the most popular form of business ownership. They account for about 70 percent of all businesses.

    Partnerships are the least popular form of business ownership, which represent about 10 percent of all businesses.

    Corporations represent about 20 percent of all businesses and thus rank second.

2. *Advantages of sole proprietorship:*
    a.   Ease and low cost of formation
    b.   All profits to the owner
    c.   Direct control of the business
    d.   Freedom from government regulation
    e.   No special taxes
    f.   Ease of dissolution

    Disadvantages of sole proprietorship:
    a.   Unlimited liability
    b.   Difficulty in raising capital
    c.   Limited managerial expertise
    d.   Personal time commitment
    e.   Unstable business life
    f.   Trouble hiring qualified employees
    g.   All losses to the owner

3. In a *general partnership*, all partners share in the management and profits.

   Limited partnerships have one or more general partners and one or more limited partners who are not active in the running of the business and whose liability is limited to their investment.

   A *master limited partnership* is taxed like a partnership, operates like a corporation, and has units that are publicly traded on a stock exchange.

4. *Advantages of partnership:*
   a. Ease of formation
   b. Availability of capital
   c. Diversity of skills and expertise
   d. Flexibility
   e. Relative freedom from government control

   Disadvantages of partnership:
   a. Unlimited liability
   b. Potential for conflict between partners
   c. Limited life
   d. Sharing of profits
   e. Difficulty in leaving partnership

5. a. Selecting a name for the firm
   b. Completing and filing the articles of incorporation
   c. Paying the required fees and taxes
   d. Holding an organizational meeting
   e. Adopting bylaws, electing directors, and passing initial operating resolutions

6. *Advantages of corporation:*
   a. Limited liability
   b. Ease of transferring ownership
   c. Unlimited life
   d. Ability to attract additional financing

   Disadvantages of corporation:
   a. Double taxation of profits
   b. Cost and complexity of formation
   c. More government restrictions than other forms

EXPERIENCING BUSINESS 6-2

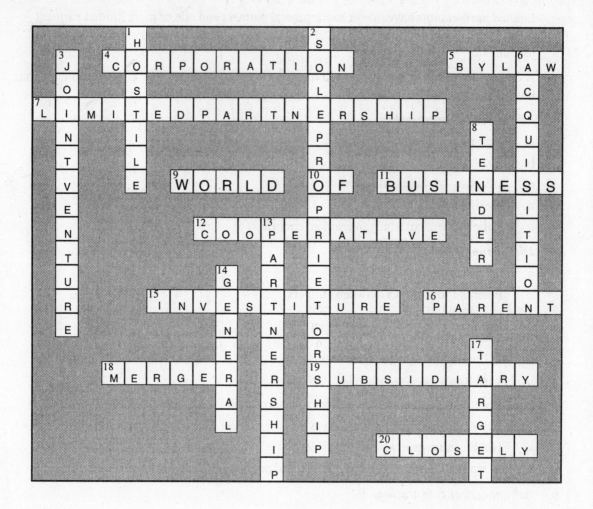

ENTREPRENEURSHIP, SMALL BUSINESS, AND FRANCHISING

OUTLINE

LEARNING GOALS

After studying this chapter, you should be able to:

1. Define entrepreneurship, discuss why people become entrepreneurs, and describe the characteristics of successful entrepreneurs.
2. Understand what a small business is, and explain the economic importance of small businesses.
3. Describe the advantages and disadvantages of small business ownership.
4. Discuss the growing importance of women and minority business owners.
5. Describe the role of the Small Business Administration.
6. Discuss start-up and management considerations.
7. Define franchising, understand its importance, and recognize its advantages and disadvantages.

TESTING YOUR KNOWLEDGE

TRUE-FALSE

Directions: *Test your knowledge of each learning goal by answering the true-false questions following each goal.*

1. Define entrepreneurship, discuss why people become entrepreneurs, and describe the characteristics of successful entrepreneurs.

    _____ a. The entrepreneur takes the risk of starting and managing a business in order to make a profit.

    _____ b. A significant majority of entrepreneurs feel that going into business for themselves is worth it and they would do it again.

    _____ c. The freedom to be independent is a big motivator for entrepreneurs.

    _____ d. Typical and common traits such as self-confidence, creativity, and willingness to take risks guarantee success for the entrepreneur.

2. Understand what a small business is, and explain the economic importance of small businesses.

    _____ a. About 98% of the businesses in the United States have fewer than 100 employees.

    _____ b. The number of employees is the definitive characteristic to determine if a business is "small."

    _____ c. The large number of small businesses gives them considerable clout (or dominance) in their respective industries.

    _____ d. Manufacturing (producing goods) is dominated by large companies and offers no opportunity for small businesses.

    _____ e. Small businesses are an important source of both jobs and new goods and services.

3. Describe the advantages and disadvantages of small business ownership.

    _____ a. Greater flexibility is a significant competitive advantage for many small businesses.

    _____ b. The principal competitive advantage for small businesses is significant profitability.

    _____ c. Since small businesses are regulated by state and local governments, they are exempt from the burden of federal governmental regulations.

4. Discuss the growing importance of women and minority business owners.

    _____ a. About a third of all businesses are now owned by women.

    _____ b. Women-owned businesses employ more people than all the Fortune 500 companies combined.

    _____ c. Minority-owned businesses tend to fail more often in their early years than other small businesses do.

5. Describe the role of the Small Business Administration.

    _____ a.   The Small Business Administration is a private association of small businesses formed to provide a broad range of support to small businesses.

    _____ b.   "Set-aside" programs refer to governmental programs that reserve loans for small businesses.

    _____ c.   The Small Business Administration provides both financial and management assistance.

6. Discuss start-up and management considerations.

    _____ a.   About two out of every three new businesses fail in the first two years.

    _____ b.   Economic factors are the most common reason for small business failures.

    _____ c.   The sole proprietorship form of organization is best for the first year of a newly formed small business or until the business becomes very profitable.

    _____ d.   A business plan can be important for many reasons, not just to help obtain financing.

    _____ e.   The size and complexity of international business operations preclude small businesses from doing business internationally.

7. Define franchising, understand its importance, and recognize its advantages and disadvantages.

    _____ a.   Most franchises offer an established business concept and the support of a large corporation.

    _____ b.   Service-oriented businesses are the fastest growing sector of franchising.

    _____ c.   Women and minorities have become the fastest growing group of franchise owners.

    _____ d.   Flexibility and freedom of operation are a popular advantage for franchisee.

    _____ e.   A franchise can provide a recognized name, product, and operating concept.

MULTIPLE-CHOICE

Directions: *Put the letter of the response that best completes each of the following statements in the blank at the left.*

_____ 1.   The person who starts a business and takes the financial and personal risks involved in keeping it going is the

a.   franchisee.
b.   venture capitalist.
c.   business planner.
d.   entrepreneur.

_____ 2.   Which of the following is *not* a realistic motive for becoming an entrepreneur?

a.   being one's own boss
b.   feeling personal satisfaction from one's work
c.   wanting lots of free time
d.   having a chance to make profits

_____ 3. According to a recent survey, one out of _____ people has a secret desire to start a company.

    a. four
    b. eight
    c. ten
    d. twenty

_____ 4. The three most important elements required of any small business owner are

    a. money, stocks, bonds.
    b. experience, debt, commitment.
    c. independence, commitment, self-sacrifice.
    d. commitment, technical knowledge, personal savings.

_____ 5. The willingness to stay with the business long enough for it to be successful takes a

    a. real commitment.
    b. little time.
    c. lot of counseling.
    d. good consultant.

_____ 6. Which of the following is *not* an advantage of operating a small business?

    a. personal touch in handling customers
    b. ability to react quickly to changes in operations
    c. survival even in limited market
    d. freedom from state and local government regulations

_____ 7. One of the disadvantages of owning a small business is

    a. flexibility.
    b. limited managerial skill.
    c. profits accrue to the owner.
    d. independence.

_____ 8. Which of the following is *not* an advantage that small businesses have over large businesses?

    a. financial backing
    b. flexibility
    c. close customer contact
    d. personal satisfaction

_____ 9. Estimates of the number of small businesses range from 4 million to _____ depending on the criteria and definition used.

    a. 5 million
    b. 20 million
    c. 1 billion
    d. unlimited

_____ 10. Which of the following businesses is dominated by large business?

     a.   construction
     b.   manufacturing
     c.   agriculture
     d.   services

_____ 11. Small businesses account for about ____ percent of the gross national product and retail sales.

     a.   40
     b.   30
     c.   20
     d.   5

_____ 12. Which of the following is *not* a disadvantage of a small business?

     a.   government regulation
     b.   fund raising
     c.   flexibility
     d.   personal commitment of the owner

_____ 13. About a ____ of all businesses are now owned by women.

     a.   fourth
     b.   half
     c.   tenth
     d.   third

_____ 14. The future opportunities for women in small business are expected to

     a.   stay the same.
     b.   decrease.
     c.   increase.
     d.   decrease at a slower rate.

_____ 15. Which of the following gives the entrepreneur a chance to fully analyze and think through the concept of the business?

     a.   entrepreneur plan
     b.   self-analysis sheet
     c.   business plan
     d.   operational guide

_____ 16. Once the business plan is complete, the next step is to

     a.   find the right business idea.
     b.   choose a form of organization.
     c.   get the needed financing.
     d.   staff the business.

_____ 17. In a franchise, the supplier of the product is the

    a. franchisee.
    b. franchisor.
    c. franchise.
    d. one who owns the inventory.

_____ 18. Which of the following would typically be the least risky investment?

    a. franchise
    b. existing business
    c. new business
    d. Each is about as risky as the others

_____ 19. Which of the following is *true*? A franchisee

    a. has complete control over the business.
    b. has complete control over the profits.
    c. has a contract with the franchisor.
    d. does not need any business management skills.

_____ 20. The most popular type of international franchises are

    a. nonfood retail stores.
    b. car rentals.
    c. business services.
    d. restaurants.

MATCHING QUESTIONS: SECTION A

a. small business
b. services
c. exporting
d. entrepreneur
e. equity
f. franchisee

g. franchiser
h. retail trade
i. managerial ability
j. business plan
k. minority-owned

MATCHING DEFINITIONS. Directions: Match the terms above with the definitions below.

_____ 1. Owned by "non-white" businesspeople.

_____ 2. Providing goods or services to international markets.

_____ 3. Funds raised through the sale of ownership interest in a business.

_____ 4. Formal, written statement which describes in detail the idea for the business and how it will be carried out.

_____ 5. An independently owned company with relatively few employees.

_____ 6. Individual or company that sells the franchised good or service in a certain area.

_____ 7. A person who takes the risk of starting and managing a business in order to make a profit.

_____ 8. Includes firms that sell goods or services directly to the end user; small businesses dominate this category.

_____ 9. Includes a wide range of businesses, which tend to be small, with output often very personal, as contrasted with production of goods.

_____ 10. Company that supplies the franchised product or format.

_____ 11. Personal competence in areas such as organization, development of operating strategy, and supervision of day-to-day activities.

MATCHING QUESTIONS: SECTION B

a.	SBA	g.	locally based
b.	debt	h.	"set-asides"
c.	franchising	i.	entrepreneurial trait
d.	franchise agreement	j.	trade association
e.	manufacturing	k.	technical knowledge
f.	business concept		

MATCHING DEFINITIONS. *Directions: Match the terms above with the definitions below.*

_____ 1. Fundamental ideas about the nature of a business, with emphasis on output and how it will be produced.

_____ 2. Specific and detailed understanding of the product or service produced.

_____ 3. The principal governmental agency that helps small businesses.

_____ 4. Firms that produce goods; a category dominated by large companies.

_____ 5. Borrowed funds that must be repaid with interest over a stated period.

_____ 6. A business arrangement between a company that supplies a good or service and the individual or company that sells the good or service in a specified area.

_____ 7. An organization that provides industry information and advice on exporting and international business.

_____ 8. One of several factors that is typical of a small business.

_____ 9. Contract authorizing the franchisee to use the franchiser's business name and its trademark and logo in exchange for payment.

_____ 10. Willingness to take moderate risk with a chance to affect the outcome.

_____ 11. Government contracts reserved for small businesses.

CHAPTER REVIEW

1. In our society, we often assume that profit or the expectation to "make a lot of money" is what drives the entrepreneur or small business owner. Is profit the most important factor? What other factors can be important?

2. What determines whether a firm is a "small business"? Is there a principal factor such as number of employees?

3. Why, in a country and economy that advocates capitalism, do we need a governmental organization such as the Small Business Administration?

4. Discuss the following statement. Explain specifically why you agree or disagree.

   "The most important aspect, the critical success factor, for starting and managing a small business is the idea or inspiration. If you have that—the magic recipe—all else will follow."

5. Pick a particular kind of business and discuss the advantages and disadvantages of franchising for that type of business enterprise.

EXPERIENCING BUSINESS 7-1 — STARTING YOUR BUSINESS (PART 1)

In this project you will take three of the key elements discussed in the text and develop a general outline from those elements. At best, the result will be an initial analysis—not in sufficient detail to really start a business, but it will take you through enough analysis that you can appreciate the rigor involved. The three elements are the idea, the form of organization, and the business plan.

To do this exercise:

1. Describe the business. Be very specific about the "product"—the good or service you will produce.

2. Describe the need. Be specific and describe the product from the perspective of your intended customer.

3. What form of organization will you choose? (The advantages of each type were discussed in Chapter 6.)

4. Describe the market. Address the demand, customers, and competition. Include some comment on how you will reach the customer (i.e., distribution).

5. How do you propose to finance the business? The plan should cover a sufficient period to deal with initial operating expenses in addition to start-up expenses.

6. What qualifications do you have to run this business?

7. What are your weaknesses? Be specific about areas in which you need help. Identify sources of advice or assistance.

EXPERIENCING BUSINESS 7-2

STARTING YOUR BUSINESS (PART 2)

This project provides a follow-up to Part 1. If you have a credible idea and the basis for a viable plan, next you will need to do your "homework."

You have many opportunities to learn from others before you start. (This may be like learning to swim. Eventually you will have to jump in the water, but why not learn from others first and maybe avoid doing something foolish or unnecessarily risky?)

The following questions are representative. Sources include someone already in this line of business or similar; the Small Business Administration (SBA) or comparable organizations; and library research. For the project pick one of those sources and answer the questions. (In a real business start-up situation, would you go to **all** the sources?)

To do this exercise:

1. What are the critical success factors—the keys to success in this particular business?

2. What type of person has been successful? Who has not?

3. What are the significant problems in this business? (If it appears easy for you to succeed, why have others not already done so?)

4. What can you expect in the future for this type of business? If you succeed, will you end up with a lot of competition?

5. How will you define success? Is this a business you have to continue to grow in order to survive; can you carve out a small niche and maintain it; etc.?

ANSWER KEY (CHAPTER 7)

TRUE-FALSE

1.	a.	T	3.	a.	T	6.	a.	F
	b.	T		b.	F		b.	T
	c.	T		c.	F		c.	F
	d.	F	4.	a.	T		d.	T
2.	a.	T		b.	T		e.	F
	b.	F		c.	T	7.	a.	T
	c.	F	5.	a.	F		b.	T
	d.	F		b.	F		c.	T
	e.	T		c.	T		d.	F
							e.	T

MULTIPLE-CHOICE

1.	d	11.	a
2.	c	12.	c
3.	b	13.	d
4.	c	14.	c
5.	a	15.	c
6.	d	16.	c
7.	b	17.	b
8.	a	18.	a
9.	b	19.	c
10.	b	20.	d

MATCHING QUESTIONS: SECTION A

1.	k	7.	d
2.	c	8.	h
3.	e	9.	b
4.	j	10.	g
5.	a	11.	i
6.	f		

MATCHING QUESTIONS: SECTION B

1.	f	7.	j
2.	k	8.	g
3.	a	9.	d
4.	e	10.	i
5.	b	11.	h
6.	c		

CHAPTER REVIEW

1. The text uses the term entrepreneurial spirit. That spirit encompasses much more than profit. There are many factors important to the prospective entrepreneur: relative independence, lifestyle, satisfaction, and image are examples.

2. A common perception is that a small business is "small" because it employs relatively few employees. However, other factors are also significant: independent management, ownership by an individual or a small group of investors, a local base, and lack of influence in the market or industry.

3. One could argue that the SBA exists specifically because our country values capitalism. Moreover, part of the "American dream" and folklore is the success of our entrepreneurs, so we choose to provide the support of a governmental organization such as the Small Business Administration.

4. Disagree! The history of business, large or small, demonstrates that the critical success factors for starting and managing a business are much more basic than good ideas, vision, or "magic recipes." Business fundamentals such as cash flow and management expertise are what counts.

5. Answers will vary. The response/comments should relate to question 4 above. The franchiser provides access to expertise in the business fundamentals and experience in the particular segment or area of operations. The franchiser provides the "lessons learned."

PART FOUR

MANAGEMENT

Part Four describes the significance of management, how the managerial process works, the dynamics of organizing a firm, and how production and operations management works. These topics survey the general organizational considerations managers deal with in setting up and running a firm.

THE MANAGERIAL PROCESS

OUTLINE

LEARNING GOALS

After studying this chapter, you should be able to:

1. Briefly explain the nature of management and the roles of managers.
2. Identify the four managerial skills, and describe their usefulness at various levels of the organization.
3. List the steps in the problem-solving process.
4. Explain the four managerial functions: planning, organizing, directing, and controlling.
5. Describe three management leadership styles.
6. Discuss management by objectives.

TESTING YOUR KNOWLEDGE

TRUE-FALSE

Directions: Test your knowledge of each learning goal by answering the true-false questions following each goal.

1.   Briefly explain the nature of management and the roles of managers.

_____   a.   A manager's job typically involves a number of planned and unplanned activities, most of which require communication.

_____   b.   Management is the process of coordinating a firm's human and other resources to achieve organizational objectives.

_____   c.   A manager's informational role involves obtaining and distributing information as well as being a spokesperson.

_____   d.   A manager's interpersonal role involves only contacts and relationships within the work group.

_____   e.   For most managers, the decisional role is a minor part of his or her job.

2.   Identify the four managerial skills, and describe their usefulness at various levels of the organization.

_____   a.   The specialized knowledge and ability that a person bring to a job are technical skills.

_____   b.   Managers often need two sets of skills: managerial plus the technical skills of a nonsupervisory position.

_____   c.   Working with people to accomplish organizational goals is generally categorized as a technical skill.

_____   d.   Conceptual skills are important only for top or upper level managers.

_____   e.   Human-relations skills include the ability of a manager to get enough power to reach his or her goals.

_____   f.   The conceptual skills of problem solving and decision making are part of a manager's normal workday.

3.   List the steps in the problem-solving process.

_____   a.   Decision making is choosing among alternatives.

_____   b.   Many problems are routine and can be solved by following set procedures.

_____   c.   The first step in problem solving is to identify alternatives.

_____   d.   With possible solutions (alternatives) identified and evaluated, the manager's next step is to choose one or more of the alternatives.

4.   Explain the four managerial functions: planning, organizing, directing, and controlling.

_____   a.   Planning begins with setting goals.

_____   b.   The planning process is the foundation for other managerial activity.

_____   c.   Proactive managers are expected to react to problems.

_____   d.   Reactive managers are considered forward-looking and able to anticipate problems and opportunities.

_____ e. Sound crisis management quickly generates answers to business problems, thereby reducing the need for contingency planning.

_____ f. The purpose of organizing is to coordinate the efforts of all parts of the company.

_____ g. Leadership, communication, and motivation are the key elements of organizing.

_____ h. Directing is guiding others to achieve specific goals.

_____ i. Controlling is important because it lets managers determine the success of their planning, organizing, and leading activities.

5. Describe three management leadership styles.

_____ a. Of the three common decision styles discussed, the combative is the most prevalent.

_____ b. The autocratic style is inappropriate, and managers cannot be successful using an autocratic style.

_____ c. Managers who share decision making with group members are using a participative decision style.

_____ d. In the "modern" workplace, the participative decision style is the most effective managerial style.

_____ e. In a free-rein (or laissez-faire) decision style, the manager turns over all authority and control to the group.

_____ f. A free-rein manager may be perceived as negligent or shirking his or her responsibility.

_____ g. A free-rein style is inappropriate because the manager does not directly control the decision process.

6. Discuss management by objectives.

_____ a. Management by objectives (MBO) is incompatible with a participative managerial decision style

_____ b. Management by objectives (MBO) will not work in a small business or organization.

_____ c. The MBO system works only for first-line supervisors and their subordinates.

_____ d. One of the principal benefits of MBO is the clearer understanding and communication that can result.

MULTIPLE-CHOICE

Directions: Put the letter of the response that best completes each of the following statements in the blank at the left.

_____ 1. The functions of management involve the cycle of:
   a. planning, organizing, controlling, directing.
   b. planning, organizing, directing, controlling.
   c. planning, decision making, directing.
   d. decision making, organizing, motivating.

_____ 2. The leadership style that involves no employee consultation is

    a. management by objectives.
    b. consultative.
    c. group-centered.
    d. autocratic.

_____ 3. When a manager makes a decision based solely on the results from a written survey of the employees' opinions, it is an example of the _____ style.

    a. people's
    b. free-rein
    c. consultative
    d. autocratic

_____ 4. The manager's role as "figurehead" is

    a. to take charge.
    b. to move the group toward the group goal.
    c. to maintain the company's resources.
    d. mostly ceremonial.

_____ 5. The proper term for setting objectives and then designing the strategies, policies, and methods needed for achieving them is

    a. planning.
    b. leading.
    c. organizing.
    d. controlling.

_____ 6. Which of the following describes the long-range, comprehensive plan and takes into account the firm's environment as well as the organization itself?

    a. strategic planning
    b. tactical planning
    c. comprehensive long-range planning
    d. planning and analysis

_____ 7. The carefully stated and explained guidelines which provide direction for managerial decision making and employee actions are called

    a. objectives.
    b. goals.
    c. policies.
    d. outlines.

_____ 8. Creating an orderly arrangement that makes use of an organization's assets in an attempt to achieve its goals is

    a. controlling.
    b. organizing.
    c. leading.
    d. planning.

_____ 9. Although all levels of managers need conceptual skills, which managers need these skills most?

a. first level managers: they need to understand the whole organization above them
b. middle managers: they must understand the operation of the levels above *and* below them
c. top-level managers: they must see the "big picture" for the success of the company
d. top and middle managers need the same amount of conceptual skills

_____ 10. Planning and organizing the workplace, assigning work duties, inspecting worker output, and closely following work rules and procedures are common traits of the

a. management-by-objectives manager.
b. job-centered leader.
c. employee-centered leader.
d. inspector.

_____ 11. The method used when communication is passed up and down the management structure is a(n)

a. ladder channel.
b. horizontal channel.
c. elevator channel.
d. vertical channel.

_____ 12. An informal system of communication is called the

a. gossip channel.
b. informal channel.
c. rumor channel.
d. grapevine.

_____ 13. In ____ channels of communication, messages are passed to people at the same organizational level.

a. formal
b. vertical
c. horizontal
d. informal

_____ 14. Leaders who permit subordinates to participate in making decisions and determining what is to be done are called.

a. job-centered leaders.
b. interpersonal leaders.
c. employee-centered leaders.
d. participating leaders.

_____ 15.   The leadership style that emphasizes a straightforward use of authority is

       a.   laissez-faire.
       b.   democratic.
       c.   liberal.
       d.   autocratic.

_____ 16.   An internal state-of-being that promotes behavior is

       a.   motivation.
       b.   leadership.
       c.   span of management.
       d.   management by objectives

_____ 17.   The activity of ensuring that operations agree with management's plans is

       a.   leadership.
       b.   planning.
       c.   organizing.
       d.   controlling.

_____ 18.   The abilities needed in working with people to successfully accomplish organizational goals are

       a.   conceptual skills.
       b.   human-relations skills.
       c.   tactical skills.
       d.   technical skills.

_____ 19.   Which of the following is *not* true?

       a.   Time pressure contributes to work-related stress.
       b.   Up to a point, stress improves performance.
       c.   Too much stress causes physical and mental problems.
       d.   A person under stress should avoid physical exercise.

_____ 20.   The process of managing by objectives was introduced by

       a.   Peter F. Drucker, in the 1950s.
       b.   Peter F. Drucker, a well-known management consultant.
       c.   Peter F. Drucker, called by some "the father of modern management."
       d.   All of the above.

MATCHING QUESTIONS: SECTION A

a.	management	i.	feedback
b.	planning	j.	mission
c.	controlling	k.	managerial skill
d.	managerial role	l.	middle managers
e.	strategic planning	m.	objectives
f.	technical skill	n.	management by objectives (MBO)
g.	human-relations skill	o.	delegation
h.	proactive managers	p.	employee-centered managers

MATCHING DEFINITIONS.   *Directions: Match the terms above with the definitions below.*

_____ 1.   The process of coordinating a firm's human and other resources to achieve an organization's objectives.

_____ 2.   An organization's general purpose or reason for existence.

_____ 3.   Deciding what needs to be done and how, when, and by whom it will be done.

_____ 4.   The specialized knowledge and ability that a person brings to a job.

_____ 5.   Measurable targets to be achieved within a certain time frame.

_____ 6.   Ability to work with people to accomplish the organization's goals.

_____ 7.   Managers who carry out the plans and policies of top managers.

_____ 8.   Program in which employees participate in setting their own goals.

_____ 9.   Set of activities or a pattern of behavior that a person is expected to perform.

_____ 10. Creating long-range, comprehensive objectives and figuring out what will need to be done and what resources will be needed.

_____ 11. The abilities needed to manage competently.

_____ 12. Information reported to management on how the system is performing.

_____ 13. Managers who tend to be more concerned about their subordinates than about the details of the tasks.

_____ 14. Managers who anticipate problems and opportunities and take advance action.

_____ 15. The process of ensuring that the organization's goals are being met.

_____ 16. Shifting and redefining authority and responsibility.

MATCHING QUESTIONS: SECTION B

a.   decision making

b.   organizing

c.   informational role

d.   directing

e.   conceptual skill

f.   contingency plans

g.   organic organization

h.   job-centered managers

i.   autocratic leadership style

j.   participative leadership style

k.   interpersonal role

l.   tactical planning

m.   political skill

n.   free-rein leadership style

o.   departmentalization

p.   performance standards

MATCHING DEFINITIONS.   *Directions: Match the terms above with the definitions below.*

_____   1.   Arranging a firm's human and material resources to carry out its plans.

_____   2.   Ability of a manager to get enough power to reach his or her goals.

_____   3.   Grouping jobs and employees into organizational units.

_____   4.   Approach wherein manager shares decision making with group members.

_____   5.   Approach wherein manager solves all problems and orders employees to implement the manager's solutions.

_____   6.   Approach wherein manager turns over all authority and control to the group.

_____   7.   Levels of performance the company wishes to attain.

_____   8.   Managers who are task-oriented and focus on what is needed to complete a task.

_____   9.   Alternative courses of actions to be taken if events undercut or preclude the intended actions.

_____   10.   Choosing among alternatives.

_____   11.   Guiding others in order to achieve specific goals.

_____   12.   Short-range, detailed planning based on overall objectives.

_____   13.   Describes an organization with little standardization and lots of adaptability.

_____   14.   Ability to view the organization as a whole and to understand how its parts fit together.

_____   15.   Manager's activities and behavior which emphasize relationships with other people.

_____   16.   Manager's activities and behavior which emphasize contacts with other people for the purpose of receiving and giving information.

CHAPTER REVIEW

1. Management is a process, typically described as activities in key areas or functions such as planning, organizing, directing, and controlling. Conceptually, all managers work in all those functional areas. Is that true, however, on a day-by-day basis, for a particular manager, in a particular organization? Explain.

2. Managers must be effective in multiple roles (informational, interpersonal, and decisional). Additionally, managers must be competent in multiple skills (technical, human-relations, conceptual, and political). Which of the skills do you consider to be most important and which role does it support?

3. Planning is often called the "primary" function of management. Many experienced managers argue that planning is the most important function. Why do you think they say that? Can any one function be more important than the others?

4. Is the function of organizing important for small business? How important is it for the smaller organization to be organized?

5. Essentially, the "third" functional area has not changed in terms of its part of the management process. For many, however, the term "directing" has become offensive. People do not want to be told what to do. When you look at the contents (leadership, communication, motivation), what do you think? Would you rename the function?

6. Performance standards are critical in the control process. Where do they come from? Give an example(s).

7. Can the employee's performance appraisal be based on how well he or she achieves the objectives set out in the management by objectives (MBO) program?

EXPERIENCING BUSINESS 8-1

LEADERSHIP STYLE

Success, even survival, as a manager depends on many factors. The needed skills (technical, human-relations, conceptual, and political) are discussed in the text. Today, skill and knowledge alone are not sufficient. Considerable emphasis is placed on "style." Leadership style, as defined in the text, is the way a leader encourages followers to accomplish a task.

The following questions are typical of what you would find in an assessment to determine if you are task-oriented (job-centered) or relationship-oriented (employee-centered).

Yes	No	
_____	_____	I encourage people to use standard procedures.
_____	_____	I allow group members to make their own decisions in solving problems.
_____	_____	I give some work-group members control over the work they do.
_____	_____	I resolve problems when they come up in the work group.
_____	_____	I will not discuss my actions with work-group members.
_____	_____	I allow the group to pace itself.

To do this exercise:

1. Answer the preceding questions.

2. How do you feel about the questions? Are they fair? Representative? What assumptions do you have to make to answer?

3. Do you consider yourself to be task-oriented (job-centered) or relationship-oriented (employee-centered)? Effective managers usually combine both approaches. Would you be able to do that?

EXPERIENCING BUSINESS 8-2

MANAGERIAL SKILLS

The text discusses four types of managerial skills: technical, human-relations, conceptual, and political.

In an "Introduction to Supervision" course, when discussing skills needed by managers, the technical, human-relations, and political skills are usually not an issue. Most new supervisors (first-line or operating-level managers) understand and accept those skills as necessary at all levels.

The one that often causes some disagreement is conceptual skill—the ability to see the organization as a whole, understanding how its parts fit together and seeing how it relates to other organizations. It is easy to relate the need for conceptual skills to top managers, who make decisions about the enterprise as a whole. But many new supervisors believe strongly that conceptual skill is not needed at the operating level. They argue that the narrow functional departmentation in their organizations does not require any broad, conceptual skill of them. Moreover, they argue that if they had it they would not be able to use it anyway; their scope of authority is very limited.

To do this exercise:

What do you think about this issue? Should conceptual skill be required at the first-line supervisor's level? Be specific, and give examples to support your opinion.

ANSWER KEY (CHAPTER 8)

TRUE-FALSE

1.	a.	T	3.	a.	T	5.	a.	F
	b.	T		b.	T		b.	F
	c.	T		c.	F		c.	T
	d.	F		d.	T		d.	F
	e.	F	4.	a.	T		e.	T
2.	a.	T		b.	T		f.	T
	b.	T		c.	F		g.	F
	c.	F		d.	F	6.	a.	F
	d.	F		e.	F		b.	F
	e.	F		f.	T		c.	F
	f.	T		g.	F		d.	T
				h.	T			
				i.	T			

MULTIPLE-CHOICE

1.	b	11.	d
2.	d	12.	d
3.	b	13.	c
4.	d	14.	c
5.	a	15.	d
6.	a	16.	a
7.	c	17.	d
8.	b	18.	b
9.	c	19.	d
10.	b	20.	d

MATCHING QUESTIONS: SECTION A

1.	a	9.	d
2.	j	10.	e
3.	b	11.	k
4.	f	12.	i
5.	m	13.	p
6.	g	14.	h
7.	l	15.	c
8.	n	16.	o

MATCHING QUESTIONS: SECTION B

1.	b	9.	f
2.	m	10.	a
3.	o	11.	d
4.	j	12.	l
5.	i	13.	g
6.	n	14.	e
7.	p	15.	k
8.	h	16.	c

CHAPTER REVIEW

1. Basically, no. Many reasons possible; some suggested:

    a. The nature of management as a group process often means sharing of the responsibilities.

    b. The nature of the business and the nature of the control systems are cyclical. Examples are (1) budgeting and forecasting for the year occurs primarily at one time of the year, and (2) employee performance appraisals are typically rendered once a year.

    c. Managers vary—their individual strengths and weaknesses will come into play. A new manager may "avoid" some areas, choosing to let others take the lead, etc.

2. It is hard and somewhat unfair to have to pick only one skill (that should tell you something about the demanding nature of managerial work). Which one skill you pick to emphasize will be very dependent on the assumptions you make. For example, we typically see a first-line supervisor as heavily involved in the technical aspects of the work and heavily involved in the informational role to train and supervise new employees.

3. As an integrated process, all the functions (planning, organizing, directing, controlling) must work in order for management to be successful. But, the planning has a different impact on the process. An organization can be well organized, a fun place to work, and cost-efficient but still go out of business. To be effective—to establish relevant objectives and attain those objectives—managers must be good at planning.

4. We all expect to find formal organizational structure in large organizations; however, some people believe that formal structure is only a burden for smaller firms. If you look at the essence of organizational structure—an understanding of who does what and how do people relate—you will find it is essential to have that understanding in all organizations.

5. Answers will vary. The issue is not so much the semantics but the perception.

6. Well-written, workable objectives often can be taken directly or with little modification to be used as standards.

    Objective: All employees will receive at least one day of classroom training in customer service skills by the end of the year.

    Objective: The hours of direct labor overtime will be reduced by at least 4% for the plant during the fiscal year.

7. Hopefully yes, and that should be a principal part of the evaluation process. To be fair, however, the supervisor/evaluator must ensure that the objectives were individually achievable and that failure to attain objectives was not due to "other" factors (for example, project funds were cut, therefore employee did not receive all the resources).

INTERNAL ORGANIZATION OF THE FIRM

OUTLINE

LEARNING GOALS

After studying this chapter, you should be able to:

1. Describe the factors to consider in building a formal organization.

2. Explain the bases for organizing departments within an organization.

3. Explain the difference between the formal and informal organization, and describe the informal organization's functions.

4. Describe organizational authority and the sources of authority.

5. Understand the roles of line and staff employees and other organizational design choices.

6. Understand how the environment affects organizational development.

TESTING YOUR KNOWLEDGE

TRUE-FALSE

Directions: *Test your knowledge of each learning goal by answering the true-false questions following each goal.*

1. Describe the factors to consider in building a formal organization.

   _____ a. Organization structure is the order and design of relationships within the "firm."

   _____ b. Organization charts provide detailed and narrative specification of the formal and informal relationships within an organization.

   _____ c. Once developed, organizational relationships are long-lasting and not changed.

   _____ d. Organization charts provide a picture of the formal relationships among people, jobs, and departments.

   _____ e. The "primary task" is the activity that forms the basis for an organization's existence.

   _____ f. Dividing work into smaller tasks and assigning the tasks to workers is "division of labor."

2. Explain the bases for organizing departments within an organization.

   _____ a. Departmentalization is grouping jobs under the authority of one manager.

   _____ b. There are many basic ways to departmentalize a firm.

   _____ c. Departmentalization by product involves arranging the work by the production process used.

   _____ d. Departmentalization by function involves grouping like resources together, such as people doing the same type of work or equipment with the same capabilities.

   _____ e. The number of employees reporting to a manager is the manager's span of control.

   _____ f. Effective organizational structure would require the same or consistent span of control throughout an organization.

   _____ g. Complex tasks and significant feedback and interaction would typically suggest a narrow span of control.

3. Explain the difference between the formal and informal organization, and describe the informal organization's functions.

   _____ a. The organization chart pictures all relationships within an organization.

   _____ b. Informal relationships develop from work-related and non-work-related activities.

   _____ c. The informal organization can help the organization achieve its goals.

   _____ d. Group norms will reinforce and support the firm's goals.

4. Describe organizational authority and the sources of authority.

    _____   a.   Authority is power granted by an organization and acknowledged by the employees.
    _____   b.   Authority can be considered the right to act.
    _____   c.   Managers have the authority; subordinates do not.
    _____   d.   Formal authority must be explicitly set forth in writing.
    _____   e.   Informal authority is inherent in every managerial position.
    _____   f.   Delegation is the sharing of job duties and authority with subordinates.
    _____   g.   Accountability is based on the responsibility and authority delegated.

5. Understand the roles of line and staff employees and other organizational design choices.

    _____   a.   All firms use a line-and-staff organization.
    _____   b.   The chief elements of the line organization are the production, marketing, and financial functions.
    _____   c.   The line managers work toward the organization's primary task.
    _____   d.   The staff specialists help the line managers through advice and specialized support services.
    _____   e.   Functional authority is a combination of line and staff authority wherein the staff member has direct authority in a specialized area.
    _____   f.   Capable line managers do not require assistance from functional specialists.
    _____   g.   Centralization is the practice of giving only limited authority to lower-level managers.
    _____   h.   Decentralization is the practice of giving a great deal of authority to lower-level managers.
    _____   i.   Effective organizational structure would require the same or consistent degree of centralization/decentralization.
    _____   j.   The size of the organization can affect the degree of centralization/decentralization.
    _____   k.   Committees are normally part of a line-and-staff organization.
    _____   l.   Matrix organization eases conflicts between horizontal and vertical authority figures.
    _____   m.   An organization wishing to promote intrapreneurial behavior would adopt a centralized structure.
    _____   n.   The virtual corporation is a parent conglomerate with many subsidiaries.

6. Understand how the environment affects organizational development.

    _____   a.   The external environment consists of social, political, economic, and technical factors that affect company operations.
    _____   b.   A firm's structure is unrelated to the rate of change in its environment.
    _____   c.   The virtual corporation is a response to rapid environmental change.

MULTIPLE-CHOICE

Directions: *Put the letter of the response that best completes each of the following statements in the blank at the left.*

_____   1.   Which of the following is *not* true concerning span of control?

a.   The more complex the task, the wider the span of control.
b.   The more locations, the narrower the span of control.
c.   The more feedback and interaction required, the narrower the span of control.
d.   The higher the skill level and motivation, the greater the span of control.

_____   2.   Redesigning business processes to improve operations is referred to as

a.   reinventing business.
b.   reengineering.
c.   span of control.
d.   formalizing the structure.

_____   3.   Most firms use a _____ organization.

a.   line
b.   matrix
c.   line-and-staff
d.   centralized

_____   4.   A(n) _____ is a picture of the relationships among tasks and those who are given the authority to do those tasks.

a.   informal organization
b.   organization chart
c.   external organization
d.   line organization

_____   5.   The order and design of relationships among employees, jobs, and departments within the organization is called a(n)

a.   line organization.
b.   firm structure.
c.   organization structure.
d.   division structure.

_____   6.   The management hierarchy has traditionally developed in a

a.   molecular fashion.
b.   pyramid fashion.
c.   box fashion.
d.   reengineered fashion.

_____ 7.   The number of employees reporting directly to a manager determines the

a.   departmentalization.
b.   specialization.
c.   division of labor.
d.   span of control.

_____ 8.   A broad span of control suggests a

a.   wide structure.
b.   tall structure.
c.   long structure.
d.   flat structure.

_____ 9.   A network of independent companies linked by information technology to share skills, costs, and access to one another's markets is referred to as a

a.   matrix organization.
b.   virtual corporation.
c.   fluid organization.
d.   databased organization.

_____ 10. A series of one-to-one authority and reporting relationships that begin with the lowest level of the organization and progress to the top level is referred to as

a.   unity of command.
b.   departmentalization.
c.   chain of command.
d.   project management.

_____ 11. An authority and responsibility relationship in which an employee reports to only one supervisor involves the concept of

a.   chain of command.
b.   staff authority.
c.   project management.
d.   unity of command.

_____ 12. The downward distribution of responsibility and authority is called

a.   delegation.
b.   staff authority.
c.   span of control.
d.   division of command.

_____ 13. Which of the following is based primarily on specialized and expert knowledge and gives the right to advise, assist, or support line managers?

a.   chain of command
b.   project management
c.   unity of command
d.   staff authority

_____ 14. Production, marketing, and financial functions of the business firm are the chief elements of the

   a. staff organization.
   b. span of control.
   c. staff authority.
   d. line organization.

_____ 15. In a _____ there are direct, clearly understood lines of authority and communication flowing from the top of the firm downward, with employees reporting to only one supervisor.

   a. virtual organization
   b. line organization
   c. tall structure
   d. flat structure

_____ 16. Decentralization is usually the best policy when

   a. the organization is small.
   b. the company is not geographically widespread.
   c. employees are willing and able to accept greater responsibility.
   d. the firm is in an industry that is slow to change.

_____ 17. Which of the following allows closer control by top management?

   a. delegation
   b. decentralization
   c. centralization
   d. authority delegation

_____ 18. Which of the following statements about intrapreneurs is *not* true?

   a. Intrapreneurs are creative, working within an organization.
   b. Intrapreneuring helps companies keep employees who otherwise might feel too confined.
   c. Intrapreneurs must regularly come up with successful products, or lose their jobs.
   d. Intrapreneurial units can be found in many major technological companies.

_____ 19. Giving a director enough authority to gather and manage the resources needed to accomplish project goals is called

   a. project management.
   b. chain of command.
   c. staff management.
   d. job enrichment.

_____ 20. A matrix organization is made of

   a. the forms of organization that are not used in today's business world.
   b. vertical and horizontal authority relationships.
   c. horizontal authority relationships.
   d. vertical authority relationships.

MATCHING QUESTIONS: SECTION A

a.	authority	g.	responsibility
b.	division of labor	h.	influence
c.	delegation	i.	line organization
d.	chain of command	j.	staff organization
e.	tall structure	k.	departmentalization
f.	flat structure	l.	centralization

MATCHING DEFINITIONS.   *Directions: Match the terms above with the definitions below.*

_____ 1.   A form of power relying on persuasion rather than command.

_____ 2.   Grouping jobs under the authority of one manager.

_____ 3.   A well-defined managerial hierarchy with clear relationships from one level to the next.

_____ 4.   The power granted by an organization and acknowledged by the employees.

_____ 5.   The practice of giving only limited authority to lower-level managers.

_____ 6.   Organization with direct, clear lines of authority flowing from top downward.

_____ 7.   The process of dividing the work and assigning tasks to workers.

_____ 8.   An obligation to take on duties and authority.

_____ 9.   The redesign of business processes to improve operations; starting over.

_____ 10. The organizational structure resulting from a wide span of control, relatively few levels.

_____ 11. Groups that provide specialized advice and assistance to managers.

_____ 12. The sharing of job duties and authority with subordinates.

MATCHING QUESTIONS: SECTION B

a.	span of control	g.	tall structure
b.	managerial hierarchy	h.	unity of command
c.	power	i.	accountability
d.	formal authority	j.	matrix
e.	specialization	k.	informal organization
f.	committee	l.	organization chart

MATCHING DEFINITIONS.   *Directions: Match the terms above with the definitions below.*

_____ 1.   The organizational structure resulting from a narrow span of control.

_____ 2.   The ability to influence others.

_____ 3.   The number of employees reporting directly to one manager.

_____ 4. The right given by one's position to influence others and request action.

_____ 5. The relationship in which an employee reports to only one person.

_____ 6. The result of delegating responsibility and authority.

_____ 7. Dividing the primary task into smaller work units that can be repeated easily and efficiently.

_____ 8. A structure in which the authority and responsibility are held by a group rather than by a single manager.

_____ 9. A permanent organization structure that brings people from different departments to work on special projects.

_____ 10. The levels of management within an organization.

_____ 11. The relationships between people that develop from work-related or non-work-related activity and that are not prescribed by management.

_____ 12. A picture of the formal relationships among people, jobs, and departments.

CHAPTER REVIEW

1. Organizational structure, the order and design of relationships within the firm, may be essential for the large organization. Is it really a concern for a small business?

2. Delegation is the sharing of job duties (responsibilities) and authority with subordinates. Yet, the ultimate accountability remains with the manager. Is that fair? Should the manager be held responsible for the failure of the subordinate?

3. The line organization is straightforward, with clear "lines" of authority and responsibility from the boss down to worker. Moreover, it relates well to the mission or primary task of the organization. Often, however, firms hire staff to provide technical help for line managers. Does that mean the line manager is not really capable of doing his/her job? Explain.

4. Should a large organization which is concerned with external environmental factors favor a centralized or decentralized approach?

5. Which is more important in the day-to-day operation of the business—the formal organization or the informal organization?

EXPERIENCING BUSINESS 9-1   ORGANIZATIONAL STRUCTURE

Organization charts do not spell out the duties and responsibilities of each position; they only show the formal relationships among people, jobs, and departments.

To do this exercise:

1. Using the list of job titles provided below, complete the organization chart on the following page by placing the title for each job in the appropriate box. You may wish to review the text material about line and staff arrangements. Some hints:

    •   This organization has seven staff departments.

    •   The list includes three divisions. These are the line elements.

(continued)

2. After you have completed the chart, answer the following:

   a. What was the basis for the departmentalization?

   b. The organization appears to have some redundancy. For example, each of the three divisions has a sales director and an accounting manager. Why would the organization break these out to each division?

   List of job titles:

   President

   Treasurer

   Controller

   Vice-President, Manufacturing Services

   Purchasing Director

   Vice-President, Marketing and Public Relations

   Corporate Secretary

   Vice-President, Personnel

   Vice-President, Cosmetics Division

   Accounting Manager, Cosmetics Division

   Purchasing Agent, Cosmetics Division

   Personnel Manager, Cosmetics Division

   Works Manager, Cosmetics Division

   Sales Director, Cosmetics Division

   Vice-President, Industrial Chemical Division

   Accounting Manager, Industrial Chemical Division

   Purchasing Agent, Industrial Chemical Division

   Personnel Manager, Industrial Chemical Division

   Works Manager, Industrial Chemical Division

   Sales Director, Industrial Chemical Division

   Vice-President, Ethical Drugs Division

   Accounting Manager, Ethical Drugs Division

   Purchasing Agent, Ethical Drugs Division

   Personnel Manager, Ethical Drugs Division

   Works Manager, Ethical Drugs Division

   Sales Director, Ethical Drugs Division

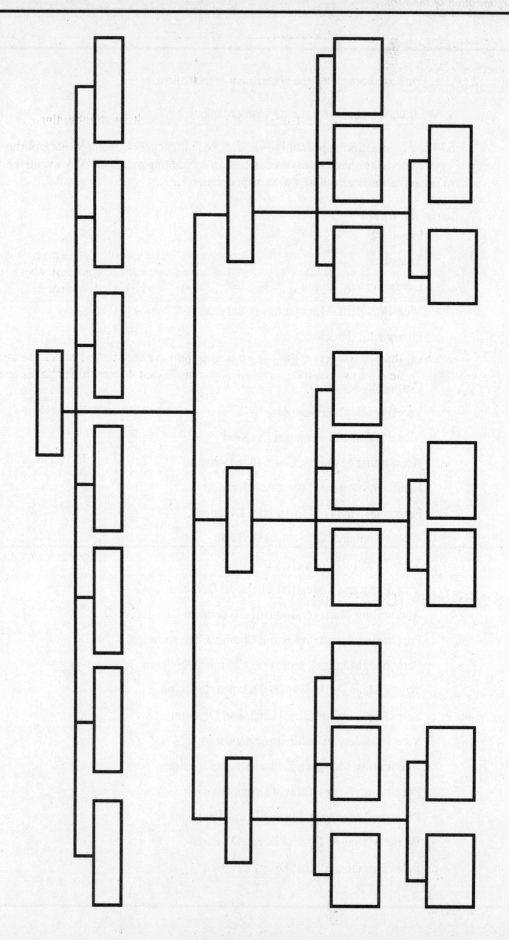

EXPERIENCING BUSINESS 9-2   DELEGATION

Delegation is the sharing of job duties (responsibilities) and authority with subordinates.

The delegation of responsibility and authority sets up the framework for accountability, a key managerial philosophy. In an organization of any size the need to delegate, to share, is obvious. As a concept it is pretty straightforward; however, in practice some managers are reluctant or unwilling to delegate.

To do this exercise:

1. What are some of the reasons that managers do not delegate, will not delegate, or cannot delegate? Without passing judgment, list as many as you can. If you think about it and discuss the question with other students, you should be able to come up with perhaps 8 to 10 reasons.

2. Having done that, take a look at the list. Typically, there are some groupings. For example, are some of the reasons due to organizational factors? What do you think should be done about those?

    Are there some reasons attributable to the individual manager? What do you think should be done about those?

ANSWER KEY (CHAPTER 9)

TRUE-FALSE

1.	a. T		c. F		4.	a. T	
	b. F		d. T			b. T	
	c. F		e. T			c. F	
	d. F		f. F			d. F	
	e. T		g. T			e. F	
	f. T	3.	a. F			f. T	
2.	a. T		b. T			g. T	
	b. T		c. T				
			d. F				

5.	a. F	g. T	m. F
	b. T	h. T	n. F
	c. T	i. F	6. a. T
	d. T	j. T	b. F
	e. T	k. T	c. T
	f. F	l. F	

MULTIPLE-CHOICE

1.	a	11.	d
2.	b	12.	a
3.	c	13.	d
4.	b	14.	d
5.	c	15.	b
6.	b	16.	c
7.	d	17.	c
8.	d	18.	c
9.	b	19.	a
10.	c	20.	b

MATCHING QUESTIONS: SECTION A

1.	h	7.	b
2.	k	8.	g
3.	d	9.	e
4.	a	10.	f
5.	l	11.	j
6.	i	12.	c

MATCHING QUESTIONS: SECTION B

1.	g	7.	e
2.	c	8.	f
3.	a	9.	j
4.	d	10.	b
5.	h	11.	k
6.	i	12.	l

CHAPTER REVIEW

1. Yes. The need may be more obvious in the large organization, but even in a small enterprise there must be an understanding of who does what and how jobs relate. The basis for delegating authority and responsibility and, in turn, establishing *accountability* are key to the success of all organizations.

2. Being a manager is, by its nature, risky. In general, you are held accountable for the successes and failures of your subordinates. Is it fair? That depends on the assumptions you make. If the failure is due to lack of training, lack of information, or lack of resources, the manager may well have a significant share of the fault. On the other hand if the failure or poor performance is due to lack of motivation, personal problems, or outside influences, the manager may not always be able to observe or predict that.

3. The increasing complexity of society places tremendous demands on the line manager. Areas such as governmental regulation (example: individual rights), complex social issues (example: drug abuse), and the like place demands on the line manager that only specialized and current resources can address. Furthermore, some staff functions, such as the mail room or corporate travel bureau, free the manager from certain routine activities and enable him or her to devote more time to line tasks and functions.

4. For the external or environmental situations where responsiveness and flexibility are desired, one could argue for *decentralization.* However, many of the external factors require very specialized knowledge/resources and only a strong *centralized* approach may succeed. The text gives examples of marketing. Consider, too, legislative or lobbying efforts, training and development, or new business ventures.

5. Answers will vary. Many likely will say that the day-to-day business depends very much on the group norms and the patterns of informal relationships. However, a strong case can be made for the importance of the formal organization and the decision making structure.

   Perhaps this question also requires some assumption about the degree of centralization versus decentralization. Would the informal organization be more important in a decentralized environment?

EXPERIENCING BUSINESS 9-1

See the organizational chart on the next page to match the corresponding number with each position below.

1   President
2   Treasurer
3   Controller
4   Vice-President, Manufacturing Services
5   Purchasing Director
6   Vice-President, Marketing and Public Relations
7   Corporate Secretary
8   Vice-President, Personnel
9   Vice-President, Cosmetics Division
10   Accounting Manager, Cosmetics Division
11   Purchasing Agent, Cosmetics Division
12   Personnel Manager, Cosmetics Division
13   Works Manager, Cosmetics Division
14   Sales Director, Cosmetics Division
15   Vice-President, Industrial Chemical Division
16   Accounting Manager, Industrial Chemical Division
17   Purchasing Agent, Industrial Chemical Division

18   Personnel Manager, Industrial Chemical Division

19   Works Manager, Industrial Chemical Division

20   Sales Director, Industrial Chemical Division

21   Vice-President, Ethical Drugs Division

22   Accounting Manager, Ethical Drugs Division

23   Purchasing Agent, Ethical Drugs Division

24   Personnel Manager, Ethical Drugs Division

25   Works Manager, Ethical Drugs Division

26   Sales Director, Ethical Drugs Division

2.   a.   Basis for the departmentalization?

The line divisions were organized based on the products, i.e. cosmetics, industrial chemicals, and ethical drugs.

b.   Redundancy?

Decentralizing the functions such as sales and accounting to each division created some cost or redundancy. However, placing these functions in the product divisions typically produces two significant benefits: (1) the functions will be more familiar with the specific products (and customers), and (2) the functions will be more responsive to the divisional managers.

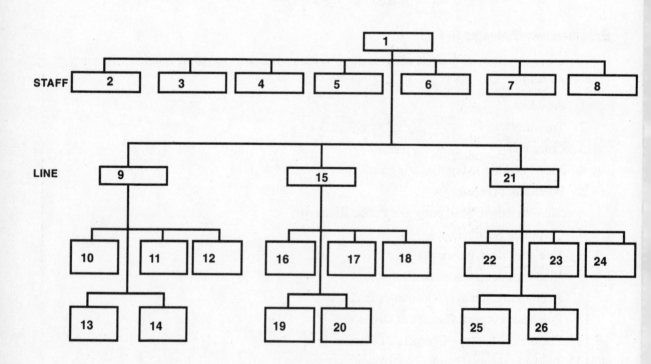

PRODUCTION AND OPERATIONS MANAGEMENT

OUTLINE

LEARNING GOALS

After studying this chapter, you should be able to:

1.   Understand why production and operations management is so important in both manufacturing and service firms.

2.   Describe the role of technology in mass production, and discuss the changing face of operations management.

3.   Discuss the various production processes.

(continued)

4. Explain how automation affects manufacturing and service industries.
5. List the factors to consider in production planning.
6. Discuss the major methods of inventory management.
7. Identify two key aspects of production control.
8. Explain how quality control affects production and operations.

TESTING YOUR KNOWLEDGE

TRUE-FALSE

Directions: Test your knowledge of each learning goal by answering the true-false questions following each goal.

1. Understand why production and operations management is so important in both manufacturing and service firms.

    _____ a.   The term "production" applies to the creation of goods and services.

    _____ b.   In both manufacturing and service firms, the production process is essentially a conversion of inputs into outputs.

    _____ c.   The production or operations function is independent of the other functions such as marketing and finance.

    _____ d.   All organizations create (produce) some type of goods or services.

2. Describe the role of technology in mass production, and discuss the changing face of manufacturing.

    _____ a.   Mass production has typically meant producing many goods at once (large-volume runs).

    _____ b.   The common definition of automation includes applications "on the plant floor," but does not include the "knowledge" applications such as design, scheduling, etc.

    _____ c.   The basic concept of standardization precludes flexible production or low volume of output.

    _____ d.   Japanese methods of lean manufacturing are having significant impact on production in the United States.

    _____ e.   Small, inexpensive changes are generally not worth making in a production process.

    _____ f.   Operations managers control about 75% of the firm's assets.

3. Discuss the various production processes.

    _____ a.   Continuous processes have the advantages of low fixed costs and scheduling flexibility.

    _____ b.   Repetitive processes are essentially assembly using standardized components and modules.

    _____ c.   Intermittent processes permit more variety in output than continuous processes.

_____ d. Traditionally, low-volume, high-variety production has been most appropriate for intermittent or job-shop systems.

_____ e. Service operations rely on standardization; therefore, the continuous process is most common for services because it promotes consistency.

4. Explain how automation affects manufacturing and service industries.

_____ a. Automation involves the use of machines to do work with minimum human intervention.

_____ b. The advantages of automation include more flexibility and reduced costs.

_____ c. CAD/CAM systems do not apply well to small firms or light manufacturing.

_____ d. A flexible manufacturing system is a broad application that encompasses automation of design and production and the applications of computer-integrated-manufacturing (CIM).

_____ e. Computer-integrated-manufacturing is a broad application that encompasses automation of design and production and the applications of flexible manufacturing systems (FMS).

_____ f. Automation has improved productivity in service businesses such as retailing and health care.

5. List the factors to consider in production planning.

_____ a. Production planning involves deciding what types and amounts of resources are needed for production.

_____ b. Production planning involves site selection.

_____ c. Qualitative factors are of little importance to high-tech companies because many of their workers telecommute.

_____ d. The main types of facilities layout from which a company must choose in production planning are process, product, and fixed-position.

_____ e. Production planning involves purchasing and sourcing decisions.

6. Discuss the major methods of inventory management.

_____ a. Inventory management involves selecting suppliers and negotiating contracts.

_____ b. Inventory management involves deciding how much stock to keep on hand and ordering, receiving, and storing it.

_____ c. A perpetual inventory approach involves a continuously updated record of inventory levels, including all gains and losses.

_____ d. Material requirements planning (MRP) relates the master schedule to the material needed for production and to inventory on hand.

_____ e. The just-in-time approach (JIT) has become a popular and cost effective replacement for MRP.

7. Identify two key aspects of production control.

_____ a. Routing is the first step in production control.

_____ b. Routing sets out the timetable for production.

_____ c. Scheduling involves specifying and controlling time for each step in the production process.

_____ d. Routing and scheduling concepts apply only to the production of physical goods or manufacturing processes.

8. Explain how quality control affects production and operations.

_____ a. Quality control involves setting standards and measuring finished goods and services against those standards.

_____ b. The way companies view and manage quality has been changing.

_____ c. Today, most companies view quality and productivity as linked.

_____ d. Quality is easier to define and measure for services than for goods because of the legal liability associated with products.

_____ e. Total quality management (TQM) focuses on the application of statistical quality control techniques.

_____ f. Statistical quality control (SQC) is applied only to manufacturing processes.

MULTIPLE-CHOICE

Directions: *Put the letter of the response that best completes each of the following statements in the blank at the left.*

_____ 1. Applying *quality principles in all aspects of a company's operations* involves considerably more than the shop floor, retail sales counter, classroom, etc. Nonetheless, the production/operation function is the "value-adding" function, and a major part of management's attention, to achieve

a. financial integrity.
b. product reliability.
c. quality.
d. total quality management.

_____ 2. Which of the following costs are *not* part of production decisions?

a. equipment
b. labor
c. advertising
d. raw material

_____ 3. Production planning focuses on all aspects of the following *except*

a. site selection.
b. facilities layout.
c. quality inspections.
d. inventory control.

_____ 4. For an intermittent process, we would expect to find the work organized around a _____ grouping/layout of the resources.

a. line or flow
b. department or functional
c. fixed-position
d. computer-integrated

_____ 5. For a repetitive process, we would expect to find the work organized around a _____ grouping/layout of the resources.

    a. line or flow
    b. departmental or functional
    c. fixed-position
    d. computer-integrated

_____ 6. The three basic types of inventory are

    a. raw materials, beginning goods, and finished goods.
    b. beginning materials, interim materials, and finished products.
    c. raw materials, work-in-process, and finished goods.
    d. beginning goods, work-in-process, and finished materials.

_____ 7. The _____ system is used to minimize inventories. It is based on the belief that materials should arrive exactly when they are needed for production.

    a. perpetual inventory
    b. work-in-process
    c. just-in-time (JIT)
    d. CPM-PERT

_____ 8. The process by which the production operations manager specifies the machines and their sequence of operation is known as

    a. perpetual inventory.
    b. deadlining.
    c. scheduling.
    d. routing.

_____ 9. Bar graphs that measure the relationship between scheduled and actual production are known as

    a. CPM-PERT charts.
    b. Gantt charts.
    c. BARS.
    d. MRP charts.

_____ 10. An important scheduling tool is the _____, which breaks projects into a sequence of events.

    a. critical path method
    b. quality-time approach
    c. lag time
    d. primary event stream

_____ 11. Small groups of workers in the same area who meet periodically to find solutions to problems are

    a. grass roots groups.
    b. quality circles.
    c. control pods.
    d. consensus groups.

_____ 12. The use of machines to perform production functions with minimum human intervention is

   a. computerization.
   b. computer-aided design (CAD).
   c. robotics.
   d. automation.

_____ 13. Benefits of cooperative relationships between corporate purchasers and vendors include *all but which* of the following?

   a. With long-term contracts, vendors can upgrade equipment.
   b. Vendors can produce to the least quality they can get away with.
   c. In general, purchasers get parts of better quality.
   d. Purchasers and vendors share information about new technologies.

_____ 14. Flexible automation systems are designed to

   a. perform the same task over and over.
   b. be programmed to do one series of tasks and then quickly be repro-grammed to perform another.
   c. replace early models of desk-top computers.
   d. simulate testing of engineering designs before they are actually placed into use.

_____ 15. Which of the following is *not* a new method for improving production?

   a. continuous improvement
   b. flexible, lean, or agile manufacturing systems
   c. computer-integrated manufacturing (CIM)
   d. fixed-position manufacturing

_____ 16. The production process is concerned with

   a. producing goods.
   b. providing services.
   c. operating systems.
   d. conversion of inputs into outputs.

_____ 17. The type of production process that typically has long production runs is _____ production.

   a. long-term
   b. continuous
   c. investment
   d. sustained

_____ 18. Many service operations find it difficult to apply a continuous process because their

   a. volume is high.
   b. standardization/uniformity is low.
   c. quality is consistently high.
   d. labor costs are low.

_____ 19. When equipment is frequently shut down or the setup changed to produce different output, the process is

    a. intermittent.
    b. continuous.
    c. determinant.
    d. consecutive.

_____ 20. How well a product serves its purpose (or fitness for use) is a

    a. customer view of quality.
    b. producer view of quality.
    c. statistician view of quality.
    d. (government) regulator view of quality.

MATCHING QUESTIONS: SECTION A

    a. work-in-process inventory   g. fixed-position layout
    b. flexible manufacturing system (FMS)   h. bill of materials
    c. perpetual inventory   i. mechanization
    d. computer-integrated manufacturing (CIM)   j. production
    e. process layout   k. production control
    f. product layout   l. assembly line

MATCHING DEFINITIONS. *Directions: Match the terms above with the definitions below.*

_____ 1. Maintaining a running balance of an item by recording all gains and losses.

_____ 2. The creation of goods and services.

_____ 3. List of the components and the quantity of each required to make a product.

_____ 4. A system that moves the work to each work station.

_____ 5. Production system incorporating automated work stations and materials/parts handling systems.

_____ 6. Layout wherein the resources necessarily move to the site.

_____ 7. Layout with like resources located together; work flow necessarily arranged to "go to" the resource.

_____ 8. Layout with the resources arranged based on the sequential nature of the tasks to be done; work flow typically a "line."

_____ 9. Production system incorporating computerized manufacturing processes with other computerized systems such as purchasing, inventory, and accounting.

_____ 10. The coordination of materials, equipment, and human resources to achieve production efficiency.

_____ 11. All items of partly-finished goods at some stage of production.

_____ 12. Accomplishing work by using machines instead of people.

Matching Questions: Section B

a. operations management	g. quality (customers' view)
b. quality (producers' view)	h. total quality management
c. quality control	i. Baldrige award
d. ISO 9000	j. statistical quality control (SQC)
e. quality circle	k. benchmarking
f. kaizen	l. concurrent engineering

MATCHING DEFINITIONS. *Directions: Match the terms above with the definitions below.*

_____ 1. System incorporating statistical techniques to control production process.

_____ 2. System that brings together small groups of employees to discuss, analyze, and recommend solutions to quality problems.

_____ 3. Managing the conversion process.

_____ 4. The degree to which the product conforms to a set of standards.

_____ 5. Creating standards and measuring finished goods and services against those standards.

_____ 6. Measuring your company's products and services against the best to identify areas for improvement.

_____ 7. The use of quality principles in all aspects of a company's operations; puts customer satisfaction first.

_____ 8. How well a product serves its purpose.

_____ 9. A set of quality requirements used increasingly for international certification.

_____ 10. A concept from Japanese manufacturing whereby teams of workers from various departments seek small, inexpensive changes to production processes.

_____ 11. The use of cross-functional teams that design both the product and its production process at the same time.

_____ 12. National recognition of quality excellence.

Matching Questions: Section C

a. just-in-time inventory (JIT)	g. continuous process
b. routing	h. repetitive process
c. computer-aided design (CAD)	i. intermittent process
d. computer-aided manufacturing (CAM)	j. MRP
e. Gantt chart	k. MRP II
f. specialization	l. robots

MATCHING DEFINITIONS. *Directions: Match the terms above with the definitions below.*

_____ 1. Production characterized by long runs (high volume) with little or no variety.

_____ 2. Production characterized by short runs with considerable variety in output.

_____ 3. Production characterized by assembly of standardized components/modules.

_____ 4. Use of computers to design, test, and modify products.

_____ 5. Use of computers to develop and control production processes.

_____ 6. Bar graphs plotted on a time line to show relationship between plan and actual work.

_____ 7. First step in production control; establish work flow.

_____ 8. Production characterized by minimum inventories of items on hand awaiting use in production.

_____ 9. Computer-controlled machines that can perform tasks independently.

_____ 10. Material requirements planning, a system to relate inventory requirements to production.

_____ 11. Manufacturing resource planning, a system that integrates data from many functional areas and generates reports to management.

_____ 12. Dividing the production process into the smallest possible activities so that each worker performs only one minor task.

CHAPTER REVIEW

1. We typically categorize operations as manufacturing or service based on the production of goods or services. In fact there are many operations that are involved with both. One example is the restaurant or food-service industry. What are some other examples? Which is more important in defining the production process—the goods or the services?

2. The text provides some examples of automation in service businesses and makes the statement that these and similar applications have improved service operations. However, can you also think of examples in which automation has "hurt the service" or negatively affected the customer?

3.   What are the key factors in the day-to-day aspects of production planning for goods? What are they for services?

4.   The just-in-time approach to inventory management has led to significant reductions of inventory as inputs to the production process. How would the concept also apply to the outputs, the finished goods?

5.   How would production control be applied in a small service system?

6.   What do you think about all the emphasis on quality? Is it a "fad"? Can it be applied as successfully in service systems as it apparently has been in manufacturing?

EXPERIENCING BUSINESS 10-1   PRODUCTIVITY AND QUALITY

To many people in the past, productivity was simply a measure of efficiency (input versus output). Today, however, most managers accept that it is more complex and that understanding productivity is important to success in business.

For years, quality and productivity were approached as separate goals. Today, management recognizes that quality and productivity are linked—indeed, successful organizations incorporate quality and productivity concerns throughout their operations management.

To do this exercise:

Consult some alternative sources such as managers or textbooks in production/operations management to answer the following questions.

1.   How do they define productivity?

2.   What factors are typically considered in the measurement of productivity?

3.   How does the goal of quality impact on the measurement of productivity?

4.   Why is productivity important? For example, how does it relate to profitability, to competitiveness?

5.   What differences do you find in dealing with productivity and quality in manufacturing industries versus service industries? For example, what approaches does management employ to improve productivity in the different sectors?

EXPERIENCING BUSINESS 10-2

WHAT IS QUALITY?

Some say:

- Quality is how well a product serves its purpose (called "fitness for use").

- Quality is how well an output conforms to a set of standards.

- Quality is value.

- Quality is perception.

The American Society for Quality Control guidelines suggest quality is the total set of features and characteristics of a product or service that bear on its ability to satisfy stated or implied needs.

This approach requires we address "absolute" and "relative" quality:

> For example, an automobile battery has a certain rating for cold-cranking. Minimum performance at that rated level would be absolute. Within that range, one can buy batteries with differing service lives—i.e., 36 months, 48 months, 60 months. Given that you pay more for the 60-month than the 48-month, etc., length of service life would also be a dimension of absolute quality.

What would be an example of relative quality for this product? Perhaps, for the same price-performance a maintenance-free versus a non-maintenance-free battery.

To do this exercise:

1. Select another product and identify aspects of absolute and relative quality for it. Answer very personally—tell how you feel about the product!

2. Now look at your answers not as an individual customer but as the manager responsible for the overall operations process to produce these outputs.

    Are these "typical" statements or expectations of quality?

    Would you expect agreement if you asked a large number of customers?

    Can you reasonably achieve these statements of quality?

    (You may find it even more challenging to repeat the exercise using a service: identify aspects of absolute and relative quality, etc.)

ANSWER KEY (CHAPTER 10)

TRUE-FALSE

1.	a.	T	4.	a.	T		d.	T
	b.	T		b.	T		e.	F
	c.	F		c.	F	7.	a.	T
	d.	T		d.	F		b.	F
2.	a.	T		e.	T		c.	T
	b.	F		f.	T		d.	F
	c.	F	5.	a.	T	8.	a.	T
	d.	T		b.	T		b.	T
	e.	F		c.	F		c.	T
	f.	T		d.	T		d.	F
3.	a.	F		e.	T		e.	F
	b.	T	6.	a.	F		f.	F
	c.	T		b.	T			
	d.	T		c.	T			
	e.	F						

MULTIPLE-CHOICE

1.	d	11.	b
2.	c	12.	d
3.	c	13.	b
4.	b	14.	b
5.	a	15.	d
6.	c	16.	d
7.	c	17.	b
8.	d	18.	b
9.	b	19.	a
10.	a	20.	a

MATCHING QUESTIONS: SECTION A

1.	c	7.	e
2.	j	8.	f
3.	h	9.	d
4.	l	10.	k
5.	b	11.	a
6.	g	12.	i

Matching Questions: Section B

1. j
2. e
3. a
4. b
5. c
6. k

7. b
8. a
9. l
10. j
11. k
12. f

Matching Questions: Section C

1. g
2. e
3. a
4. b
5. c
6. k

7. b
8. g
9. d
10. f
11. l
12. i

Chapter Review

1. Answers will vary. For the restaurant example: the food served may be secondary to the dining experience, or to atmosphere.

   For automobile repair: the parts and material may be secondary to the technical expertise and the warranty.

   For a discount retailer: the amenities of service, display, and availability, etc. may be secondary to the bargain-priced merchandise.

2. In many areas automation or "depersonalization" has affected the service; however, it is a tradeoff. For example, you cannot accomplish as much on an automated-teller-machine (ATM) as with a bank teller, and if you have a problem it can be very upsetting to try to resolve later. Still, consider the opportunity you now have to conduct business at extended times and locations—much more accessible than the old days with lobby hours of 9:00 AM to 2:00 PM.

3. For production of goods, the planning starts with the master schedule which shows the particular good(s) by time period. The planning then deals with the resources such as people and equipment and the materials required.

   For production of services, there are some significant differences. Some services balance demand; scheduling appointments is an example. For most services, however, the key factors are the highly variable demand and the fact that services cannot be stored. Therefore, staffing levels are a major consideration in production planning for service businesses.

4. Many firms produce "to stock," that is, they produce goods and store them in advance of customer orders. This can include seasonal demand, annual model runs, etc. The JIT concept does not apply here.

   Some firms, such as a small machine shop, may be producing for a large customer such as an automobile assembly plant that uses JIT. With that JIT delivery schedule, the small firm may have some opportunity to reduce their finished-goods inventory. But it is unlikely that the small firm can pace their output exactly to the input of the large firm.

5. The emphasis is typically on scheduling. The routing is usually not an issue. For example, a visit to the dentist for routine cleaning and screening involves several set procedures. The "control" is on scheduling appointments.

6. Answers will vary.

   To the second part: The setting of standards and management of services is clearly more difficult. So much of the "product" is intangible, is affected by customer perception, etc.

PART FIVE

HUMAN RESOURCES

Part Five introduces a human behavior dimension to the study of business. It covers the nature of worker motivation and leadership and examines group behavior. It looks at the functions of human-resource planning in the organization and, finally, considers the history and environment of labor-management relations in the United States.

MOTIVATION, LEADERSHIP, AND GROUP BEHAVIOR

OUTLINE

LEARNING GOALS

After studying this chapter, you should be able to:

1. Understand Taylor's concept of scientific management.
2. Describe what Mayo's Hawthorne studies revealed about worker motivation.
3. Discuss Maslow's hierarchy of needs.
4. Describe Theory X, Theory Y, and Theory Z.
5. Explain job motivators, job-maintenance factors, worker expectations, and equity theory.
6. Distinguish between job enlargement and job enrichment, and explain their effects on workers.
7. Explain the nature of work groups, group socialization, and group cohesiveness.
8. Discuss the importance of group leadership.

TESTING YOUR KNOWLEDGE

TRUE-FALSE

*Directions: Test your knowledge of each learning goal by answering the true-false questions
following each goal.*

1.   Understand Taylor's concept of scientific management.

_____   a.   Taylor's approach assumed there was a basic technical measure of a day's
work.

_____   b.   Taylor believed that if a person could be taught a better way to work and be
paid for increased productivity, everyone would profit.

_____   c.   Taylor's ideas led to significant increases in workplace morale and job
satisfaction.

_____   d.   Taylor's ideas led to dramatic increases in productivity where he worked
(the Midvale Steel plant).

2.   Describe what Mayo's Hawthorne studies revealed about worker motivation.

_____   a.   Mayo's studies led to the recognition of the "Hawthorne effect," the insight
that improved attitude can lead to improved work performance.

_____   b.   Mayo's studies proved that workers are motivated by money alone.

_____   c.   Mayo's studies proved that money is a strong motivator.

3.   Discuss Maslow's hierarchy of needs.

_____   a.   Maslow's needs hierarchy accurately explains all peoples' behavior.

_____   b.   Maslow's proposed theory of motivation is based on common or "universal"
human needs.

_____   c.   Maslow's theory assumes that unsatisfied needs motivate behavior.

_____   d.   Maslow's hierarchy of needs places safety at the top—attained after all
others.

_____   e.   Maslow's hierarchy assumes self-actualization is the most basic need.

4.   Describe Theory X, Theory Y, and Theory Z.

_____   a.   McGregor's study was based on Taylor's concept of scientific management.

_____   b.   A Theory X assumption: the average person dislikes work and will avoid it
if possible.

_____   c.   A Theory Y assumption: the average person prefers to be directed and
avoids responsibility.

_____   d.   Theory X managers tell people what to do and are very directive.

_____   e.   Theory X managers recognize individual differences and encourage workers
to learn and develop their skills.

_____   f.   Theory Z has many Japanese (management style) elements, but it reflects
U.S. cultural values.

5. Explain job motivators, job-maintenance factors, and equity theory.

    _____ a. Herzberg considered job satisfiers those factors that satisfy and motivate workers.

    _____ b. Job satisfiers include achievement and the work itself.

    _____ c. Job satisfiers include pay and working conditions.

    _____ d. Herzberg considered job-maintenance factors those aspects of the work environment that lie outside of the job.

    _____ e. Job-maintenance factors can help satisfy worker's physiological, safety, and social needs.

    _____ f. Good attitudes toward work and good job performance usually bring about job satisfaction.

    _____ g. Equity theory provides a useful explanation of worker motivation based on equality in pay between co-workers.

    _____ h. Equity in "equity theory" means perceived fairness of rewards or treatment at work.

6. Distinguish between job enlargement and job enrichment, and explain their effects on workers.

    _____ a. Job enlargement involves making jobs more pleasant, to motivate workers to perform better.

    _____ b. Job enlargement is the expansion of the number of tasks involved in a job.

    _____ c. Job enrichment is the redesign of jobs to provide more authority, responsibility, challenge, and opportunity for more personal achievement.

    _____ d. Job rotation is equally assigning employees to work less desirable schedules, such as night shifts.

7. Explain the nature of work groups, group specialization, and group cohesiveness.

    _____ a. Work groups are formal groups created to accomplish a specific task.

    _____ b. Some work groups are informal groups.

    _____ c. Work norms are conveyed through the formal procedures and policies of the organization.

    _____ d. Socialization is the process of conveying group norms.

    _____ e. Norms refers to the degree to which group members want to stay in the group and the tendency of the group to resist outside influences.

    _____ f. The goals of the work group affect the group's cohesiveness.

8. Discuss the importance of group leadership.

    _____ a. Effective leadership is the ability to influence and direct others for the purpose of attaining specific goals.

    _____ b. Effective leadership may require working to strengthen ties among group members, to build cohesiveness.

    _____ c. Formal leaders are more effective at building cohesiveness than informal leaders.

    _____ d. Informal leaders are typically appointed by management to build cohesiveness.

    _____ e. Informal leaders are typically appointed by management to improve communication.

MULTIPLE-CHOICE

Directions: *Put the letter of the response that best completes each of the following statements in the blank at the left.*

_____   1.   The study of the importance of individuals as they interact on the job is called

      a.   human relations.
      b.   job maintenance.
      c.   job satisfiers.
      d.   esteem needs.

_____   2.   _____ is well known for his studies and contributions to the founding of scientific management.

      a.   Elton Mayo
      b.   Frederick Taylor
      c.   Abraham Maslow
      d.   Victor Vroom

_____   3.   The pioneering work that found elements of the social system of work to have an impact on employee motivation is known as the

      a.   Hawthorne studies.
      b.   Maslow hierarchies.
      c.   Mayo clinics.
      d.   Taylor studies.

_____   4.   The management policy that treats work as being as natural as rest or play and that promotes positive motivation of employees is called

      a.   Theory M.
      b.   Theory X.
      c.   Theory Y.
      d.   Theory Z.

_____   5.   Which of the following is *not* assumed by a Theory Y manager?

      a.   Work is as natural as play.
      b.   The threat of punishment is not the only way to get people to work.
      c.   Most workers are creative and willing to help solve problems.
      d.   Workers want security over all else.

_____   6.   Who developed the concepts of Theory X and Theory Y?

      a.   Taylor
      b.   Maslow
      c.   Mayo
      d.   McGregor

_____   7.   According to Theory Y, the average worker under proper conditions will actually

      a.   come to work late.
      b.   sleep on the job.
      c.   ask for a raise.
      d.   seek responsibility.

_____ 8. The Theory Z management approach was proposed by

   a. Ouchi.
   b. McGregor.
   c. Mayo.
   d. Taylor.

_____ 9. The most basic human needs are _____ needs.

   a. physiological
   b. safety
   c. social
   d. pay

_____ 10. According to _____, peoples' needs are arranged in a hierarchy.

   a. Maslow
   b. McGregor
   c. Mayo
   d. Herzberg

_____ 11. The categories of human needs that Maslow developed for his motivational theory are referred to as

   a. social needs.
   b. motivating needs.
   c. the hierarchy of needs.
   d. the principal needs.

_____ 12. According to needs-based theory, a satisfied need is not

   a. a lack.
   b. the element.
   c. an objective.
   d. a motivator.

_____ 13. According to needs-based theory, what happens after one need has been at least partially satisfied?

   a. Another need emerges.
   b. Other needs seem less urgent.
   c. People feel lost.
   d. People can relate to aspirations better.

_____ 14. That job satisfiers will satisfy and motivate workers was the idea of

   a. Maslow.
   b. Herzberg.
   c. McGregor.
   d. Hawthorne.

_____   15.   Which of the following is *not* a job satisfier?

    a.   achievement
    b.   recognition
    c.   working conditions
    d.   growth

_____   16.   Things that are required to keep a worker on the job, such as good working conditions, are referred to as

    a.   maintenance factors.
    b.   motivators.
    c.   task factors.
    d.   elements.

_____   17.   The management theory that motivation and job performance depend on how employers view their workers is

    a.   corporate culture.
    b.   equity theory.
    c.   leadership theory.
    d.   expectancy theory.

_____   18.   The management theory that motivation depends on workers' perceptions of how fairly they are treated compared with co-workers is

    a.   corporate culture.
    b.   equity theory.
    c.   leadership theory.
    d.   expectancy theory.

_____   19.   The standards that determine whether an informal group member's actions are acceptable to the group are

    a.   policy and procedures.
    b.   standard operating procedure (SOP).
    c.   norms.
    d.   corporate culture.

_____   20.   Work group norms are conveyed through the process of

    a.   inclusion.
    b.   policy and procedures.
    c.   socialization.
    d.   career development.

MATCHING QUESTIONS: SECTION A

a.	Theory X	g.	equity theory
b.	organizational behavior	h.	job enlargement
c.	corporate culture	i.	Hawthorne effect
d.	job-maintenance factors	j.	hierarchy of needs
e.	norms	k.	esteem needs
f.	informal leader	l.	job rotation

MATCHING DEFINITIONS. *Directions:* *Match the terms above with the definitions below.*

_____ 1. Expansion of the number of tasks involved in a job.

_____ 2. Aspects of the work environment that lie outside of the job itself.

_____ 3. Assignment of workers to several jobs over time.

_____ 4. Human behavior in an organized setting.

_____ 5. Influential group member displaying leadership but not appointed by management.

_____ 6. Needs for the respect of others and for a sense of accomplishment and achievement.

_____ 7. Theory of what motivates workers based on negative stereotypes such as people dislike work and will avoid it if possible.

_____ 8. Theory of motivation based on workers' perceptions of how fairly they are treated compared with co-workers.

_____ 9. Maslow's proposed sequence of needs.

_____ 10. The standards used to determine whether a group member's actions are acceptable.

_____ 11. The phenomenon of an improved attitude leading to improved behavior.

_____ 12. The set of attitudes, values, and standards of accepted behavior that distinguishes one organization from another.

MATCHING QUESTIONS: SECTION B

a.	Theory Y	g.	social needs
b.	work groups	h.	group cohesiveness
c.	socialization	i.	job enrichment
d.	self-actualization	j.	safety needs
e.	job satisfiers	k.	needs theory of motivation
f.	physiological needs	l.	quality-of-work-life programs

MATCHING DEFINITIONS. *Directions:* *Match the terms above with the definitions below.*

_____ 1. The factors that satisfy and motivate workers.

_____ 2. The redesign of jobs to provide workers more authority, responsibility, and challenge.

_____ 3. Needs for food, shelter, and clothing.

_____ 4. Needs for belonging and for acceptance by others.

_____ 5. Inclusive term for efforts intended to enhance job performance and worker commitment to the organization.

_____ 6. Theory of what motivates workers based on positive stereotypes, such as people will be self-directed and try to achieve organizational goals if they believe in them.

_____ 7. The degree to which group members want to stay in the group and the tendency of the group to resist outside influence.

_____ 8. The process by which work norms are conveyed to new group members.

_____ 9. Needs to feel secure and to avoid the unexpected.

_____ 10. Units created to accomplish a specific task.

_____ 11. Needs for fulfillment and for living up to one's potential.

_____ 12. Theory based on premise that behavior is motivated by unsatisfied needs.

MATCHING QUESTIONS: SECTION C

a.	Theory Z	f.	motivation
b.	mentoring	g.	decisions by consensus
c.	networking	h.	baseball team culture
d.	morale	i.	expectancy theory
e.	psychological contract	j.	leadership

MATCHING DEFINITIONS: *Directions:*   *Match the terms above with the definitions below.*

_____ 1. Approach to motivating workers based on long-term employment, career development, concern for workers, group decision making, and individual responsibility.

_____ 2. Theory that motivation and job performance depend on how employers view their workers.

_____ 3. Teaching a newer employee about the organization.

_____ 4. Unwritten expectations of an employee or an employer.

_____ 5. Corporate environment that seeks out talent of all ages and experience; emphasis is on short-term results.

_____ 6. The desire to put forth effort to achieve organizational objectives.

_____ 7. Ability to influence and direct others for the purpose of attaining specific goals.

_____ 8. Mental attitude toward work and people.

_____ 9. Using informal contacts inside and outside an organization.

_____ 10. More than participation, involving all who would be affected by a decision.

CHAPTER REVIEW

1. What was Taylor's concept of management?

2. What did Mayo's Hawthorne studies reveal?

3. What does it mean to say that Maslow's theory of motivation is a "needs-based" approach?

4. How do Theories X and Y relate to Theory Z?

5. Why is Herzberg's theory so important to the technique of job enrichment?

6. The text says that the concepts of job enlargement and job enrichment are closely related. Explain.

7.   Why are norms important to work groups and to the motivation of individual members?

8.   Assume you are the newly appointed manager (formal leader) of a strongly cohesive group. What might you expect?

EXPERIENCING BUSINESS 11-1   ATTITUDES AND EXPECTATIONS

According to Greek mythology, King Pygmalion of Cyprus sculpted his version of the perfect woman in ivory, then fell in love with her. Aphrodite, goddess of love, gave life to Pygmalion's statue. From the story we get the term "the Pygmalion effect," which is commonly referred to as a self-fulfilling prophecy. Whether you believe in the myth or not, there is sufficient experience in real life of the power of suggestion/expectation to influence people's behavior that the self-fulfilling prophecy is a "real" consideration.

This exercise is intended to help understand Douglas McGregor's Theory X and Theory Y categorization of one's view of human nature, and in particular to consider how either expectation would affect a manager's approach to typical supervisory situations.

To do this exercise:

For each of the following, what approach would you expect a Theory-X manager to take? A Theory-Y manager?

1.   Setting goals

2.   Evaluating performance

3.   Resolving conflict (on the job)

4.   Praising and recognizing special achievement

EXPERIENCING BUSINESS 11-2

NEEDS

PART ONE: *A matching exercise*

How do you categorize the following examples of needs according to Maslow's hierarchy?

Maslow's hierarchy:

P	Physiological	SL	Social	SA	Self-actualization
SY	Safety	E	Esteem		

Representative needs:

____ 1. water	____ 6. promotion	____ 11. trusted friends
____ 2. recognition	____ 7. belonging	____ 12. food
____ 3. savings	____ 8. to be informed	____ 13. personal growth
____ 4. shelter	____ 9. reputation	____ 14. self-fulfillment
____ 5. insurance	____ 10. prestige	____ 15. job tenure

PART TWO:

Provide an example of what an organization might do to motivate an employee, by category of need. For example: job enrichment—the redesign of jobs to provide more authority, responsibility, and opportunity for achievement. Where might that apply?

1. Physiological

2. Safety

3. Social

4. Esteem

5. Self-actualization

(Answers to this exercise are provided at the end of the chapter.)

ANSWER KEY (CHAPTER 11)

TRUE-FALSE

1. a. T	4. a. F	6. a. F
b. T	b. T	b. T
c. F	c. F	c. T
d. T	d. T	d. F
2. a. T	e. F	7. a. T
b. F	f. T	b. F
c. F	5. a. T	c. F
3. a. F	b. T	d. T
b. T	c. F	e. F
c. T	d. T	f. T
d. F	e. T	8. a. T
e. F	f. T	b. T
	g. T	c. F
	h. T	d. F
		e. F

MULTIPLE-CHOICE

1.	a	11.	c
2.	b	12.	d
3.	a	13.	a
4.	c	14.	b
5.	d	15.	c
6.	d	16.	a
7.	d	17.	d
8.	a	18.	b
9.	a	19.	c
10.	a	20.	c

MATCHING QUESTIONS: SECTION A

1.	h	7.	a
2.	d	8.	g
3.	l	9.	j
4.	b	10.	e
5.	f	11.	i
6.	k	12.	c

MATCHING QUESTIONS: SECTION B

1.	e	7.	h
2.	i	8.	c
3.	f	9.	j
4.	g	10.	b
5.	l	11.	d
6.	a	12.	k

MATCHING QUESTIONS: SECTION C

1.	a	6.	f
2.	i	7.	j
3.	b	8.	d
4.	3	9.	c
5.	h	10.	g

CHAPTER REVIEW

1. Taylor's attempt to bring order and precision to the workplace was an important part of the scientific management period and approach. Taylor and other management "pioneers" focused on the one best way to do a job with emphasis on efficiency.

2. Mayo, often called the first industrial psychologist, revealed through his studies that the work group was important to the employees. Moreover, the involvement of the employees was a positive motivational factor. The "Hawthorne effect" was a general observation that improved attitude could lead to improved performance.

3. Theories of motivation, which are based on needs, assume that human behavior is driven by unsatisfied needs. Maslow structured that assumption into a sequence or hierarchy of needs to consider the relative importance of different categories.

4. Theories X and Y are different views of human nature and are often used to relate the behavior of individual managers. Theory Z is a broader theory that attempts to combine much of traditional U.S. management style with Japanese management style. In general Theory Z involves the entire organization—it is more of a cultural consideration of an organization.

5. The entire notion of job enrichment—to redesign jobs to provide more authority, responsibility, and challenge—is based on the same premise as Herzberg's two-factor theory. The premise is that only job satisfiers can truly motivate, and one must look to the job itself to provide the motivation. This was quite a departure from the traditional reliance on pay, security, etc. to motivate workers.

6. Realistically, job enlargement will not provide much relief to a boring, repetitive job. Broadening the job to provide more tasks sounds good, but in many situations the limit is quickly reached. And, just adding to the task-set can be frustrating, thereby self-defeating as a motivational approach. On the other hand, the involvement that results from enrichment could also be described as making the job bigger, but it makes the job bigger "vertically" by adding responsibility.

7. The patterns of individual behavior which are acceptable have a major effect on the day-to-day behavior of the individual. They thus relate to Maslow's needs—the social need for belonging, the esteem need for the respect of others—and help determine worker satisfaction.

8. Answers will vary. Typically: could expect resistance to "outsider" taking over; could expect some reluctance to accept varying opinions or suggestions.

EXPERIENCING BUSINESS 11-2

PART ONE

P	1.	water
E	2.	recognition
SY	3.	savings
P	4.	shelter
SY	5.	insurance
SA	6.	promotion
SL	7.	belonging
SL	8.	to be informed
E	9.	reputation
E	10.	prestige
SL	11.	trusted friends
P	12.	food
SA	13.	personal growth
SA	14.	self-fulfillment
SY	15.	job tenure

PART TWO

1.	Physiological	supplemental benefits program
2.	Safety	job security
3.	Social	team approach to work process
4.	Esteem	job enrichment, redesigning jobs to provide more authority
5.	Self-actualization	using senior employees as mentors

HUMAN-RESOURCE MANAGEMENT

OUTLINE

(continued)

LEARNING GOALS

After studying this chapter, you should be able to:

1. Describe the human-resource function.
2. Describe the federal laws and agencies that affect human-resource management.
3. Discuss human-resource planning.
4. Explain how employees are recruited and selected.
5. Describe how employees are trained and developed.
6. Explain how performance appraisals and career development are used in human-resource management.
7. Explain the forms of compensation and fringe benefits available to employees.
8. Discuss promotions, transfers, and separations.
9. Describe key human-resource issues of the 1990s.

TESTING YOUR KNOWLEDGE

TRUE-FALSE

Directions: Test your knowledge of each learning goal by answering the true-false questions following each goal.

1. Describe the human-resource function.

   _____ a. Human-resource management is the process of hiring, developing, motivating, and evaluating people in order to achieve organizational goals.

   _____ b. Human-resource management recognizes that employees are an asset, not just a cost.

   _____ c. Recruiting and selection are line functions and do not involve the human-resource management function.

   _____ d. The human-resource function is typically the focal point for dealing with labor relations.

   _____ e. The human-resource function is a line function.

   _____ f. Since human-resource specialists are the technical experts, they should have the final say in human-resource management planning and execution.

   _____ g. Lower-level or operating managers typically rely on the specific programs and procedures developed by the human-resource function.

2. Describe the federal laws and agencies that affect human-resource management.

   _____ a. Federal laws help ensure that job applicants and employees are treated fairly and not discriminated against.

   _____ b. In general, federal law prohibits discrimination based on age, race, sex, color, national origin, or religion.

_____ c. Federal law does not deal with discrimination based on disability.

_____ d. Laws governing wages, pensions, and unemployment compensation are left to the states.

_____ e. The federal agency OSHA administers the federal portion of Student Health programs.

3. Discuss human-resource planning.

_____ a. Creating a strategy for meeting future human-resource needs is called human-resource planning.

_____ b. The job description spells out the skills, knowledge, and abilities one must have to fill a job.

_____ c. The job specification lists the tasks and responsibilities of a job.

_____ d. Scheduling work is an important part of human-resource planning.

_____ e. The job description and job specification are products of job evaluation.

4. Explain how employees are recruited and selected.

_____ a. The process of attempting to find and attract qualified applicants is called selection.

_____ b. The two sources of job applicants are the internal and external labor markets.

_____ c. Recruiting primarily deals with the external labor market.

_____ d. After people have been recruited and have applied, the selection process begins.

_____ e. Employment tests are often controversial.

5. Describe how employees are trained and developed.

_____ a. Orientation programs acquaint new employees with the organization.

_____ b. The new employee's supervisor can play a significant role in the orientation.

_____ c. Formal training is separate from orientation.

6. Explain how performance appraisals and career development are used in human-resource management.

_____ a. Performance appraisals are typically part of the employment testing process to evaluate applicant skills.

_____ b. Human-resource managers assess employee performance.

_____ c. Career planning is up to the individual employee.

7. Explain the forms of compensation and fringe benefits available to employees.

_____ a. Employees are usually paid based on time, output, or some combination of both.

_____ b. Piecework payment is tied to part-time hours of temporary employees.

_____ c. Comparable worth is an issue of compensation.

_____ d. Fringe benefits include insurance, pension plans, and paid sick leave.

_____ e. Employee services as a fringe benefit could include day care or incentive pay.

8. Discuss promotions, transfers, and separations.

_____ a. Promotion is an upward move in an organization.

_____ b. Transfer is a sideways move in an organization.

_____ c. Separation could be for reasons of resignation, layoff, termination, or retirement.

_____ d. Layoff is the term a sensitive supervisor uses to tell an employee he or she is being fired.

9. Describe key human-resource issues of the 1990s.

_____ a. Wellness programs help employees reduce stress.

_____ b. A cafeteria benefits plan refers to better menu items in the company cafeteria.

_____ c. A cafeteria benefits plan is one way of controlling health care and other benefits costs.

MULTIPLE-CHOICE

Directions: *Put the letter of the response that best completes each of the following statements in the blank at the left.*

_____ . 1.   The personnel (human resource) function is primarily concerned with

a.   forecasting for human resource needs.
b.   training line managers.
c.   effective management of human resources.
d.   selection of new employees.

_____ 2.   Maximizing worker satisfaction, improving worker efficiency, and ensuring a sufficient number of quality employees to meet organizational objectives is the job of

a.   human-resource management.
b.   an executive team.
c.   line or operating managers.
d.   worker compensation.

_____ 3.   Creating a strategy for meeting future human-resource needs is called

a.   employee training.
b.   objectives planning.
c.   forecasting for human-resource needs.
d.   human-resource planning.

_____ 4.   The skills, knowledge, and abilities necessary for a job are included in the

a.   job description.
b.   job evaluation.
c.   job specification.
d.   control unit sample.

_____   5.   Staffing a new position or an existing job within the organization utilizes the
                ____ labor market.

                a.   external
                b.   vertical
                c.   horizontal
                d.   internal

_____   6.   The scheduling of 40 hours of normal work into less than five days is called a(n)

                a.   compressed workweek.
                b.   abnormal work schedule.
                c.   flextime schedule.
                d.   "killer" schedule.

_____   7.   For entry-level positions that require specialized skill and knowledge, many
                firms look to

                a.   their personnel department.
                b.   employment agencies.
                c.   college campuses.
                d.   executive search firms.

_____   8.   Of the following, which attempts to locate and attract qualified and compatible
                applicants from the external labor market?

                a.   human-resource planning
                b.   recruitment
                c.   selection
                d.   promotion

_____   9.   The two steps in most initial screenings are

                a.   preliminary interview and work sample.
                b.   employment application and preliminary interview.
                c.   preliminary interview and selection interview.
                d.   testing and selection interview.

_____   10.   Which of the following would *not* be an appropriate consideration in employ-
                ment testing to screen job applicants?

                a.   skills and knowledge
                b.   general intelligence and knowledge
                c.   attitudes and personality
                d.   loyalty and lifestyle preference

_____   11.   Which of the following is used as an in-depth discussion about an applicant's
                work experience, skills and abilities, education, and personal interests?

                a.   selection interview
                b.   initial screening
                c.   performance appraisal
                d.   reference checking

_____ 12. Programs that attempt to increase the knowledge and skills of the employees fall in the category of

    a. development analyses.
    b. job analyses.
    c. training and development.
    d. affirmative action quotas.

_____ 13. Comparing actual performance with expected performance is a

    a. job specification.
    b. job analysis.
    c. performance appraisal.
    d. job description.

_____ 14. A systematic comparison of jobs on the basis of their required skills, responsibility, and experience with the purpose to set wages and salaries is

    a. a job evaluation.
    b. comparable worth.
    c. a performance appraisal.
    d. human-resource planning.

_____ 15. A benefit package that allows employees to pick their own benefits is called

    a. cafeteria-style.
    b. merit.
    c. flexicomp.
    d. piecework.

_____ 16. The _____ Act sets the minimum wage.

    a. Pension Reform
    b. Fair Labor Standards
    c. Wage Standards and Uniform Classification
    d. Taft-Hartley

_____ 17. The _____ Act restricts the use of child labor.

    a. Pension Reform
    b. Fair Labor Standards
    c. Wage Standards and Uniform Classification
    d. Taft-Hartley

_____ 18. The _____ Act prohibits discrimination based on mental or physical "handicap."

    a. Americans with Disabilities
    b. Fair Labor Standards
    c. Family and Medical Leave
    d. Civil Rights (Title VII)

_____ 19. The ____ Act requires employers to provide unpaid leave for childbirth or adoption.

    a. Americans with Disabilities
    b. Fair Labor Standards
    c. Family and Medical Leave
    d. Civil Rights (Title VII)

_____ 20. ____ refers to the principle that employees should be paid the same for jobs that are similar in worth to the employer.

    a. Comparable worth
    b. Equal pay for equal work
    c. Union scale
    d. Worth-and-value analysis

MATCHING QUESTIONS: SECTION A

a.	dehiring	g.	assessment center
b.	fringe benefits	h.	comparable worth
c.	transfer	i.	job description
d.	flextime	j.	cafeteria benefits plan
e.	altered workweeks	k.	employee services
f.	job analysis	l.	on-the-job training

MATCHING DEFINITIONS. *Directions: Match the terms above with the definitions below.*

_____ 1. Compensation approach whereby employees have choice of benefits.

_____ 2. Form of compensation that includes such "extras" as social/recreational programs, free parking, tuition reimbursement, and merchandise discounts.

_____ 3. A sideways move in an organization.

_____ 4. A series of tasks, such as interviews, discussions, exercises, and job simulations.

_____ 5. A method of termination whereby the employer gets the employee to quit.

_____ 6. Concept that employees should be paid the same for jobs that are similar in worth to the employer.

_____ 7. Work scheduling to get away from the eight-hour-a-day, five-day-a-week schedule.

_____ 8. Study of the tasks required to do a job well.

_____ 9. Work scheduling system whereby the employee works a core period but can vary other times.

_____ 10. Compensation in the form of insurance, pension plans, and paid sick leave.

_____ 11. The statement of tasks and responsibilities of a job.

_____ 12. Training the employees in the workplace.

MATCHING QUESTIONS: SECTION B

a.	recruitment	g.	human-resource management
b.	selection	h.	job evaluation
c.	promotion	i.	job specification
d.	termination	j.	performance appraisals
e.	separation	k.	affirmative action programs
f.	vestibule training	l.	off-the-job training

MATCHING DEFINITIONS.   *Directions: Match the terms above with the definitions below.*

_____ 1. The process of hiring, developing, motivating, and evaluating people in order to achieve organizational goals.

_____ 2. Programs to expand opportunities for women and minorities.

_____ 3. An employee leaving the company due to resignation, layoff, or retirement.

_____ 4. An upward move in an organization.

_____ 5. Teaching employees off the job how to operate specific equipment they will use on the job.

_____ 6. Training the employees away from the workplace.

_____ 7. The attempt to find and attract qualified applicants in the external labor market.

_____ 8. Review of applicants to identify one best suited to fill the job.

_____ 9. A permanent separation arranged by the employer.

_____ 10. A systematic comparison of jobs based on required skills, responsibility, and experience.

_____ 11. The statement of skills, knowledge, and abilities required for a job.

_____ 12. Comparison of actual performance with expected performance.

CHAPTER REVIEW

1. Federal laws help ensure that job applicants and employees are treated fairly and not discriminated against. Discuss.

2. The large organization may be able to hire full-time, qualified specialists in human-resource management. What would human resource management be like in the small organization?

3. How do you feel about the federal government's involvement in the human-resource management area?

4. Why are alternatives such as flextime and altered workweeks important elements of an organization's human-resource strategy?

5. Many of the tests used in employment screening are controversial. As a prospective employee, how would you feel about being tested for drugs, for AIDS, for other "lifestyle"-related concerns?

   As the employer faced with a hiring decision, how would you feel about those same areas?

6. What should be covered during the "initial" orientation of new employees? Is it possible to cover too much?

7. The text says that career planning is up to the individual. Do you agree?

8.   For many years working managers and those who study management have debated whether
     money motivates. The development of financial incentive systems, such as piecework pay-
     ment, has largely been based on money as a motivator. Do you believe that money is a
     motivator? Is it the most important motivator?

9.   In today's society is money as important as it may have been? Increasingly, "pay" is being
     separated from "benefits." Is it reasonable that someone may actually take a job more for
     the benefits than the pay?

10. What do you think about dehiring, that is, getting an employee to quit? What are some of the
     problems that could come up?

EXPERIENCING BUSINESS 12-1

JOB SPECIFICATIONS AND JOB DESCRIPTIONS

A job specification and the job description are two very different tools. Not only are they different in content, but they also are very different in the application and the intent. As a student of business you should understand the distinction and the application of each.

The job specification is the statement of skill, knowledge, etc. required for the job. It lists what you are looking for when you fill the job, what the specific requirements are to be eligible for the job.

The job description is the statement of the duties and responsibilities of the job. It lists what you expect the person hired to perform.

In practice, however, it is common to have the parts of the two components or documents mixed together. That may serve a purpose, but the distinction is still important. When advertising a vacant position (part of recruitment) the announcement typically combines elements of both sources.

To do this exercise:

1. Look at the following examples. What is part of the specification? What is part of the description? What other information is provided?

   Traffic Manager
   > Individual must have a minimum of 5 years experience, a degree in transportation preferred. Monitor all incoming bills, control inbound and outbound freight.

   Machine Repair Person
   > Seeking a self-motivated individual who takes pride in his/her job responsibilities. Should possess working knowledge of NC/CNC electronics, mechanics, and hydraulics. Work involves travel to multiple locations. Excellent work references are required along with a pre-employment physical examination including drug and alcohol screening. We are a growing company and provide an excellent opportunity for growth and offer an excellent benefits program.

2. Select your own example from local newspaper or job postings.

(Answers to this exercise are provided at the end of the chapter.)

EXPERIENCING BUSINESS 12-2

LEGAL ENVIRONMENT FOR HUMAN-RESOURCE MANAGEMENT

In many cases the title of the law/regulation/order is pretty indicative of the content. The purpose of the following exercise is primarily to show the scope of some of the federal legal environment. However, you should also note the dates. Some of the significant legislation is longstanding; some is fairly new!

To do this exercise:

Match the legislation with the relevant area(s).
(At least one of the sources has multiple matches)

1. Fair Labor Standards Act (1938)
2. Equal Pay Act (1963)
3. Civil Rights Act (1964), Title VII
4. Age Discrimination in Employment Act (1967)
5. Occupational Safety and Health Act (1970)
6. Pension Reform Act (Employee Retirement Income Security Act, 1974)
7. Pregnancy Discrimination Act (1978)
8. Americans with Disabilities Act (1990)
9. Family and Medical Leave Act (1993)

_____ Sets the minimum wage.

_____ Requires employers to provide unpaid leave for childbirth, adoption, or illness.

_____ Regulates pension plans.

_____ Prohibits employment discrimination based on mental or physical disabilities.

_____ Declares it illegal to discriminate in employment because of race, color, religion, gender, or national origin.

_____ Forbids discrimination in compensation and employment on account of age.

_____ Regulates overtime pay for non-managerial employees.

_____ Regulates child labor.

_____ Eliminates pay differentials based on gender.

_____ Requires federal government to set health and safety standards.

_____ Protects the retirement income of employees and retirees.

_____ Prohibits discrimination in employment based on pregnancy.

(Answers to this exercise are provided at the end of the chapter.)

ANSWER KEY (CHAPTER 12)

TRUE-FALSE

1	a.	T		c.	F		7.	a.	T
	b.	T		d.	T			b.	F
	c.	F		e.	F			c.	T
	d.	T	4.	a.	F			d.	T
	e.	F		b.	T			e.	F
	f.	F		c.	T	8.	a.	T
	g.	T		d.	T			b.	T
2.	a.	T		e.	T			c.	T
	b.	T	5.	a.	T			d.	F
	c.	F		b.	T	9.	a.	T
	d.	F		c.	T			b.	F
	e.	F	6.	a.	F			c.	T
3.	a.	T		b.	F				
	b.	F		c.	T				

MULTIPLE-CHOICE

1.	c	11.	a
2.	a	12.	c
3.	d	13.	c
4.	c	14.	a
5.	d	15.	a
6.	a	16.	b
7.	c	17.	b
8.	b	18.	a
9.	b	19.	c
10.	d	20.	a

MATCHING QUESTIONS: SECTION A

1.	j	7.	e
2.	k	8.	f
3.	c	9.	d
4.	g	10.	b
5.	a	11.	i
6.	h	12.	l

Matching Questions: Section B

1.	g	7.	a
2.	k	8.	b
3.	e	9.	d
4.	c	10.	h
5.	f	11.	i
6.	l	12.	j

Chapter Review

1. In general, federal laws prohibit discrimination based on age, race, gender, color, national origin, religion, and disability.

2. The human-resource function is often a part-time or shared responsibility in a small organization. Additionally, much of the day-to-day management falls on the operating/line supervisors.

3. Answers will vary.

4. These options could be significant not only in increasing productivity and reducing absenteeism, as discussed in the text for existing employees, but also in attracting new employees. With trends such as single-parent households or both spouses working, many people are looking for some flexibility to balance their personal life with their jobs.

5. Answers will vary.

    Note: As the employer you have to be very aware of and current on legal issues, such as the restriction on the use of polygraph (lie detectors) in employment screening.

6. Much of the initial orientation will focus on administrative matters such as pay, parking, and enrollment in benefits programs. The employee may be somewhat overwhelmed and not familiar enough with the job specifics to fully appreciate the job, mission, and corporate culture aspects. On the other hand, first impressions are crucial and that initial orientation can be a significant opportunity to communicate and reinforce organizational values.

7. Answers will vary.

8. Answers will vary.

9. Answers will vary, although, considering the trends and issues for the 1990s, the answer is essentially, yes. Some individuals with "family" responsibilities will be more concerned with access to non-pay benefits than with the actual pay or salary.

10. This practice has probably been around a long time in various forms, some subtle and some not so subtle. Putting pressure on an unwanted employee could lead to charges of discrimination.

EXPERIENCING BUSINESS 12-1

Traffic Manager

  Specification: minimum of 5 years experience, a degree in transportation

  Description: monitor all incoming bills, control inbound and outbound freight.

Machine Repair Person

  Specification: self-motivated individual who takes pride in his/her job responsibilities; working knowledge of NC/CNC electronics, mechanics, and hydraulics

  Description: travel to multiple locations

  Other: excellent work references, a pre-employment physical examination including drug and alcohol screening

  growing company, opportunity for growth, benefits program

EXPERIENCING BUSINESS 12-2

1. Fair Labor Standards Act (1938)
2. Equal Pay Act (1963)
3. Civil Rights Act (1964), Title VII
4. Age Discrimination in Employment Act (1967)
5. Occupational Safety and Health Act (1970)
6. Pension Reform Act (Employee Retirement Income Security Act, 1974)
7. Pregnancy Discrimination Act (1978)
8. Americans with Disabilities Act (1990)
9. Family and Medical Leave Act (1993)

1   Sets the minimum wage.

9   Requires employers to provide unpaid leave for childbirth, adoption, or illness.

6   Regulates pension plans.

8   Prohibits employment discrimination based on mental or physical disabilities.

3   Declares it illegal to discriminate in employment because of race, color, religion, gender, or national origin.

4   Forbids discrimination in compensation and employment on account of age.

1   Regulates overtime pay for nonmanagerial employees.

1   Regulates child labor.

2   Eliminates pay differentials based on gender.

5   Requires federal government to set health and safety standards.

6   Protects the retirement income of employees and retirees.

7   Prohibits discrimination in employment based on pregnancy.

LABOR-MANAGEMENT RELATIONS

OUTLINE

LEARNING GOALS

After studying this chapter, you should be able to:

1. Understand the history of the U.S. union movement, and describe labor organizations today.

2. Understand the role of federal legislation in the growth of unionism and collective bargaining.

3. Explain the union organizing process.

4. Explain the collective bargaining process.

5. Understand the important issues and items in labor agreements.

6. Discuss the grievance procedure.

7. Identify and describe the economic weapons of unions and management.

8. Discuss trends affecting the American workforce and labor-management relations.

TESTING YOUR KNOWLEDGE

TRUE-FALSE

Directions: Test your knowledge of each learning goal by answering the true-false questions following each goal.

1.   Understand the history of the U.S. union movement, and describe labor organizations today.

    _____ a.   The forerunners of unions began to develop toward the end of the 1700s based on guilds or societies of skilled craftsmen.

    _____ b.   The Knights of Labor was the first major national labor organization in the United States.

    _____ c.   The American Federation of Labor (AFL) was formed by craft groups and organized by skilled trade or craft.

    _____ d.   The Congress of Industrial Organizations (CIO) competed with the American Federation of Labor (AFL) to organize workers by craft.

    _____ e.   Today, the AFL-CIO is the umbrella organization for all U.S. labor unions.

    _____ f.   Today, the percentage of all workers who belong to unions is lower than it has been for decades.

    _____ g.   The main functions of the local union are collective bargaining, worker relations and member services, and community and political activities.

2.   Understand the role of federal legislation in the growth of unionism and collective bargaining.

    _____ a.   Before 1932 (the Norris LaGuardia Act) a company faced with striking workers could obtain a court order (injunction) to order them back to work.

    _____ b.   The National Labor Relations Act (Wagner Act) was significant because it encouraged the formation of unions and collective bargaining.

    _____ c.   The National Labor Relations Board (NLRB) enforces the Wagner Act.

    _____ d.   The 1947 Taft-Hartley Act repealed the Wagner Act.

    _____ e.   The 1947 Taft-Hartley Act included emergency strike procedures.

    _____ f.   In 1959 Congress passed the Internal Affairs Act to deal with internal affairs of labor unions such as rules for electing union officials and safeguards to help make unions financially sound.

3.   Explain the union organizing process.

    _____ a.   Unions can gain new members in two ways: a unionized employer hires more workers or the employees of a nonunion employer form or join a union.

    _____ b.   A nonunion employer becomes organized through a bargaining campaign.

    _____ c.   A union must get authorization cards from at least 30 percent of the employees in order for the NLRB to hold a certification election.

    _____ d.   The bargaining unit consists of the employees who will be represented by a particular union.

    _____ e.   Before a union certificate election, the union can campaign with speeches, memos, and meetings, but the employer is not allowed to do so.

    _____ f.   A decertification election allows workers to vote out a union. .

4. Explain the collective bargaining process.

　　　　　　a.　Collective bargaining is the process of negotiating, administering, and interpreting labor contracts.

　　　　　　b.　The bargaining agenda lists the issues that will be discussed during the bargaining process.

　　　　　　c.　Collective bargaining is administered by the National Labor Bureau.

5. Understand the important issues and the items in labor agreements.

　　　　　　a.　The most common form of union security today is the agency shop.

　　　　　　b.　Typically, much negotiating effort goes into wage increases and fringe-benefit improvements.

　　　　　　c.　Basic items for negotiation are wages, hours, and working conditions.

　　　　　　d.　Seniority is an established right and no longer an issue for collective bargaining.

　　　　　　e.　A management-rights clause may be included in the union contract to protect management prerogatives.

　　　　　　f.　Three-quarters of the U.S. states have right-to-work laws.

6. Discuss the grievance procedure.

　　　　　　a.　A grievance is a formal complaint, by an employee or by the union, that management has violated some part of the contract.

　　　　　　b.　A grievance is a formal complaint, by a supervisor or by the company, that the union has violated some part of the contract.

　　　　　　c.　Arbitration is the settling of a labor-management dispute between the two parties.

　　　　　　d.　A decision from arbitration may sometimes be appealed through the courts.

7. Identify and describe the economic weapons of unions and management.

　　　　　　a.　The strike is the most often used union weapon.

　　　　　　b.　A boycott is the union's effort to keep people from doing business with a firm involved in a labor dispute.

　　　　　　c.　Secondary boycotts are illegal since the 1989 Landrum-Griffin Act.

　　　　　　d.　Lockout is the term for management's action to refuse workers entry to the workplace.

　　　　　　e.　A company can file for bankruptcy in the face of a strike.

8. Discuss trends affecting the American workforce and labor-management relations.

　　　　　　a.　The changing mix of ages, sexes, and races in the labor force is affecting union membership.

　　　　　　b.　The changing technology in the workplace is affecting both the workers and the relationship between labor and management

　　　　　　c.　Union membership has been a top priority for "split-shift parents"—those working weekends or evenings in dual-income families.

MULTIPLE-CHOICE

Directions: Put the letter of the response that best completes each of the following statements in the blank at the left.

_____ 1. In recent years, union membership as a percentage of the workforce has

    a. increased slightly.
    b. increased significantly.
    c. declined.
    d. been cyclical.

_____ 2. Labor unions whose members work in government agencies are called

    a. employee associations.
    b. governmental unions.
    c. governmental-charted associations.
    d. employee-mutual federations.

_____ 3. The union officials who represent union members to management at the lowest level are

    a. field officers.
    b. labor leaders.
    c. foremen.
    d. shop stewards.

_____ 4. The forerunners of unions—guilds and societies—began toward the end of the

    a. 1600s.
    b. 1700s.
    c. 1800s.
    d. 1930s.

_____ 5. The Knights of Labor was first organized by a group of

    a. clothing workers.
    b. miners.
    c. railroad workers.
    d. Knights of Columbus.

_____ 6. The next major force on the labor scene after the Knights of Labor was the

    a. CIO.
    b. AFL.
    c. NLRB.
    d. UMW.

_____   7.   Which of the following is *not* true?

   a.   From 1935 to the 1950s, the AFL and CIO were fierce rivals.
   b.   John L. Lewis and his union, the United Mine Workers, broke away from the AFL to form the CIO.
   c.   In 1955, the AFL and the CIO merged into one union.
   d.   Samuel Adams was the first president of the AFL-CIO.

_____   8.   Prior to the passage of the _____ Act, a company faced with a strike could get the courts to require the employees to return to work.

   a.   Norris-LaGuardia
   b.   Landrum-Griffin
   c.   Wagner
   d.   Consolidated Practices

_____   9.   The act that gave workers the right to organize and bargain collectively was the _____ Act.

   a.   Norris-LaGuardia
   b.   Landrum-Griffin
   c.   Wagner
   d.   Consolidated Practices.

_____   10.   A set of unfair union practices was designated by the

   a.   Wagner Act.
   b.   Taft-Hartley Act.
   c.   NLRB.
   d.   Consolidated Practices Act.

_____   11.   Collective bargaining is overseen by the

   a.   Wagner Act.
   b.   Taft-Hartley Act.
   c.   NLRB.
   d.   Consolidated Practices Act.

_____   12.   Once contact has been made between employees and a representative of a union, the next step in an organizing campaign is

   a.   the employer's counter campaign.
   b.   signing authorization cards.
   c.   petitioning the NLRB for a certification election.
   d.   defining the bargaining unit.

_____   13.   A right-to-work provision says that

   a.   a state can make all forms of union security illegal.
   b.   union shops are illegal.
   c.   federal law guarantees to any worker who qualifies for a job but objects to union membership, the right to work without joining the union.
   d.   management guarantees the right to work by vetoing the union.

_____ 14. The management rights clause in a labor agreement specifies the area of

    a. union affairs that management can vote in.
    b. union affairs that management may not participate in.
    c. management control and operation free of any union consideration.
    d. management control subject to joint approval from the union.

_____ 15. The cost of living (COLA) adjustment clause is usually tied to the

    a. profit potential of the company.
    b. actual year-end profits of the company.
    c. consumer price index.
    d. prime interest rate.

_____ 16. Higher pay for less desirable work shifts, payments for certain nonwork times, and income maintenance plans are all examples of

    a. cost-of-living adjustments.
    b. fringe benefits.
    c. management rights area.
    d. supplementary unemployment benefits.

_____ 17. Mediators are assigned by the ____ to help settle labor disputes.

    a. Federal Labor Board
    b. Federal Mediation and Conciliation Service
    c. National Labor Relations Board
    d. National Labor Disputes Board

_____ 18. A(n) ____ shop is a place where only union members may be hired.

    a. union
    b. closed
    c. agency
    d. open

_____ 19. A weapon *not* used by unions in a labor dispute is the

    a. mutual aid pact.
    b. primary boycott.
    c. secondary boycott.
    d. corporate campaign.

_____ 20. Which of the following is *not* a weapon used by management in a labor dispute?

    a. mutual aid pact
    b. lockout
    c. strikebreakers
    d. corporate campaign

MATCHING QUESTIONS: SECTION A

a. agency shop   g. bargaining unit
b. arbitration   h. international union
c. closed shop   i. collective bargaining
d. conglomerate union   j. industrial union
e. craft union   k. right-to-work laws
f. Wagner Act   l. employee associations

MATCHING DEFINITIONS.   *Directions: Match the terms above with the definitions below.*

_____   1.   Settling of labor-management disputes by third party.

_____   2.   Represents a wide variety of workers and industries.

_____   3.   Represents workers in a single industry, regardless of their skill level or occupation.

_____   4.   Only union members can be hired.

_____   5.   Represents workers in a single occupation or craft.

_____   6.   Labor organizations whose members work in government.

_____   7.   Established the National Labor Relations Board in 1935; encouraged the formation of unions and collective bargaining.

_____   8.   The process of negotiating labor agreements between union members and management.

_____   9.   Employees can work at unionized company without having to join the union.

_____ 10.   Workers do not have to join union but they must pay the union a fee.

_____ 11.   A national union with membership outside the United States.

_____ 12.   Those eligible to vote for union certification.

MATCHING QUESTIONS: SECTION B

a. labor union   g. benefit rights
b. mediation   h. job rights
c. national union   i. open shop
d. union shop   j. primary boycott
e. secondary boycott   k. shop stewards
f. grievance   l. union certification election

MATCHING DEFINITIONS.   *Directions: Match the terms above with the definitions below.*

_____   1.   Union's effort to keep people from doing business with a firm involved in a labor dispute.

_____   2.   Based on seniority, related to job choice, shift preference, overtime work, and job transfers.

_____ 3. An organization that represents workers in their disputes with management over wages, hours, and working conditions.

_____ 4. Nonunion people can be hired but they must join the union.

_____ 5. Workers do not have to join union, and they do not have to pay fees or dues.

_____ 6. Targets companies doing business with a firm that is the subject of a primary boycott.

_____ 7. A group of many unions, within an industry, a skilled trade, or geographic area.

_____ 8. Based on seniority, related to areas such as vacation eligibility, severance pay, and pensions.

_____ 9. Union representatives in the plant.

_____ 10. Administered by the National Labor Relations Board (NLRB) to determine whether the employees want to be represented by a union.

_____ 11. A process wherein a specialist employs communication and persuasion with union and management negotiators to seek agreement.

_____ 12. Formal complaint, by an employee or the union, that management has violated some part of the contract.

CHAPTER REVIEW

1. What power and authority does a national union have?

2. Which of the cited laws (legal environment) do you consider most significant?

3. The number of union members may be high in absolute terms, but the membership as a percentage of the workforce has dropped dramatically. How can unions increase membership in today's environment?

4. What are management rights?

5. Does the fact that a dispute has to go to arbitration mean the management process has "failed"?

6. What is the difference between primary and secondary boycotts?

7. The traditional industrial relations system—based on collective bargaining, the grievance procedure, and seniority systems—was developed in a period of U.S. economic dominance and growth. Now the economy is global, and the United States must deal with increasing competition. How does that affect the future for labor-management relations?

EXPERIENCING BUSINESS 13-1   UNION VALUES

Organizational (or corporate) culture is "the set of attitudes, values, and standards of accepted behavior that distinguishes one organization from another."

Unions are formal organizations which must be "businesslike" and well managed to succeed. The labor movement is an integral part of our U.S. history, and as individuals we learn about unions through many sources. Assuming that we individually have opinions about unions and what they stand for, how valid and complete are our opinions and impressions?

Increasingly, unions are doing what other well-managed organizations are doing—explicitly setting down their values as part of the recorded culture for their members. The following are quoted from the constitution of the International Union, United Automobile, Aerospace, and Agricultural Implement Workers of America (the UAW):

> "The precepts of democracy require that workers through their union participate meaningfully in making decisions affecting their welfare and that of the communities in which they live."

> "Essential to the UAW's purpose is to afford the opportunity for workers to master their work environment; to achieve not only improvement in their economic status but, of equal importance, to gain from their labors a greater measure of dignity, of self-fulfillment and self-worth."

To do this exercise:

Contact a local union and obtain some literature by the local or their national union.

What are some of the key values set forth there? How do they define the union's purpose and mission?

EXPERIENCING BUSINESS 13-2 — BILL OF RIGHTS

From around 1930 to the 1960s, public policy came to be based on the "labor law approach." This was the period that largely shaped unionism as we think of it today.

One of the significant pieces of legislation, the Landrum-Griffin Act (Labor-Management Reporting and Disclosure Act) of 1959 dealt mostly with internal affairs and sought two broad objectives:

> To make union officials more responsible for the proper use of union funds by establishing detailed reporting requirements.

> To make unions more democratic by providing members with certain rights.

One section, Title I, is generally referred to as the union member's "bill of rights." If a worker has a complaint about the union, the employer's personnel department need not get involved. The worker can contact the nearest office of the Department of Labor, which will investigate the complaint.

To do this exercise:

Answer the following questions.

1. What was the union member's "bill of rights"?

2. Why was such legislation considered necessary?

This exercise can be readily completed in a college library. However, if you have access to someone knowledgeable in labor relations or union history, it may be interesting to discuss it with them.

(Answers are provided at the end of the chapter.)

ANSWER KEY (CHAPTER 13)

TRUE-FALSE

1.	a.	T	3.	a.	T		e.	T
	b.	T		b.	F		f.	F
	c.	T		c.	T	6.	a.	T
	d.	F		d.	T		b.	F
	e.	F		e.	F		c.	F
	f.	T		f.	T		d.	T
	g.	T	4.	a.	T	7.	a.	F
2.	a.	T		b.	T		b.	T
	b.	T		c.	F		c.	F
	c.	T	5.	a.	F		d.	T
	d.	F		b.	T		e.	T
	e.	T		c.	T	8.	a.	T
	f.	F		d.	F		b.	T
							c.	F

MULTIPLE-CHOICE

1. c	11. c
`2. a	12. b
3. d	13. a
4. b	14. c
5. a	15. c
6. b	16. b
7. d	17. b
8. a	18. b
9. c	19. a
10. b	20. d

MATCHING QUESTIONS: SECTION A

1. b	7. f
2. d	8. i
3. j	9. k
4. c	10. a
5. e	11. h
6. l	12. g

MATCHING QUESTIONS: SECTION B

1. j	7. c
2. h	8. g
3. a	9. k
4. d	10. l
5. i	11. b
6. e	12. f

CHAPTER REVIEW

1. The local unions have the significant power of collective bargaining. However, the national union can be a strong leader, as is the UAW in the auto industry. In a more general sense, the national unions have the significant clout to lobby for legislation, consideration, etc.

2. Answers will vary. However, the Wagner Act (National Labor Relations Act) was a watershed, creating a new environment for labor and signaling a shift in public policy.

3. Unions will have to target the service industries and more white-collar jobs. Union success may hinge on what value they can offer to these categories of prospects.

4. The traditional right to decide and direct all areas of the work tasks, quality standards, employee supervision, and work environment. These rights often conflict with union positions on such issues as seniority and craft classification.

5. Answers will vary. Many would say yes, but consider the mechanism and the orderly and equitable resolution that arbitration offers. In a broad sense arbitration may be considered part of the "management process" when parties are too close to an issue to be objective; the use of arbitration may be the best recourse.

6. A primary boycott is directed against the company involved in a labor dispute. A secondary boycott is directed against companies that do business with a company targeted in a primary boycott.

7. A broad question. Many comments are possible, but key is the increasing pressure for "partnership" with more cooperation—a "sink or swim together" approach. This need for cooperation affects the work rules and work conditions of individual jobs to look for such changes as productivity improvement or union give-backs.

EXPERIENCING BUSINESS 13-2

1. What was that "bill of rights"?

    Title I of the Landrum-Griffin Act (Labor-Management Reporting and Disclosure Act) of 1959 created a bill of rights for union members in dealing with their unions. It assured members equal rights, freedom of speech and assembly, the right to sue the union, and other safeguards.

2. Why was such legislation considered necessary?

    During the twelve years following passage of the Labor-Management Relations Act (Taft-Hartley) in 1947, it became evident that some union leaders were not properly representing their members' interests. As the shift in public policy was toward a "labor law approach," it was consistent to address the concern with legislation.

PART SIX

MARKETING MANAGEMENT

Part Six explores the world of marketing. Marketing theory and process are examined using the elements of the marketing mix: product and price, distribution, and promotional strategies.

THE MARKETING PROCESS AND MARKETING RESEARCH

OUTLINE

LEARNING GOALS

After studying this chapter, you should be able to:

1. Explain the marketing concept.

2. Describe the four elements of the marketing mix.

3. Understand how the marketing environment can affect marketing decisions.

4. Explain how consumers make decisions.

5. Explain how markets can be segmented.

6. Understand how marketing research is used to minimize marketing risk.

TESTING YOUR KNOWLEDGE

TRUE-FALSE

Directions: Test your knowledge of each learning goal by answering the true-false questions following each goal.

1.   Explain the marketing concept.

_____   a.   The marketing concept began right after the Industrial Revolution.

_____   b.   The marketing concept focuses on raising output and producing goods of uniform quality.

_____   c.   The first aspect of the marketing concept is goal orientation.

_____   d.   The marketing concept is applied by the firm's marketing department.

_____   e.   A firm should be consumer oriented only to the extent that it also achieves organizational goals.

2.   Describe the four elements of the marketing mix.

_____   a.   McDonald's and Wendy's have roughly the same marketing mix.

_____   b.   Marketing strategy typically starts with the product.

_____   c.   Marketers believe that a good product can be sold successfully anywhere.

_____   d.   Pricing strategy is based on production cost and on demand.

_____   e.   Public relations plays a special role in promotion.

_____   f.   Marketing strategies for consumer and industrial products are very similar.

3.   Understand how the marketing environment can affect marketing decisions.

_____   a.   Today, barely a third of all grocery shoppers read labels on food.

_____   b.   The slowing rate of U.S. population growth will send marketers looking for new ways to increase sales.

_____   c.   Marketers need not focus on consumers over age 50, because they don't have much money to spend.

_____   d.   Growing regions of the country, such as the Far West and the Mountain states, offer good marketing opportunities.

_____   e.   Low inflation always results in lots of consumer spending.

_____   f.   Most managers in not-for-profit organizations have little or no background in marketing but must generate and manage large sums of money.

_____   g.   Selling tickets for charity balls and dinners is the goal of social marketing.

4.   Explain how consumers make decisions.

_____   a.   Individual and social factors can influence the consumer decision-making process.

_____   b.   A buying decision starts with problem recognition.

_____   c.   Family is one of the key social factors affecting decision making.

5.   Explain how markets can be segmented.

_____   a.   Psychographics provide the skeleton for consumer needs, but demographics add meat to the bones.

_____ b. Benefit segmentation is based on consumer characteristics rather than on what a product will do.

_____ c. Heavy users often account for a very large portion of a product's sales.

_____ d. Demographic segmentation is the most common form of market segmentation.

_____ e. Advertising airplane fares to Florida from New York in February is an example of geographic segmentation.

6. Understand how marketing research is used to minimize marketing risk.

_____ a. Primary marketing research data has been collected primarily for a project other than the current one.

_____ b. Those firms using mall-intercept interviews are gathering primary data.

_____ c. Telephone interviews are more expensive than door-to-door interviews.

_____ d. Single-source research uses electronic monitoring tools to test marketing effectiveness.

MULTIPLE-CHOICE

Directions: *Put the letter of the response that best completes each of the following statements in the blank at the left.*

_____ 1. When marketing managers identify the groups of those people who are most likely to buy their products, they have a

   a. consumer orientation.
   b. production orientation.
   c. decision making.
   d. goal orientation.

_____ 2. Which of the following is *not* a specialty of marketing?

   a. product and service offerings
   b. a distribution system created to reach a certain group
   c. producing and assembling
   d. pricing

_____ 3. The marketing concept is

   a. finding out what the consumer wants and producing it at a reasonable profit.
   b. goal orientation.
   c. consumer orientation.
   d. promotion.

_____ 4. The unique blend of product and service offerings, a distribution system designed to reach a target market, pricing, and promotion is known as

   a. advertising.
   b. publicity.
   c. promotion.
   d. the marketing mix.

5. The process of separating, identifying, and evaluating various strata or layers of a market is called

    a. demographics.
    b. lifestyle.
    c. market segmentation.
    d. utility.

6. The element of the marketing mix that uses coupons, catalogs, premiums, contests, and other special offers is

    a. public relations.
    b. advertising.
    c. sales promotion.
    d. personal selling.

7. Which of the following is *not* an example of social marketing?

    a. an ad campaign for use of auto safety belts
    b. a grocery store accepting plastic bags and bottles for recycling
    c. the state highway patrol offering free coffee for drivers over a holiday weekend
    d. a candidate for political office speaking at a state fair

8. Psychographics refers to the development of

    a. regional, urban, or rural profiles.
    b. psychological profiles of consumers and their lifestyles.
    c. distinctive lifestyles.
    d. age, sex, and income profiles.

9. A demographic profile would contain data on

    a. age, region, and lifestyle.
    b. personality, lifestyle, and values.
    c. distinctive lifestyles.
    d. vital statistics such as age, birth, death, gender, and race.

10. Field research services often utilize this method of interviewing to cut costs:

    a. mail
    b. door-to-door
    c. focus group
    d. mall intercept

11. What form of interviewing uses one-way mirrors for client observers, is held in a conference room setting, and is led by a moderator?

    a. focus group
    b. mall interviewing
    c. mail
    d. phone

_____ 12.   ____ utility means having the product where consumers would like to buy it or use it.

    a.   Form
    b.   Place
    c.   Time
    d.   Possession

_____ 13.   _____ utility is created by storage.

    a.   Place
    b.   Form
    c.   Time
    d.   Possession

_____ 14.   One aspect of _____ strategy is deciding how many stores will handle the product in a geographic area.

    a.   product
    b.   distribution
    c.   pricing
    d.   promotion

_____ 15.   Many people feel that ____ is the most exciting part of the marketing mix.

    a.   promotion
    b.   pricing
    c.   distribution
    d.   product strategy

_____ 16.   About ____ percent of U.S. consumers regard themselves as environmentalists.

    a.   50
    b.   60
    c.   70
    d.   80

_____ 17.   The average age of today's consumer is moving toward _____.

    a.   25
    b.   35
    c.   40
    d.   45

_____ 18.   Which of the following is the first step in the decision-making process?

    a.   problem recognition
    b.   stimulus
    c.   information
    d.   outcome expectation
    e.   quality evaluation

_____ 19. Crest toothpaste has a product that prevents cavities and another that stops tartar buildup. These products are targeted by _____ segmentation.

    a. volume
    b. benefit
    c. psychographic
    d. demographic

_____ 20. The greatest concern to marketers is (are)

    a. the distribution of consumer income.
    b. inflation.
    c. recession.
    d. All are concerns.

MATCHING QUESTIONS: SECTION A

a. form utility
b. target market
c. product strategy
d. possession utility
e. distribution strategy
f. promotion strategy
g. consumer orientation
h. place utility
i. exchange

j. utility
k. marketing concept
l. goal orientation
m. product orientation
n. pricing strategy
o. marketing mix
p. time utility
q. marketing

MATCHING DEFINITIONS.   *Directions: Match the term above with the definitions below.*

_____ 1. Planning and executing the conception, pricing, promotion, and distribution of ideas, goods, and services.

_____ 2. Takes place when the consumer trades money for desired goods or services.

_____ 3. The ability of a good or service to satisfy consumer desires.

_____ 4. When a good or service is transformed into something more desirable or usable.

_____ 5. Having the product where consumers want it.

_____ 6. Having the good or service available when the consumer wants it.

_____ 7. Making it possible for the consumer to complete a transaction and use the product.

_____ 8. Identifying and producing goods or services that the consumer wants.

_____ 9. Assumes that people want to buy products at the lowest possible price, so the firm should produce what it does best.

_____ 10. Identifying a firm's customers and producing something that meets their needs and wants.

_____ 11. Achieving corporate goals such as profit.

_____ 12. A specific group of consumers toward which a firm directs its marketing efforts.

_____ 13. Pricing, promotion, distribution and product offering.

_____ 14. Choosing a brand name, packaging and service program.

_____ 15. Deciding how many stores can handle the product in an area.

_____ 16. Is based on demand and cost.

_____ 17. Personal selling, advertising, public relations, and sales promotion.

MATCHING QUESTION: SECTION B

a. demography   i. consumer products
b. social marketing   j. geographic segmentation
c. demographic segmentation   k. volume segmentation
d. benefit segmentation   l. secondary data
e. focus group   m. market segmentation
f. psychographic segmentation   n. marketing research
g. consumer behavior   o. primary data
h. industrial products

MATCHING DEFINITIONS.   *Directions: Match the terms above with the definitions below.*

_____ 1. Products and services bought by the end user.

_____ 2. Products bought for use in producing other products.

_____ 3. The study of vital statistics.

_____ 4. The application of marketing to social issues.

_____ 5. The actions people take in buying goods and services.

_____ 6. Separating, identifying, and evaluating layers of a market.

_____ 7. Age, education, gender, and income.

_____ 8. Segmenting markets by region.

_____ 9. Segmentation by personality or lifestyle.

_____ 10. Is based on what a product will do.

_____ 11. Is based on the amount purchased.

_____ 12. Involves collecting, recording, and analyzing data.

_____ 13. Collected from the original source.

_____ 14. Collected for a product other than the current one.

_____ 15. Brings together people from a target market to discuss specific products and brands.

CHAPTER REVIEW

1. Explain the marketing concept.

2. List and describe the four elements of the marketing mix.

    a.

    b.

    c.

    d.

3. Identify and describe five environments that affect the overall marketing environment.

4. How do consumers make decisions?

5. Identify and describe the five basic forms of market segmentation.

   a.

   b.

   c.

   d.

   e.

6. What is the difference between primary and secondary data?

EXPERIENCING BUSINESS 14-1

MARKETING TERMS

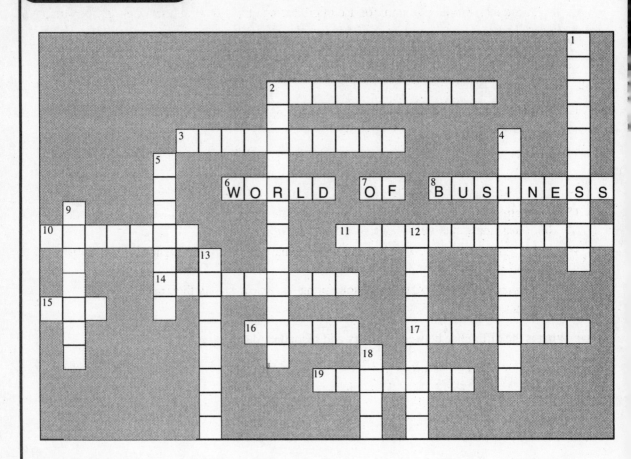

ACROSS

2 Study of vital statistics, such as ages and locations of people.

3 ___ products: Products bought for use in producing other goods and services, or operating a business.

6 WORLD

7 OF

8 BUSINESS

10 _____ strategy: Decisions about specific elements of a product or service, such as brand names, packaging, etc.

11 Market _____: Process of separating, identifying, and evaluating the layers of a market in order to design a marketing mix.

14 _____ strategy: Decisions about how to advertise and sell a good or service.

15 Marketing _____: Blend of product offering, pricing, promotional methods, and distribution systems that will reach a specific group of customers.

16 _____ groups: Groups of people from target markets who are brought together to discuss products and other marketing ideas.

17 Process in which two parties give something of value to satisfy their needs.

19 The ability of a good or service to satisfy customer desires.

DOWN

1 _____ utility: Making it possible for consumers to complete a transaction and gain the right to use the product.

2 _____ strategy: Decisions about how to deliver a good or service to the consumer.

4 (two words) Research data collected directly from the original source for the current project.

5 Marketing _____: Idea that a firm first identifies consumer needs and then produces goods or services that satisfy the needs.

9 _____ strategy: Decisions about how to price a good or service, determined by demand and cost.

12 Process of planning and executing the conception, pricing, promotion, and distribution of goods and services to create exchanges that satisfy individual and organizational objectives.

13 _____ products: Goods and services purchased and used by the end user.

18 _____ utility: Having a good or service available when consumers would like to buy or use it.

(Solution is provided at the end of the chapter.)

EXPERIENCING BUSINESS 14-2

MARKETING MIX

The marketing mix is the blend of product offering, pricing, promotional methods, and distribution system (place) that will reach a specific group of customers.

To do this exercise:

Choose an organization for each of the following general areas. Consider the basic product of the organization. Fill in the "4 Ps" matrix for a basic marketing mix.

The organization	A for-profit, goods producer, private sector (an auto maker?)	A not-for-profit, service-oriented, private sector (a hospital?)	A not-for-profit, service-oriented, public sector (a city?)
Product			
Price			
Promotion			
Place			

ANSWER KEY (CHAPTER 14)

TRUE-FALSE

1.	a.	F	3.	a.	F	5.	a.	F
	b.	F		b.	T		b.	F
	c.	F		c.	F		c.	T
	d.	T		d.	T		d.	T
	e.	T		e.	F		e.	T
2.	a.	F		f.	T	6.	a.	F
	b.	T		g.	F		b.	T
	c.	F	4.	a.	T		c.	F
	d.	T		b.	F		d.	T
	e.	T		c.	T			
	f.	F						

MULTIPLE-CHOICE

1.	a	11.	a
2.	c	12.	b
3.	a	13.	c
4.	d	14.	b
5.	c	15.	a
6.	c	16.	d
7.	d	17.	c
8.	b	18.	b
9.	d	19.	b
10.	d	20.	d

MATCHING QUESTIONS: SECTION A

1.	q	7.	d	13.	o
2.	i	8.	k	14.	c
3.	j	9.	m	15.	e
4.	a	10.	g	16.	n
5.	h	11.	l	17.	f
6.	p	12.	b		

MATCHING QUESTIONS: SECTION B

1.	i	6.	m	11.	k
2.	h	7.	c	12.	n
3.	a	8.	j	13.	o
4.	b	9.	f	14.	l
5.	g	10.	d	15.	e

CHAPTER REVIEW

1. The marketing concept is the process of getting the right goods or services to the right people at the right place, time, and price, using the right promotion techniques. This is not as simple as it might seem. All professional sports teams have the same number of players and similar equipment, yet some win more games than others. Why? It's how they put them all together—execution.

2. a. Giving the consumer the *good* or *service* that he/she wants is the first part of the marketing mix.

   b. *Pricing* the good or service (not too high or too low) is a second ingredient to the formula.

   c. *Promotion,* a third part of the mix, involves personal selling, advertising, public relations, and sales promotion such as coupons, premiums, or games.

   d. Last, the firm must decide on the distribution (*place*) of the good or service—what stores and how many should sell the product.

3. The *social/cultural environment* shapes the values of society and groups within society. This influences what the marketing people produce and advertise. For example, dual-career families have more money but less time, so they may want quick meals.

    The *demographic environment* of the U.S. is changing. We are getting older as a society. The number of minority-group families is increasing.

    The *economic environment* is of great concern to people in marketing. Consumer buying is decreased by recessions and unemployment.

    The *technological environment* is constantly changing. Marketers must keep up to date.

    We live in a free enterprise system which makes the *competitive environment* very fierce.

4. A buying decision starts with a stimulus. The stimulus leads to problem recognition. The consumer next gets information about the purchase. He or she then weighs the options and decides whether to make a purchase. The consumer has certain expectations if the purchase is made. Finally, he or she evaluates the quality of the item purchased.

5. a. *Demographic* segmentation uses age, education, gender, income, and family size.

    b. *Geographic* segmentation means segmenting markets by region, city, county, state, or climate.

    c. *Psychographic* segmentation is market segmentation by lifestyles or personality.

    d. *Benefit* segmentation is based on what a product will do rather than on consumer characteristics.

    e. *Volume* segmentation is based on the amount of products purchased.

6. Primary data are collected from the original source to solve a problem. Secondary data have already been collected for a product other than the current one.

EXPERIENCING BUSINESS 14-1

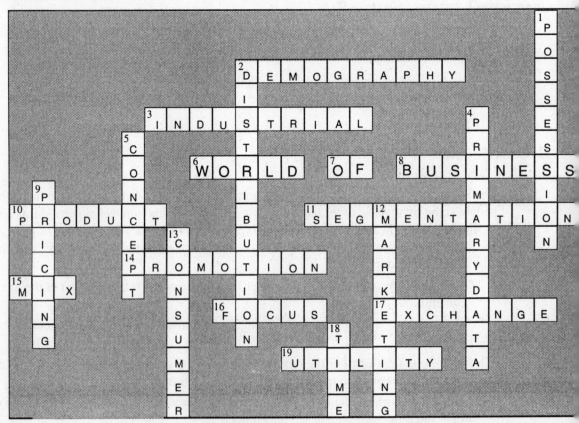

PRODUCT AND PRICE STRATEGIES

OUTLINE

LEARNING GOALS

After studying this chapter, you should be able to:

1. Explain the product concept.
2. Describe a product classification system for consumer and industrial goods.
3. Explain the roles of branding, packaging, and labeling in creating a product.
4. Explain the process of new-product development.
5. List the stages of the product life cycle.
6. Describe the role of pricing in marketing.
7. Explain how prices can be set.
8. Explain price skimming and penetration pricing.
9. Understand the pricing tactics used by marketers to maintain a competitive position.

TESTING YOUR KNOWLEDGE

TRUE-FALSE

Directions: Test your knowledge of each learning goal by answering the true-false questions following each goal.

1.   Explain the product concept.

_____   a.   The creation of a marketing mix normally begins with the product.

_____   b.   A product is any good or service that satisfies wants along with its perceived attributes and benefits.

_____   c.   Products are often a blend of goods and services.

_____   d.   Consumer nondurables are products with poor performance records.

2.   Describe a product classification system for consumer and industrial goods.

_____   a.   Soft drinks, candy bars, and milk are examples of shopping products.

_____   b.   Consumers search hard and long for specialty products.

_____   c.   Expense items are usually large, expensive items with a long life span.

_____   d.   Accessories have the same long-run impact on the firm as installations.

_____   e.   Raw materials are not expense items.

_____   f.   Services are used to plan or support company operations.

3.   Explain the roles of branding, packaging, and labeling in creating a product.

_____   a.   Most industrial and consumer products have a brand name.

_____   b.   Manufacturer brands are sometimes called national brands.

_____   c.   Profit margins are lower on dealer brands than manufacturer brands.

_____   d.   Brand loyalty lets consumers buy with less time, thought, and risk.

_____   e.   Very few new packaging methods have been developed recently.

_____   f.   Federal laws dealing with product labeling date back to 1906.

4.   Explain the process of new-product development.

_____   a.   Creating new products is fairly easy.

_____   b.   Diet Cherry Coke and caffeine-free Coke are line extensions.

_____   c.   Larger firms usually depend solely on employees, customers, investors, and distributors for new ideas.

_____   d.   As new ideas emerge, they are screened against the firm's long- and short-range strategies.

_____   e.   In new product development, actual production of the product is usually the least expensive step.

5.   List the stages of the product life cycle.

_____   a.   Sony turntables are an example of a product in the maturity stage.

_____   b.   Profits are lowest near the end of the growth stage.

_____   c.   Death of a product in the decline stage is inevitable.

6. Describe the role of pricing in marketing.

_____ a. Price can be anything with perceived value.

_____ b. Trade exchanges—barter—is most popular with larger firms.

_____ c. Price is important in determining how much a firm earns.

_____ d. Value marketing means offering customers high quality at high prices.

7. Explain how prices can be set.

_____ a. The most common form of cost-based pricing is markup pricing.

_____ b. Traditionally department stores used a 40 percent markup.

_____ c. Tradition, competition, store image, and stock turnover influence markups.

_____ d. Increasing a firm's sales lowers the break-even point and expands profits.

8. Explain price skimming and penetration pricing.

_____ a. For most products, skimming is a long-range strategy.

_____ b. Penetration pricing may discourage competitors from entering the market.

_____ c. Price skimming is often used with a product that uses a new technology.

9. Understand the pricing tactics used by marketers to maintain a competitive position.

_____ a. Items that are leader priced are usually not well known.

_____ b. Department stores rarely use leader pricing.

_____ c. Odd prices are used to imply bargains.

_____ d. Psychology plays a big role in how consumers view prices.

MULTIPLE-CHOICE

Directions: Put the letter of the response that best completes each of the following statements in the blank at the left.

_____ 1. What is a name, term, symbol, or design used to identify a company's products and differentiate them from a competitor's products?

     a. trade symbol
     b. brand
     c. copyright
     d. patent

_____ 2. What is the legally protected design, name, or other identifying mark associated with a company or its product?

     a. brand
     b. generic name
     c. trademark
     d. family name

_____ 3. Brands that carry the wholesaler's or retailer's name rather than that of the manufacturer are

     a. dealer brands.
     b. national brands.
     c. family brands.
     d. generic brands.

_____ 4. What is the term for products sold at low cost, in packages bearing only the name of the product?

    a. standard products
    b. private brands
    c. generic products
    d. designer products

_____ 5. Convenience products are

    a. usually expensive.
    b. relatively inexpensive.
    c. hard to find.
    d. specific goods.

_____ 6. Which of the following is *not* an example of a capital product?

    a. buildings
    b. paper
    c. large machines
    d. airplanes

_____ 7. Which one of the following is *not* a stage in the product life cycle?

    a. decline stage
    b. maturity stage
    c. level stage
    d. introductory stage

_____ 8. Profits are highest near the end of the _____ stage.

    a. introductory
    b. maturity
    c. growth
    d. decline

_____ 9. When sales begin to fall permanently, the decline stage has set in. The rate of decline is governed by

    a. poor advertising.
    b. poor packaging.
    c. need for new positioning.
    d. how rapidly consumer taste is changing.

_____ 10. The second stage in a product life cycle is the _____ stage.

    a. growth
    b. level
    c. introductory
    d. maturity

_____ 11. What is the term for the stage of a product life cycle when sales rise for a while and eventually level off?

   a. introductory stage
   b. decline stage
   c. level stage
   d. maturity stage

_____ 12. Which of the following is the last stage in a product life cycle after it reaches the market?

   a. maturity
   b. decline
   c. growth
   d. introduction

_____ 13. Which one of the following is *not* a characteristic of the introductory stage?

   a. high profits
   b. little competition
   c. frequent product modification
   d. limited distribution

_____ 14. Which of the following is realized by a firm that continues to produce units of output as long as the revenue is greater than the cost?

   a. prestige profit
   b. profit maximization
   c. profit margin
   d. profit target

_____ 15. A target return on investment is used by a company to

   a. maximize sales.
   b. sell a good at the highest price.
   c. pay for bills outstanding.
   d. determine the price that will give it a desired profitability.

_____ 16. If a company estimates that it will cost $1 million to develop, launch, and market a new product, and the net profit is forecast to be $100,000, the return on investment will be _____ percent.

   a. 1
   b. 5
   c. 10
   d. 20

_____ 17. Which of the following can be a way to test the market to find what buyers are willing to pay?

   a. leader pricing
   b. price lining
   c. price skimming
   d. penetration pricing

18. The practice of lowering an item's price as it moves through the product life cycle is called

    a. price lining.
    b. profit maximization.
    c. penetration pricing.
    d. price skimming.

19. The practice of offering items at mass-market prices with the expected return of a large sales volume is called

    a. odd-even pricing.
    b. penetration pricing.
    c. leader pricing.
    d. bait-and-switch.

20. The psychological tactic of offering items for sale at prices slightly below whole-dollar figures is called

    a. bait-and-switch.
    b. leader pricing.
    c. below-dollar-value pricing.
    d. odd-even pricing.

MATCHING QUESTIONS: SECTION A

a. specialty products		i. shopping products
b. expense items		j. brand loyalty
c. dealer brands		k. value marketing
d. capital products		l. trademark
e. manufacturer brand		m. warranty
f. generic products		n. express warranty
g. full warranty		o. brand
h. convenience products		p. product

MATCHING DEFINITIONS.   *Directions:*   *Match the terms above with the definitions or examples below.*

1. Any good or service that satisfies wants.

2. Soft drinks, candy bars, and milk.

3. Expensive jewelry and designer clothing.

4. Furniture and automobiles.

5. Buildings and large machines.

6. Printer ribbon and paper.

7. The product identifier for a company.

8. Legally exclusive design or name.

9. Also known as national brands.

_____ 10. Craftsman, Diehard, and Kenmore.

_____ 11. Carry no brand names.

_____ 12. Preference for a particular brand.

_____ 13. Guarantees the quality of a good or service.

_____ 14. "100 percent cotton."

_____ 15. Means the manufacturer must meet certain minimum federal standards.

_____ 16. Offering a product of high quality at a fair price.

MATCHING QUESTIONS: SECTION B

a.	line extension	i.	flanker brands
b.	price	j.	innovative maturity
c.	brainstorming	k.	target return on investment
d.	product life cycle	l.	breakeven point
e.	profit maximization	m.	total profit
f.	markup pricing	n.	total cost
g.	franchise extension	o.	screening
h.	new product		

MATCHING DEFINITIONS.   *Directions: Match the terms above with the definitions or examples below.*

_____ 1. Simplesse by Nutra Sweet Company.

_____ 2. Hampton Inns and Embassy Suites.

_____ 3. Diet Coke and caffeine-free Coke.

_____ 4. Reynolds plastic wrap.

_____ 5. Used to generate new-product ideas.

_____ 6. Checking ideas against the firm's new-product goals and its long range strategies.

_____ 7. A pattern of sales and profits over some period.

_____ 8. The use of creative marketing to prolong the life of a product.

_____ 9. The perceived value that is exchanged for something else.

_____ 10. Sum of total variable costs plus total fixed costs.

_____ 11. The goal is to get the largest profit.

_____ 12. Used by 3M, P&G, GE, and DuPont.

_____ 13. The most common form of cost-based pricing.

_____ 14. The point at which costs are covered and additional sales result in profit.

_____ 15. Total revenue minus total cost.

MATCHING QUESTIONS: SECTION C

a.	fixed cost contribution	i.	variable costs
b.	leader pricing	j.	penetration pricing
c.	total revenue	k.	cash rebate
d.	bundling	l.	prestige pricing
e.	unbundling	m.	odd-even pricing
f.	loss leader	n.	fixed costs
g.	economies of scale	o.	price skimming
h.	total cost		

MATCHING DEFINITIONS.   *Directions: Match the terms above with the definitions below.*

_____ 1. Costs that do not vary with output.

_____ 2. Costs that change with output.

_____ 3. The selling price per unit minus the variable cost per unit.

_____ 4. The selling price per unit times the number of units sold.

_____ 5. The total of the variable costs and the fixed costs.

_____ 6. Charging a high price for a new product.

_____ 7. Selling new products at low prices.

_____ 8. Cost per unit decreases when large quantities are produced.

_____ 9. Pricing well-known items low enough to attract many customers.

_____ 10. A product priced below cost.

_____ 11. Grouping two or more items together and pricing them as one.

_____ 12. Price reductions made after products are purchased.

_____ 13. Department stores charging for gift wrapping.

_____ 14. Pricing an item at $499.95 or $495.

_____ 15. Raising the price of a product so consumers will perceive it as being of higher quality, status, or value.

CHAPTER REVIEW

1.   What is a product?

2. Identify and give examples of the three categories of consumer products and five types of industrial products.

    Consumer Products

    a.

    b.

    c.

    Industrial Products

    a.

    b.

    c.

    d.

    e.

3. What is the difference between a brand and a trademark?

4. How are flanker brands and line extensions used in marketing?

5. List the four stages of the product life cycle.

    a.

    b.

    c.

    d.

6.   What is price strategy and how is it used?

7.   Explain the role of psychology in how consumers view prices.

EXPERIENCING BUSINESS 15-1   PRODUCT ATTRIBUTES

A product is any want-satisfying good or service, along with its perceived tangible and intangible attributes and benefits. Consumers typically associate multiple attributes with products. Examples of attributes individuals associate with an automobile:

Product	*Attributes*
automobile	purchase price
	warranty
	availability of service
	cost of service/repair
	image

To do this exercise:

Identify some typical attributes associated with the following products.

Product	*Attributes*
1. a soft drink (e.g., Coke)	
2. a beer (e.g., Bud Light)	
3. cable television	
4. air travel	
5. name-brand clothing (e.g., Guess, Levi)	
6. college courses	
7. a college degree	

EXPERIENCING BUSINESS 15-2

PRICING

To do this exercise:

Assume you are the marketing manager of an enterprise in each of the following situations. You have to determine (1) what your pricing objective should be and (2) how to determine what price to charge. You will have to make some assumptions here—make the assumptions you believe are realistic. (One example is provided; what could be another objective for that situation?)

	(1)	(2)
Business/product	Pricing Objective	Basis for setting the price
1. retail clothier/ name-brand clothes	a. meet the competition	comparison shopping, competitors' advertisements, offer to "match" any price
	b. (another?)	
2. electronics sales/ video recorders		
3. tax preparer/ individual tax returns		
4. janitorial services/ cleaning commercial sites		
5. state college or university/ college courses in business		

ANSWER KEY (CHAPTER 15)

TRUE-FALSE

1.	a.	T		e.	F	7.	a.	T
	b.	T		f.	T		b.	T
	c.	T	4.	a.	F		c.	T
	d.	F		b.	T		d.	F
2.	a.	F		c.	F	8.	a.	F
	b.	T		d.	T		b.	T
	c.	F		e.	T		c.	T
	d.	F	5.	a.	F	9.	a.	F
	e.	F		b.	F		b.	F
	f.	T		c.	F		c.	T
3.	a.	T	6.	a.	T		d.	T
	b.	T		b.	F			
	c.	F		c.	T			
	d.	T		d.	F			

MULTIPLE-CHOICE

1.	b		11.	d
2.	c		12.	b
3.	a		13.	a
4.	c		14.	b
5.	b		15.	d
6.	b		16.	c
7.	c		17.	c
8.	c		18.	d
9.	d		19.	b
10.	a		20.	d

MATCHING QUESTIONS: SECTION A

1.	p		9.	e
2.	h		10.	c
3.	a		11.	f
4.	i		12.	j
5.	d		13.	m
6.	b		14.	n
7.	o		15.	g
8.	l		16.	k

MATCHING QUESTIONS: SECTION B

1.	h	9.	b
2.	i	10.	n
3.	a	11.	e
4.	g	12.	k
5.	c	13.	f
6.	o	14.	l
7.	d	15.	m
8.	j		

MATCHING QUESTIONS: SECTION C

1.	n	9.	b
2.	i	10.	f
3.	a	11.	d
4.	c	12.	k
5.	h	13.	e
6.	o	14.	m
7.	j	15.	l
8.	g		

CHAPTER REVIEW

1. A product is any good or service that satisfies wants, along with its perceived attributes and benefits.

2. *Consumer Products*
   a. Convenience products: soft drinks, candy bars, milk, bread, small hardware items
   b. Shopping products: furniture, automobiles, some clothing
   c. Specialty products: expensive jewelry, designer clothing, gourmet dinners

   Industrial Products
   a. Installations: GM's Saturn plant
   b. Accessories: copy machines, computer terminals, table drills
   c. Component parts and materials: a case for a computer, a steering assembly, computer terminals
   d. Raw materials: lumber, coal, copper
   e. Supplies: paper, pencils, paper clips

3. Brands appear in the form of words, names, symbols, designs, or any combination. A trademark is the *legally* exclusive design, name, or other identifying mark associated with a company brand.

4. Flanker brands are used when the company introduces a new brand in an area where it already has products, thus capitalizing on the success of the original product.

5.   a.   Introduction
     b.   Growth
     c.   Maturity
     d.   Decline

6.   Price is important in determining how much a firm earns. It must not be too high or too low. The most common form of cost-based pricing is to add a certain percentage to the cost. Sometimes a firm will charge a high introductory price for a new product. In other cases, a company may sell a new product at low prices in hopes of obtaining a large sales volume. In still other cases, a product may be sold at or below cost to attract customers.

7.   Retailers may use odd-even pricing to attract customers. Instead of offering a television for sale at $600, they advertise it at $595.00.

     In many cases, customers relate quality to price. It is for this reason that some retailers *raise* their prices to give the appearance of quality, status, or prestige.

DISTRIBUTION MANAGEMENT

OUTLINE

LEARNING GOALS

After studying this chapter, you should be able to:

1. Describe the role of distribution channels.

2. Explain why different channels are used for consumer products and industrial products.

3. Decide when a marketer would use exclusive, selective, or intensive distribution.

4. Discuss the functions of wholesalers and their relationships to manufacturers and others in the distribution channels.

5. Distinguish among the types of wholesalers.

6. Contrast the different kinds of retail operations.

7. Explain the goals and functions of physical distribution.

TESTING YOUR KNOWLEDGE

TRUE-FALSE

*Directions: Test your knowledge of each learning goal by answering the true-false questions
following each goal.*

1. Describe the role of distribution channels.

_____ a. A distribution channel is a series of production entities through which goods
and services pass on their way from producers to end users.

_____ b. Distribution facilitators serve to move items in the channel but do not
perform negotiating functions.

_____ c. Channels simplify distribution by reducing the number of transactions to get
a product from manufacturer to the consumer.

_____ d. Sorting out is a channel function that makes decisions about quality of end
items.

_____ e. Accumulation is a channel function that provides working capital to wholesalers.

_____ f. Allocating is a channel function that breaks similar products into smaller
and smaller lots.

_____ g. Functions performed by channel members (middlemen) help increase the
efficiency of the channel.

_____ h. Channel members can be eliminated but their functions cannot.

2. Explain why different channels are used for consumer products and industrial products.

_____ a. Industrial distributors are independent wholesalers that buy related product
lines from many manufacturers and sell them to industrial users.

_____ b. Wholesalers are sales representatives of manufacturers.

_____ c. Consumer product channels tend to be less complex than industrial product
channels.

_____ d. Vertical marketing systems are aligned in a hierarchy of manufacturer to
wholesaler to retailer.

3. Decide when a marketer would use exclusive, selective, or intensive distribution.

_____ a. Market coverage involves how many dealers will be used to distribute the
product in a particular area.

_____ b. The type of product determines the intensity of market coverage.

_____ c. Exclusive distribution means general distribution of exclusive, high-value,
glamour products.

_____ d. Selective distribution means a limited number of dealers in an area.

_____ e. Selective distribution means dealers handle only part of a manufacturer's line.

_____ f. Intensive distribution means broad coverage to sell products everywhere
there are potential customers.

4. Discuss the functions of wholesalers and their relationships to manufacturers and others in the distribution channels.

    _____ a. Wholesalers are brokers that bring together buyers and sellers.

    _____ b. Wholesalers are middlemen that buy finished products from manufacturers and sell them to retailers.

    _____ c. Wholesalers sometimes sell products to manufacturers.

5. Distinguish among the various types of wholesalers.

    _____ a. The three main types of wholesalers include merchant wholesalers, institutions, and brokers.

    _____ b. Manufacturing sales branches, owned and completely controlled by manufacturers, are the fastest-growing form of wholesaling.

    _____ c. Manufacturers' representatives (also called manufacturers' agents) are wholesalers.

6. Contrast the different kinds of retail operations.

    _____ a. In-store retailing includes people who come to the store as well as direct response through media such as television.

    _____ b. Nonstore retailing includes vending, direct selling, and direct response marketing.

    _____ c. Half of all retail sales come from fewer than 10 percent of all retail businesses.

    _____ d. The first step in creating a retail strategy is to choose and buy products to offer consumers.

7. Explain the goals and functions of physical distribution.

    _____ a. Physical distribution consists of all activities concerned with transporting raw materials, component parts, and finished inventory to arrive when needed in usable condition.

    _____ b. Physical distribution has two main goals: good service and timeliness.

    _____ c. Simply cutting distribution costs can be a bad idea.

    _____ d. Order cycle time is the time between placing the order and confirmation of shipment/release.

    _____ e. Physical distribution includes inventory control.

MULTIPLE-CHOICE

Directions: *Put the letter of the response that best completes each of the following statements in the blank at the left.*

_____   1.   A channel of distribution is a

   a.   stage of the marketing sequence.
   b.   sequence of marketing entities through which a product passes on its way from the producer to the final user.
   c.   wholesaler.
   d.   definitive arrangement which distributes all products in an industry through a set channel.

_____   2.   Which of the following are the two basic channels of distribution?

   a.   luxury items and convenience goods
   b.   industrial and short channels
   c.   consumer goods and industrial goods
   d.   custom made and consumer goods

_____   3.   Market coverage can be thought of in three basic degrees:

   a.   exclusive, broker, and speciality store.
   b.   intensive, selective, and exclusive.
   c.   industrial, consumer, and selective.
   d.   intensive, retailer, and manufacturer's representative.

_____   4.   The channel members who buy products either for resale or for industrial use and sell them to others are

   a.   wholesalers.
   b.   retailers.
   c.   agents.
   d.   brokers.

_____   5.   About _____ of all wholesalers offer financing for their customers.

   a.   ten percent.
   b.   a fourth
   c.   half
   d.   two thirds

_____   6.   Independent wholesalers who buy goods from manufacturers on their own account and then resell them to other businesses are called

   a.   manufacturers' sales branches.
   b.   merchant wholesalers.
   c.   manufacturers' representatives.
   d.   discount stores.

_____ 7. The most rapidly growing form of wholesaling is

    a. full service wholesaling.
    b. merchant wholesalers.
    c. manufacturers' sales branches.
    d. manufacturers' agents.

_____ 8. ____ sell finished goods to institutions.

    a. Agents
    b. Brokers
    c. Wholesalers
    d. Retailers

_____ 9. Which of the following are representatives of manufacturers and wholesalers?

    a. agents
    b. distributors
    c. industrial distributors
    d. proxy dealers

_____ 10. About ____ Americans work in retailing.

    a. 5 million
    b. 15 million
    c. 30 million
    d. 53 million

_____ 11. The first task in creating a retail strategy is

    a. defining the market to be served.
    b. developing a product offering.
    c. creating an image.
    d. figuring out where to put the store.

_____ 12. Stores such as Sears, Wal-Mart, J.C. Penney, and K-Mart dominate the

    a. brokerage firms.
    b. manufacturers' sales branches.
    c. wholesale market.
    d. retail market.

_____ 13. Direct response marketing means

    a. door-to-door selling.
    b. selling through catalogs, telephone, and direct mail.
    c. across-the-counter selling.
    d. sales person to customer.

_____ 14. The main advantage of air transportation is

    a. cost.
    b. dependability.
    c. flexibility.
    d. speed.

_____ 15. ____ are the most flexible way to move freight.

    a. Airplanes
    b. Railroads
    c. Trucks
    d. Pipelines

_____ 16. The success of distribution service is measured by

    a. time of arrival.
    b. speed of arrival.
    c. method of transportation.
    d. order cycle time.

_____ 17. The major goals of physical distribution are

    a. quality service and public relations.
    b. cost minimization and repeat sales.
    c. cost minimization and quality service.
    d. quality service and new customers.

_____ 18. Which of the following is the slowest mode of transportation?

    a. water
    b. pipelines
    c. rail
    d. air

_____ 19. The use of large, uniform-sized containers for shipping goods is called

    a. containerization.
    b. container utilization.
    c. piggyback.
    d. standard usage.

_____ 20. Which of the following is *not* a function of physical distribution?

    a. choosing warehouse location and type
    b. setting up systems for materials-handling, inventory, and order processing
    c. choosing modes of transportation
    d. sending out sales representatives to book orders

MATCHING QUESTIONS: SECTION A

a.	agents	h.	backward integration
b.	brokers	i.	contractual distribution system
c.	distribution channel	j.	breaking bulk
d.	physical distribution	k.	industrial distributors
e.	retailers	l.	manufacturers' sales branches
f.	market coverage	m.	order cycle time
g.	sorting out	n.	selective distribution

MATCHING DEFINITIONS.   *Directions: Match the terms above with the definitions below.*

_____   1.   Wholesalers that perform many of the same functions as full-service merchant wholesalers but that are owned and controlled by manufacturers.

_____   2.   A network of independent firms at different levels that coordinates their distribution activities through a written contract.

_____   3.   A series of marketing entities through which goods and services pass on their way from producers to end users.

_____   4.   Sales representatives of manufacturers and wholesalers.

_____   5.   When a wholesaler or retailer gains control over the production process.

_____   6.   Breaking many different items into separate stocks that are similar.

_____   7.   Arrangement wherein a manufacturer chooses a limited number of dealers in an area (but more than one or two).

_____   8.   Parties that bring together buyers and sellers.

_____   9.   Independent wholesalers that buy related product lines from many manufacturers and sell them to industrial users.

_____   10.   Breaking down large shipments into smaller, more usable quantities that can be sold to retailers.

_____   11.   Firms that sell goods to consumers and to industrial users for their own consumption.

_____   12.   All activities concerned with transporting raw materials, component parts, and finished inventory so that they arrive when needed in usable condition.

_____   13.   The pattern of dealers used to distribute a product in a particular area.

_____   14.   The time between placing an order and receiving it in good condition.

MATCHING QUESTIONS: SECTION B

a.	accumulation	h.	distribution facilitators
b.	allocating	i.	nonstore retailing
c.	wholesalers	j.	administrative distribution system
d.	merchant wholesalers	k.	manufacturers' representatives
e.	forward integration	l.	intensive distribution
f.	distribution centers	m.	exclusive distribution
g.	vertical marketing system	n.	corporate distribution system

MATCHING DEFINITIONS. *Directions: Match the terms above with the definitions below.*

_____ 1. Wholesalers who represent noncompeting manufacturers, do not take title or possession, and work on commission.

_____ 2. Organizations that help move merchandise but are not members of the distribution channels and do not perform negotiating functions.

_____ 3. Intent to sell product everywhere there are potential customers.

_____ 4. Includes vending, direct selling, and direct response marketing.

_____ 5. Arrangement wherein a strong organization takes over as leader and sets channel policies.

_____ 6. Arrangement wherein a manufacturer selects one or two dealers per area to market products.

_____ 7. Independent wholesalers that buy goods from manufacturers on their own account and then resell them to other businesses.

_____ 8. Bringing similar stocks together into a larger quantity.

_____ 9. One firm owns the entire channel of distribution.

_____ 10. Firms aligned in a hierarchy to increase the efficiency of distribution channels (manufacturer to wholesaler to retailer).

_____ 11. When a manufacturer acquires a middleman closer to the target market, such as a wholesaler or retailer.

_____ 12. Breaking similar products into smaller and smaller lots.

_____ 13. Firms that sell finished goods to retailers, manufacturers, and institutions.

_____ 14. A special form of warehouse that specializes in changing shipment size but not in storing goods.

CHAPTER REVIEW

1. The text provides examples of distribution facilitators, i.e. organizations that help move merchandise through the channel but do not perform negotiating functions (truck line, banks, and market-research firms). What are some other examples?

2. The text says "although channel members can be eliminated, their functions cannot." What does that mean?

3. Why are manufacturers' sales branches the fastest growing form of wholesaling?

4. What are some advantages of nonstore retailing?

5. What are the basic modes of transportation? Cite an advantage of each.

EXPERIENCING BUSINESS 16-1   DISTRIBUTION STRATEGY, GOODS

Distribution is important; for some products it may be a primary basis for the competitive situation. This exercise will challenge you to relate the principles of distribution, as presented in the chapter, to the marketing of different goods.

Notes:

In Chapter 14, the text comments on distribution strategy as a part of overall marketing strategy and provides an example of cosmetics and different distribution approaches.

In Chapter 15, the text discusses consumer products based on the amount of effort consumers are willing to make to acquire them (convenience, shopping, and speciality).

To do this exercise:

1. For each category—convenience, shopping, and speciality products—provide at least two examples of goods. Example: Clinique cosmetics.

    (We are assuming here that some cosmetics are a "shopping" product, selected after brand-to-brand comparison. You could come up with different answers for other cosmetics.)

Convenience	*Shopping*	*Speciality*
	Clinique cosmetics	

2. For each of your categories/examples above, what would be an appropriate distribution channel? Example: cans of Maxwell House coffee.

    (Example is specific—for a convenience item—because some coffee is a speciality item. At least one coffee company direct mails to consumers.)

Product	*Distribution channel*
Maxwell House coffee	manufacturer-wholesaler-retailer-consumer

(Your recommendations here should be based on the marketing-competitive advantage of the channel. For example, some channels allow the producer to retain control over the goods. For what category of product could that be an advantage?)

EXPERIENCING BUSINESS 16-2

DISTRIBUTION STRATEGY, SERVICES

Several chapters address the importance of services—pure services as well as combinations wherein the service is integral to the consumption of the good.

Building on the previous exercise, this exercise challenges you to apply the concept of convenience, shopping, and speciality products to "services" and consider distribution strategy for services.

To do this exercise:

1. For each category—convenience, shopping, and speciality products—provide at least two examples of services. Example: Allstate automobile insurance.

   (We are assuming here that some insurance is a "shopping" product, selected after brand-to-brand comparison.)

Convenience	*Shopping*	*Speciality*
	Allstate automobile insurance	

2. For each of your categories/examples above, what would be an appropriate distribution channel? Example: warranty service on new Geo (automobile).

Service	*Distribution channel*
Geo warranty service	manufacturer-retailer-consumer

ANSWER KEY (CHAPTER 16)

TRUE-FALSE

1.	a.	F	3.	a.	T	5.	a.	F
	b.	T		b.	T		b.	T
	c.	T		c.	F		c.	T
	d.	F		d.	T	6.	a.	F
	e.	F		e.	F		b.	T
	f.	T		f.	T		c.	T
	g.	T	4.	a.	F		d.	F
	h.	T		b.	T	7.	a.	T
2.	a.	T		c.	T		b.	F
	b.	F					c.	T
	c.	F					d.	F
	d.	T					e.	T

MULTIPLE-CHOICE

1.	b	11.	a
2.	c	12.	d
3.	b	13.	b
4.	a	14.	d
5.	c	15.	c
6.	b	16.	d
7.	c	17.	c
8.	c	18.	b
9.	a	19.	a
10.	c	20.	d

MATCHING QUESTIONS: SECTION A

1.	l	8.	b
2.	i	9.	k
3.	c	10.	j
4.	a	11.	e
5.	h	12.	d
6.	g	13.	f
7.	n	14.	m

MATCHING QUESTIONS: SECTION B

1.	k	8.	a
2.	h	9.	n
3.	l	10.	g
4.	i	11.	e
5.	j	12.	b
6.	m	13.	c
7.	d	14.	f

CHAPTER REVIEW

1. Answers will vary. Some examples could be delivery services, the U.S. Postal service, advertising firms.

2. The manufacturer/producer either must perform the functions of the channel member or find new ways of getting them carried out. In some cases this may be achieved by increasing customer involvement, such as self-service pickup.

3. Some manufacturers are dissatisfied with merchant wholesalers; some may want more control over promotion or inventory.

4. Answers will vary. Typically, advantages include flexibility in location, extended service hours, and consolidated physical distribution.

5. Air: fastest   Water: low cost for bulk
   Highway: most flexible   Pipeline: can be low cost; is continuous
   Rail: low cost for bulk

PROMOTIONAL STRATEGIES

OUTLINE

LEARNING GOALS

After studying this chapter, you should be able to:

1. Describe the goals of promotional strategy.
2. Define the promotional mix, and explain its elements.
3. Describe the types of advertising.
4. Evaluate the media that advertisers use.
5. Describe the selling process.
6. Distinguish among the various types of sales promotion.
7. Understand how public relations fits into the promotional mix.
8. Discuss the factors that affect promotional mix.

TESTING YOUR KNOWLEDGE

TRUE-FALSE

*Directions: Test your knowledge of each learning goal by answering the true-false questions
following each goal.*

1.   Describe the goals of promotional strategy.

_____ a.   Most firms undertake promotion of some sort.

_____ b.   Informative promotion is more common in the late stages of the product life
cycle.

_____ c.   Promotion helps find customers.

_____ d.   Promotion can be used to help ease a firm's public relations problems.

_____ e.   Promotional materials that reach a product's current users are a waste of the
promotional budget.

2.   Define the promotional mix, and explain its elements.

_____ a.   The elements of the promotional mix are advertising, personal selling, sales
promotion, and public relations.

_____ b.   Personal selling is a paid form of nonpersonal promotion.

_____ c.   Sales promotion includes personal selling and public relations.

3.   Describe the types of advertising.

_____ a.   Comparative advertising creates a positive picture of a company.

_____ b.   Reminder advertising is sometimes used during the maturity stage of the
product life cycle.

_____ c.   Advocacy advertising is a form of institutional advertising.

4.   Evaluate the media that advertisers use.

_____ a.   The most popular advertising medium in the United States is television.

_____ b.   Newspapers are an excellent medium for selling products in local markets.

_____ c.   An expensive medium with great flexibility is outdoor advertising.

_____ d.   A strength of radio advertising is its short lead time.

_____ e.   Advertising costs are usually quoted in terms of CPM, costs per medium.

5.   Describe the selling process.

_____ a.   Few sales people find it pays off to spend time qualifying sales prospects.

_____ b.   Canned presentations are often used in industrial sales.

_____ c.   Almost every sales presentation meets with some objections.

_____ d.   The last step in the selling process is the close.

6.   Distinguish among the various types of sales promotion.

_____ a.   Over 90% of U.S. households use coupons regularly.

_____ b.   Sweepstakes are skilled competitive events among consumers for prizes.

_____ c.   Coupons are best for getting nonusers to try a brand.

_____ d.   Trade shows and conventions are an insignificant part of sales promotion.

7. Understand how public relations fits into the promotional mix.

   _____   a.   Publicity can be good or bad.

   _____   b.   Public relations activities are confined to large companies.

   _____   c.   The main tool of the public relations department is the press release.

8. Discuss the factors that affect promotional mix.

   _____   a.   Promotional mixes vary only slightly from one product and industry to the next.

   _____   b.   Selling toothpaste is not very different from selling overhead industrial cranes.

   _____   c.   Money is one of the biggest influences on the promotional mix.

   _____   d.   The nature of the market determines the promotional mix.

   _____   e.   The pull strategy relies on extensive selling to wholesalers and retailers.

Multiple-Choice

Directions: *Put the letter of the response that best completes each of the following statements in the blank at the left.*

   _____   1.   Any paid form of sales or promotional efforts made on behalf of goods, services, or ideas by an identified sponsor is called

       a.   sales promotion.
       b.   advertising.
       c.   personal sales.
       d.   publicity.

   _____   2.   Promotion is made up of personal selling, advertising, sales promotion, and publicity. This is known as

       a.   the marketing mix.
       b.   sales promotion.
       c.   the promotional mix.
       d.   publicity.

   _____   3.   Advertising that builds a desired image and goodwill for a company is known as _____ advertising.

       a.   advocacy
       b.   institutional
       c.   persuasive
       d.   informative

   _____   4.   Advertising used to maintain consumer awareness of a product or service is ____ advertising.

       a.   subliminal
       b.   reminder
       c.   advocacy
       d.   comparative

_____ 5. When specific products, mentioned by name, are contrasted in terms of quality and functional utility, the marketing agent is using _____ advertising.

    a. pioneering
    b. informative
    c. comparative
    d. advocacy

_____ 6. Advertising that takes a stand on specific issues is called _____ advertising.

    a. pioneering
    b. informative
    c. comparative
    d. advocacy

_____ 7. Advertising of a specific good or service is called _____ advertising.

    a. product
    b. advocacy
    c. point-of-purchase
    d. informative

_____ 8. _____ is/are second only to _____ in the share of advertising dollars.

    a. Magazines; newspapers
    b. Newspapers; television
    c. Television; newspapers
    d. Direct mail; television

_____ 9. An advertising agency that furnishes a wide range of services for its accounts is called a

    a. publicity agency.
    b. retail agency.
    c. marketing firm.
    d. full-service agency.

_____ 10. The _____ is the federal agency that oversees advertising of products sold across state lines.

    a. National Advertising Division (NAD)
    b. National Advertising Review Board (NARB)
    c. Food and Drug Administration (FDA)
    d. Federal Trade Commission (FTC)

_____ 11. A person who understands every aspect of the product line and who knows how to present the product creatively to meet the needs of the potential buyer is known as a(n)

    a. professional salesperson.
    b. cashier.
    c. sales clerk.
    d. army recruiter.

12. The process of identifying those firms and persons most likely to buy the seller's offerings is called

    a. organized presentation.
    b. closing the sale.
    c. the selling process.
    d. prospecting.

13. After the persons or businesses most likely to purchase have been identified, the next step is

    a. the closing.
    b. handling objections.
    c. the approach.
    d. the presentation.

14. Industrial salespersons often employ

    a. a canned presentation.
    b. an organized presentation.
    c. informative advertising.
    d. pioneer advertising.

15. Being able to _____ shows the salesperson's confidence in the product.

    a. take sales orders
    b. be pushy
    c. call in a supervisor for help
    d. handle objections

16. The final step in the selling process is

    a. closing the sale.
    b. objection handling.
    c. demonstration.
    d. follow up.

17. Bonuses offered to people who use a specific product are called

    a. premiums.
    b. publicity.
    c. bribes.
    d. promotion.

18. A catch-all category that includes trade shows, catalogs, premiums, coupons, contests, and games is called

    a. sales promotion.
    b. publicity.
    c. consumer orientation.
    d. marketing mix.

_____ 19. A news story about the reliability of a Chevrolet pickup in *The New York Times* is an example of

    a. advertising.
    b. personal selling.
    c. organized presentation.
    d. public relations.

_____ 20. Promotional material (displays, printed material, etc.) placed inside retail stores, usually next to the advertiser's goods, is referred to as

    a. point-of-purchase advertising (POP).
    b. sales material.
    c. publicity gimmicks.
    d. consumer information.

MATCHING QUESTIONS: SECTION A

a.	promotional mix	j.	differential advantage
b.	reminder advertising	k.	institutional advertising
c.	advertising media	l.	sales prospects
d.	CPM	m.	qualifying questions
e.	advertising	n.	product advertising
f.	personal selling	o.	sales leads
g.	prospecting	p.	advertising agency
h.	direct marketing	q.	comparative advertising
i.	promotion	r.	promotional strategy

MATCHING DEFINITIONS. *Directions: Match the term above with the definitions below.*

_____ 1. Builds demand for products.

_____ 2. Unique features that makes a product better than the competition.

_____ 3. The plan for informing, persuading, or reminding the target market about a product.

_____ 4. Advertising, personal selling, sales promotion, and public relations.

_____ 5. Paid form of nonpersonal presentation.

_____ 6. Features a specific good or service.

_____ 7. Compares competing named products.

_____ 8. Used to keep the product in the public's mind.

_____ 9. Creates a positive picture of a company.

_____ 10. The channels through which advertising is carried to prospective customers.

_____ 11. How advertising costs are usually quoted.

_____ 12. Promoting a product directly to a buyer.

_____ 13. A company that creates ads.

_____ 14. A face-to-face sales presentation.

_____ 15. Those people most likely to buy.

_____ 16. Looking for those people most likely to buy.

_____ 17. Also known as inquiries.

_____ 18. Used to separate prospects from those who do not have the potential to buy.

MATCHING QUESTIONS: SECTION B

a. sales promotion   h. samples
b. sweepstakes   i. coupons
c. public relations   j. POP displays
d. premiums   k. contests
e. pull strategy   l. push strategy
f. detailing   m. canned presentations
g. trade shows

MATCHING DEFINITIONS.   *Directions: Match the terms above with the definitions below.*

_____ 1. Presentations that are memorized.

_____ 2. Marketing events that stimulate consumer buying.

_____ 3. Price reductions designed to bring an immediate sale.

_____ 4. Free gifts of a product distributed to build public acceptance.

_____ 5. Prizes to people that buy a product.

_____ 6. Skilled competition among consumers for prizes.

_____ 7. Competitions whose winners are picked by chance.

_____ 8. Manufacturers and wholesalers display their wares here.

_____ 9. About the least costly kind of sales promotion.

_____ 10. A news story about a new personal computer.

_____ 11. The physical stocking of merchandise.

_____ 12. Using personal selling and advertising on a wholesaler or retailer.

_____ 13. Stimulates consumer demand to get products distributed.

CHAPTER REVIEW

1. What is the problem with using comparative ads?

2. Describe how advertising messages are developed.

3. Identify the steps in the personal selling process.

4. List five of the most popular forms of sales promotion.

    a.

    b.

    c.

    d.

    e.

5. How is publicity different from advertising?

6. Identify and describe the elements of the promotional mix.

EXPERIENCING BUSINESS 17-1

DIFFERENTIAL ADVANTAGE

Differential advantage is the set of unique features that the target market perceives as important to and better than the competition. Promotion is the means to convince the target customers of the differential advantage.

To do this exercise:

Consider automobiles.

You may use (1) independent sources, such as *Consumer Reports* magazine, (2) industry-specific materials, such as *Car and Driver* magazine, or (3) company sources, such as advertising materials from Chrysler for the Jeep Cherokee. In this product area:

1.   What features define "advantage"?

2.   What companies/models have the differential advantage now?

        (Japanese, American, other?)

3.   Is the differential advantage real or perceived?

EXPERIENCING BUSINESS 17-2

PROMOTIONAL TERMS

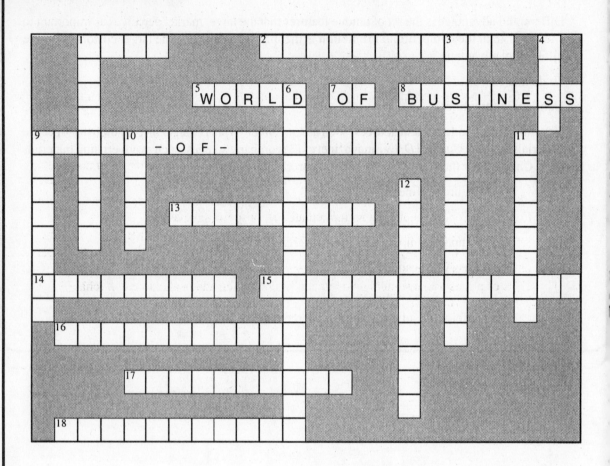

ACROSS

1   _____ strategy: Manufacturer's attempt to stimulate consumer demand to get wider distribution of a product.

2   Any paid form of nonpersonal presentation by an identified sponsor.

5   WORLD

7   OF

8   BUSINESS

9   (compound word, XXXXX-OF-XXXXXXXX) _____ displays: Promotional devices designed to stimulate immediate sales.

13 Marketing activity that stimulates demand for a firm's goods and services.

14 Differential _____: A set of unique features that the target market perceives as important and better than the competition.

15 (two words) Combination of advertising, personal selling, sales promotion, and public relations used to promote a product.

(continued)

16 _____ advertising: Product advertising in which the company's product is compared with competing, named products.

17 _____ advertising: Advertising run to correct the false impressions left by previous advertisements.

18 Looking for sales prospects.

DOWN

1 Information about a company or product that appears in the news media and is not directly paid for by the company.

3 _____ advertising: Advertising that creates a favorable picture of a company and its ideals, services, and roles in the community.

4 _____ strategy: Manufacturer's use of aggressive selling and advertising to convince a wholesaler or retailer to carry its merchandise.

6 (two words) Variety of approaches, such as catalogs, direct mail, and telephone sales, used to promote a product and get an immediate response from the buyer.

9 _____ selling: Face-to-face sales presentation to a prospective customer.

10 _____ shows: Meetings that give manufacturers and wholesalers the chance to display their products to a large audience of potential buyers.

11 Gifts or prizes to consumers who buy a product, which adds value to the purchase.

12 _____ questions: Questions used by salespeople to find genuine sales prospects.

(Solution is provided at the end of the chapter.)

ANSWER KEY (CHAPTER 17)

TRUE-FALSE

1.	a.	T	4.	a.	F		c.	T
	b.	F		b.	T		d.	F
	c.	T		c.	F	7.	a.	T
	d.	T		d.	T		b.	F
	e.	F		e.	F		c.	T
2.	a.	T	5.	a.	F	8.	a.	F
	b.	F		b.	F		b.	F
	c.	F		c.	T		c.	T
3.	a.	F		d.	F		d.	T
	b.	T	6.	a.	T		e.	F
	c.	T		b.	F			

MULTIPLE-CHOICE

1.	b	11.	a
2.	c	12.	d
3.	b	13.	c
4.	b	14.	b
5.	c	15.	d
6.	d	16.	d
7.	a	17.	a
8.	c	18.	a
9.	d	19.	d
10.	d	20.	a

MATCHING QUESTIONS: SECTION A

1.	i	10.	c
2.	j	11.	d
3.	r	12.	h
4.	a	13.	p
5.	e	14.	f
6.	n	15.	l
7.	q	16.	g
8.	b	17.	o
9.	k	18.	m

MATCHING QUESTIONS: SECTION B

1.	m	8.	g
2.	a	9.	j
3.	i	10.	c
4.	h	11.	f
5.	d	12.	l
6.	k	13.	e
7.	b		

CHAPTER REVIEW

1. In many cases, the consumer remembers the other brand or is confused as to the sponsor—i.e., Was it Goodyear or Goodrich? Was it Duracel or Eveready?

2. Advertising messages are developed in three stages: (1) generation, (2) evaluation, and (3) execution. *Message generation* is the creative development of things to say about the product. *Message evaluation* normally involves market research to find the best theme among those that have been developed. *Message execution* means developing copy and illustrations for the campaign.

3. The process consists of prospecting for and qualifying customers, approaching customers, presenting and demonstrating the product, handling objections, closing the sale, and following up on the sale.

4. a. coupons

    b. samples

    c. premiums

    d. contests

    e. sweepstakes

5. Publicity is information about a company or product that appears in the news media and is not directly paid for by the company. Advertising is a paid form of nonpersonal presentation.

6. Advertising, personal selling, sales promotion, and public relations make up what is known as the promotional mix. Advertising is any paid form of nonpersonal promotion by an identified sponsor. Personal selling consists of a face-to-face presentation. Sales promotion includes coupons and samples, displays, shows, exhibitions, and demonstrations. Public relations is any communication or activity designed to win goodwill or prestige for a company or a person.

EXPERIENCING BUSINESS 17-2

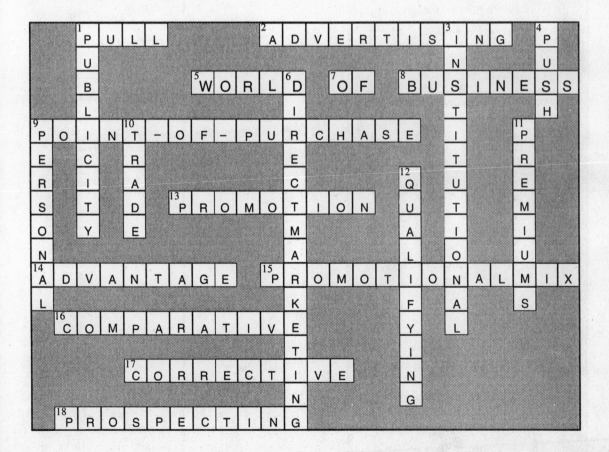

PART SEVEN

MANAGEMENT INFORMATION TOOLS

Part Seven looks at the tools businesses use to maintain control over financial and information data in the course of doing business—computers and information systems, and accounting systems.

COMPUTERS AND INFORMATION SYSTEMS

OUTLINE

LEARNING GOALS

After studying this chapter, you should be able to:

1. Describe the role of information in decision making.

2. Explain the four size categories of computers.

3. Name the parts of a computerized information system.

4. Describe what commonly used microcomputer software does.

5. Discuss the role of computer networks in business information systems.

6. Describe the structure of a typical management information system.

7. Discuss how companies should address the issues of computer security, computer crime, and privacy.

TESTING YOUR KNOWLEDGE

TRUE-FALSE

Directions: Test your knowledge of each learning goal by answering the true-false questions following each goal.

1. Describe the role of information in decision making.

    _____ a. Managers use information systems, procedures, and equipment to obtain what they need to make decisions.

    _____ b. To be relevant, information must be economical to obtain.

    _____ c. Partial information may be a problem or limitation.

    _____ d. Timeliness is desirable for information in decision making.

    _____ e. Four general qualities for "good" information are relevance, accuracy, completeness, and timeliness.

2. Explain the four size categories of computers.

    _____ a. Most experts today divide computers into four categories by cost.

    _____ b. The smallest is the microcomputer, commonly called a personal computer.

    _____ c. The second, the minicomputer, is small enough to fit in an office.

    _____ d. The third and fourth categories are mainframe and supercomputer, respectively.

    _____ e. The size of a computer and its power are directly related.

3. Name the parts of a computerized information system.

    _____ a. The two main parts of a computerized information system are the hardware and the software.

    _____ b. In computerized business systems data entry is typically the most predictable, least expensive process.

    _____ c. A CD-ROM holds lots of data but is difficult to access.

    _____ d. Businesses are typically reluctant to add to the cost of data entry by adding devices such as optical scanners and touch-screen display units.

    _____ e. Auxiliary storage systems provide long-term storage for programs and data.

4. Describe what commonly used microcomputer software does.

    _____ a. Microcomputer applications are limited to generic, common business tasks.

    _____ b. Word processing is text-oriented software for correspondence, letters, reports, etc.

    _____ c. Spreadsheets are essentially software oriented to calculation and organization of data.

    _____ d. Database software primarily provides graphics and presentation support.

    _____ e. The communications software now available can link individual microcomputers with company mainframes.

5. Discuss the role of computer networks in business information systems.

    _____ a. A trend in business computing is the use of networks to deliver information to managers.

_____ b. Microcomputers have made networking much more popular.

_____ c. Local area networks link a group of computers within one site.

_____ d. A network that connects computers at different sites is commonly called a TLK (Telecommunications Link).

_____ e. The "E-mail" service provides only for emergency or urgent communications.

6. Describe the structure of a typical management information system.

_____ a. A management information system (MIS) collects and stores key data and produces information for analysis, control, and decision making.

_____ b. A typical component of a MIS is a data-processing system to collect and update records.

_____ c. A typical component of a MIS is a management reporting system to collect the reports prepared by the managers.

_____ d. A typical component of a MIS is a decision support system which lets managers get the information they want on demand.

_____ e. A typical component of a MIS is an office automation system, to eliminate word processing and internal communications processing.

_____ f. Another component of a MIS is an expert system to apply "artificial intelligence" techniques in providing "advice" to users.

7. Discuss how companies should address the important issues of computer security, computer crime, and privacy.

_____ a. The most common computer crimes are software piracy and misuse of communications software.

_____ b. The crime of unauthorized access and use could involve something as "simple" as using a computer at work to prepare a term paper for class.

MULTIPLE-CHOICE

Directions: *Put the letter of the response that best completes each of the following statements in the blank at the left.*

_____ 1. Which of the following is *not* an input device?

     a. mouse
     b. optical scanner
     c. touch screen display
     d. printer

_____ 2. The basic purpose of systems software is to permit the computer to

     a. execute several jobs simultaneously.
     b. quickly and accurately do repetitive tasks.
     c. count differently than humans count.
     d. access data used in processing.

_____ 3. BASIC, FORTRAN, and C are languages used in

      a. system software.
      b. computer manuals.
      c. application programs.
      d. compiler programs.

_____ 4. Commonly used operating systems include all of the following *except*

      a. MS-DOS.
      b. Microsoft Windows.
      c. IBM's OS/2.
      d. Apple's SAUCE.

_____ 5. Which of the following would be too large to fit on a desktop but appropriate for an office application?

      a. microcomputer
      b. notebook computer
      c. laptop computer
      d. minicomputer

_____ 6. Computer-based systems for maintaining company records, reporting on company activities, and tracking flow of money and work through the company are

      a. flowcharts.
      b. data processing systems.
      c. data-based management.
      d. interfacing systems.

_____ 7. On-line processing

      a. costs less than batch processing.
      b. requires little computing power.
      c. keeps data current.
      d. is well suited to payroll applications.

_____ 8. Popular spreadsheet programs include

      a. Lotus 1-2-3.
      b. Quattro.
      c. Excel.
      d. All of the above.

_____ 9. A(n) _____ enables a group of computers within one site to exchange data.

      a. local area network
      b. wide area network
      c. modem
      d. electronic mail system

_____ 10. A(n) ____ enables a group of computers at different sites to exchange data.

    a. local area network
    b. wide area network
    c. modem
    d. electronic mail system

_____ 11. A(n) ____ allows messages to be recorded and transmitted throughout a network.

    a. local area network
    b. wide area network
    c. modem
    d. electronic mail system

_____ 12. The ____ is essentially a global E-mail service.

    a. USPS
    b. CommWorld System
    c. Internet
    d. G-mail

_____ 13. The key application for human-resource management is the ____ system.

    a. payroll
    b. accounts payable
    c. directory
    d. E-mail

_____ 14. The most common applications in sales are ____ and processing.

    a. payroll
    b. order entry
    c. distributor locator
    d. E-mail

_____ 15. The key application for manufacturing MIS is

    a. order entry.
    b. sales forecasting.
    c. inventory and production scheduling.
    d. E-mail.

_____ 16. A decision support system is a

    a. log of day-to-day production reports.
    b. tool for answering "what if " questions.
    c. substitution of technology for production data.
    d. source of external validation.

_____ 17. Essentially, an office automation system is a(n)

    a. word processor.
    b. electronic mail system.
    c. communications tool.
    d. order entry system.

_____ 18. If the authors of this study guide could stay at home and keep in touch with the office through computers and communications technology, they would be

   a.   data processing.
   b.   using E-mail.
   c.   working on flextime.
   d.   telecommuting.

_____ 19. A(n) _____ system gives managers advice like they would get from a human consultant.

   a.   expert
   b.   decision support
   c.   management reporting
   d.   desktop publishing

_____ 20. A(n) _____ system uses collected data to produce decision-making information in the form of reports.

   a.   expert
   b.   decision support
   c.   management reporting
   d.   desktop publishing

MATCHING QUESTIONS: SECTION A

   a.   cyberspace   h.   artificial intelligence
   b.   system software   i.   decision support system
   c.   database software   j.   desktop publishing software
   d.   networks   k.   auxiliary storage system
   e.   information systems   l.   wide area network (WAN)
   f.   mainframe computer   m.   management information system (MIS)
   g.   office automation system   n.   on-line processing

MATCHING DEFINITIONS.   *Directions: Match the terms above with the definitions below.*

_____ 1. Collects and stores data and produces information needed for analysis, control, and decision making.

_____ 2. Application that lets a computer system solve problems more or less as humans do.

_____ 3. Data are processed as they become available.

_____ 4. Provides long-term storage for programs and data.

_____ 5. Provides several kinds of decision-making information and allows its users to ask "what if " questions.

_____ 6. Program routines that are needed by all applications.

_____ 7. The sphere in which people interact by way of computer networks.

_____ 8. Microcomputer software to record and organize data.

_____ 9. Procedures and equipment that provide information about a firm's operations.

_____ 10. Microcomputer software to design and produce brochures, catalogs, and newsletters.

_____ 11. Terminals, computers, and other equipment that use communications channels to share data.

_____ 12. A network that connects computers at different sites.

_____ 13. A communications tool, providing key elements such as word processing, E-mail, and administrative support.

_____ 14. Computer that can serve many users at the same time, typically requiring a separate facility and relatively extensive installation/support.

MATCHING QUESTIONS: SECTION B

a.	data	h.	application software
b.	hardware	i.	management reporting system
c.	word processing	j.	spreadsheet software
d.	minicomputers	k.	electronic mail
e.	information	l.	central processing unit
f.	expert system	m.	batch processing
g.	operating system	n.	local area network (LAN)

MATCHING DEFINITIONS. *Directions: Match the terms above with the definitions below.*

_____ 1. The heart of a computer system.

_____ 2. Microcomputer software that provides for text processing such as letters, reports, etc.

_____ 3. Microcomputer software that provides for calculation and organization of data.

_____ 4. Periodically updating records based on collecting data over some time.

_____ 5. Connects computers within one site.

_____ 6. Larger than microcomputers; can serve several users at the same time.

_____ 7. Uses data collected by the data processing system to produce reports that managers can use for decision making.

_____ 8. Application of artificial intelligence to give advice.

_____ 9. The equipment comprising a computer system.

_____ 10. The programs that make the computer do specific work for its individual users.

_____ 11. Electronic recording and transmission of messages over a network.

_____ 12. The basic facts that describe the company's status.

_____ 13. A meaningful and useful summary of data.

_____ 14. Basic collection of program routines that handles general functioning of the computer.

CHAPTER REVIEW

1. How could you use the individual course entries as recorded on your college transcript to illustrate the distinction between data and information?

2. What types of computer(s) would you expect to find in a small business?

3. One could argue that when we think of a computer, we often think of the hardware, but when we think of an information system, we more often think of the software. How would you explain that?

4. In our society today, educators are concerned with "computer literacy." In college this is shifting to familiarity with some of the microcomputer applications, such as word processing, desktop publishing, spreadsheets, database systems, graphics, or communications. Do you think this emphasis on applications as opposed to understanding the theory is correct?

5. How can a network help an individual manager?

6. Management information systems existed before computers. Therefore, it is not just the automation that makes a system a MIS. What might be an example(s) of applications a business might still choose not to automate?

7. As a manager in an organization with significant access to company data, what would be your responsibility toward that data? Toward the information?

EXPERIENCING BUSINESS 18-1

BUSINESS SYSTEM APPLICATIONS

To do this exercise:

Following are four common business applications of microcomputer software. For each, (1) select the appropriate description from the list below, (2) identify a particular product/brand of software, and (3) identify at least one feature of that product/brand.

Description:

A. Software to write, edit, and format correspondence and reports.
B. Software to design and produce brochures, catalogs, and newsletters.
C. Software to organize data, to perform arithmetic and statistical calculations, and to present data in tabular or graphic formats.
D. Software to store, organize, and present/retrieve data in alternative formats.

Applications:

I. *Spreadsheets*

   1. description:

   2. product/brand name:

   3. feature:

II. *Word processing*

   1. description:

   2. product/brand name:

   3. feature:

III. *Databases (database management)*

   1. description:

   2. product/brand name:

   3. feature:

IV. *Desktop publishing*

   1. description:

   2. product/brand name:

   3. feature:

EXPERIENCING BUSINESS 18-2

SMALL BUSINESS APPLICATIONS

The processing capability of microcomputers has increased dramatically in recent years. For many small businesses, the microcomputer provides adequate capacity for their applications.

To do this exercise:

Visit a small business that uses a computer and observe what applications they are running.

Some suggested questions:

What is the computer? The capacity?

What applications are being used? Individual packages or integrated under one package?

Is the software generic software (such as a commercial spreadsheet) or a specific application package (such as general ledger accounting)?

What would they like to have that they do not have now?

ANSWER KEY (CHAPTER 18)

TRUE-FALSE

1.	a.	T	3.	a.	T		c.	T
	b.	F		b.	T		d.	F
	c.	T		c.	F		e.	F
	d.	T		d.	F	6.	a.	T
	e.	T		e.	T		b.	T
2.	a.	F	4.	a.	F		c.	F
	b.	T		b.	T		d.	T
	c.	T		c.	T		e.	F
	d.	T		d.	F		f.	T
	e.	F		e.	T	7.	a.	F
			5.	a.	T		b.	T
				b.	T			

MULTIPLE-CHOICE

1.	d	11.	d
2.	b	12.	c
3.	c	13.	a
4.	d	14.	b
5.	d	15.	c
6.	b	16.	b
7.	c	17.	c
8.	d	18.	d
9.	a	19.	a
10.	b	20.	c

MATCHING QUESTIONS: SECTION A

1.	m	8.	c
2.	h	9.	e
3.	n	10.	j
4.	k	11.	d
5.	i	12.	l
6.	b	13.	g
7.	a	14.	f

MATCHING QUESTIONS: SECTION B

1.	l	8.	f
2.	c	9.	b
3.	j	10.	h
4.	m	11.	k
5.	n	12.	a
6.	d	13.	e
7.	i	14.	g

CHAPTER REVIEW

1. Individual courses with their entries are data. The data can be summarized many ways. They could be ordered and compared with a degree plan to verify eligibility for graduation. They could be summarized as grade-point-average. They could be used in part to verify prerequisite requirements for an advanced course. All of these represent data processed into information.

2. The microcomputer would handle a surprising amount of applications for a small business. Think of examples, such as small retailers, personal services, and professional services. As the text points out, the power is not dependent on the size. Even a "large" small business could likely get by with a minicomputer.

3. For many computer users, the physical aspects or hardware are relatively unimportant. These people would not be concerned with "bits and bytes" but with the processing capabilities. The ability to manipulate data, to tailor the information as needed, are managerial aspects and express more about the information system than about a particular piece of hardware/ software.

4. Answers will vary. The key assumption is that the skill-building in applications is appropriate because the tool applies in so many course areas, and later in so many job areas.

5. A network leverages the capability of an individual user by providing access to other users (example: E-mail), access to software on a shared basis, and access to data that any one user could not obtain or manage.

6. Small businesses may choose to continue with many functions "off-line." Even in a larger enterprise, where some data manipulation and analysis, such as spreadsheets, are computerized, it would not be surprising to find the collection before and the control afterwards remaining off-line.

7. Answers will vary. Mostly a question of ethics. Also touches on issues of proprietary data.

ACCOUNTING

OUTLINE

LEARNING GOALS

After studying this chapter, you should be able to:

1. Understand the role and uses of accounting information.

2. Distinguish between financial and managerial accounting and public and private accountants.

3. Discuss the accounting equation, double-entry bookkeeping, and the accounting cycle.

4. Describe the balance sheet and its key parts.

5. Describe the income statement and its key parts.

6. Understand the role of the statement of cash flows.

7. Explain how common-size financial statements and ratio analysis can be used to spot a firm's financial strengths and weaknesses.

TESTING YOUR KNOWLEDGE

TRUE-FALSE

*Directions: Test your knowledge of each learning goal by answering the true-false questions
following each goal.*

1.   Understand the role and uses of accounting information.

_____   a.   Accounting is the process of collecting, recording, classifying, summarizing,
reporting, and analyzing marketing data.

_____   b.   The accounting system converts the details of financial transactions into a
form that people can use to make decisions.

_____   c.   Financial reports include financial statements and special reports.

_____   d.   Financial reports are prepared solely for the internal use of the company.

_____   e.   Financial statements are prepared solely for the internal use of the company.

_____   f.   Bookkeeping is typically much broader than accounting.

2.   Distinguish between financial and managerial accounting and private and public accountants.

_____   a.   Financial accounting focuses on preparing the financial reports.

_____   b.   Managerial accounting describes the progression of accountants into supervisory and managerial duties.

_____   c.   Providing financial information that can be used to evaluate and make decisions about current and future operations is called operations accounting.

_____   d.   Public accountants are employed by governmental (federal, state, local)
organizations.

_____   e.   Private accountants are in independent or private practice to serve individuals
or organizations for a fee.

_____   f.   Accountants employed within organizations are called private accountants.

3.   Discuss the accounting equation, double-entry bookkeeping, and the accounting cycle.

_____   a.   The relationship among assets, liabilities, and owners' equity is the basis for
the accounting equation.

_____   b.   To keep the accounting equation in balance, every transaction must be recorded as two entries.

_____   c.   The accounting cycle starts with the analysis of activities with a financial
impact on the firm.

_____   d.   The accounting cycle includes recording the transactions with financial impact and posting them to specific accounts.

_____   e.   The final step in the accounting cycle is the preparation of the trial balance
which confirms the accuracy of the figures.

4.   Describe the balance sheet and its key parts.

_____   a.   The balance sheet summarizes the firm's financial position at a specific point
in time.

_____   b.   The balance sheet summarizes the revenue and expenses over some period.

_____ c. Assets are categorized into current, fixed, and intangible.

_____ d. Intangible assets are long-term with no physical existence, such as patents and copyrights.

_____ e. Liabilities are the amounts a firm owes to its creditors.

_____ f. Long-term liabilities must add up to the total of intangible assets.

_____ g. Owners' equity is the owners' total investment in the business.

5. Describe the income statement and its key parts.

_____ a. The income statement summarizes the firm's financial position at a specific point in time.

_____ b. The income statement summarizes the assets and liabilities over some period.

_____ c. The three key parts of the income statement are the revenues, expenses, and net profit/loss.

_____ d. Expenses are the cost of generating revenues.

_____ e. Cost of goods sold relates only to the cost of producing goods, not services.

_____ f. The income statement is prepared only if the firm can show a net profit in its bottom line.

_____ g. Accounting techniques like depreciation and inventory valuation can produce different profit/loss numbers on the income statement.

6. Understand the role of the statement of cash flows.

_____ a. A firm's profit is the amount by which its cash account increases.

_____ b. A statement of cash flows is a summary of money flowing into and out of the firm.

_____ c. Operating flows are those directly related to the production of the firm's output, including labor costs, material costs, and investment on fixed assets.

7. Explain how common-size financial statements and ratio analysis can be used to spot a firm's financial strengths and weaknesses.

_____ a. Common-size income statements express each item as a percentage of some given base, such as sales.

_____ b. In trend analysis the ratios are compared over time, typically years, to spot trends.

_____ c. Cross-sectional analysis involves comparison of the same elements for two or more similar firms.

_____ d. Liquidity ratios measure a firm's ability to pay short-term debts.

_____ e. Activity ratios measure how well a firm reacts to payment of long-term debt.

_____ f. Earnings per share is an activity ratio that is an important sign of the firm's financial success.

MULTIPLE-CHOICE

Directions: *Put the letter of the response that best completes each of the following statements in the blank at the left.*

_____   1.   The money owed the firm for goods and services it has sold is classified as

     a.   receivables.
     b.   liabilities.
     c.   payables.
     d.   bad debts.

_____   2.   A firm with assets of $8 million and liabilities of $7 million would have ____ in owners' equity.

     a. $15 million
     b. $7.5 million
     c. $8 million
     d. $1 million

_____   3.   LIFO stands for

     a.   last in, first outcome.
     b.   last input, first operation.
     c.   last in, first out.
     d.   liabilities input, financial output.

_____   4.   Assets, liabilities, and owners' equity appear in that order on the

     a.   income statement.
     b.   annual report.
     c.   balance sheet.
     d.   GAAP statement.

_____   5.   Amounts owed to a firm by customers who bought its goods or services and who were granted an extension of time to pay are

     a.   prepaid expenses.
     b.   accounts receivable.
     c.   accrued expenses.
     d.   accounts payable.

_____   6.   Obligations that the company has incurred but not yet paid for are

     a.   prepaid expenses.
     b.   accounts receivable.
     c.   accrued expenses.
     d.   accounts payable.

_____ 7. Current liabilities are those due

    a. now.
    b. within 6 months.
    c. within 1 year of the date of the balance sheet.
    d. within 1 year of the date it was incurred.

_____ 8. Patents are classified as a(n)

    a. intangible asset.
    b. long-term liability.
    c. capital account.
    d. direct investment.

_____ 9. A summary of the revenues and expenses of a firm over a specified period of time is a(n)

    a. trend analysis.
    b. ratio analysis.
    c. income statement.
    d. GAAP statement of flows.

_____ 10. Rent, as an expense to a firm, would appear on which of the following statements?

    a. time-series analysis
    b. income statement
    c. balance sheet
    d. summary of receivables

_____ 11. For manufacturers, labor and overhead are considered part of

    a. revenue.
    b. direct material.
    c. the profitability ratio.
    d. cost of goods sold.

_____ 12. Net profit is found

    a. by subtracting expenses from net income.
    b. by subtracting expenses from revenue.
    c. from cross-sectional analysis.
    d. from the GAAP Handbook.

_____ 13. Profit and cash are different because

    a. double-entry bookkeeping requires profit be expressed in non-dollar terms.
    b. GAAP requires depreciation be charged as a non-dollar-valued expense.
    c. most firms recognize revenue at the time of sale, not when they are paid.
    d. some organizations are not-for-profit enterprises.

_____ 14.   Common-size income statements express each item as a(n) _____ of some given base.

     a.   percentage
     b.   set amount
     c.   pre-determined valuation
     d.   industry average

_____ 15.   Comparing the same set of ratios for four consecutive years is a _____ analysis.

     a.   trend
     b.   comparative ratio
     c.   net profit and loss
     d.   cross-sectional

_____ 16.   A number of regularly published industry averages are available and aid in _____ analysis.

     a.   trend
     b.   comparative ratio
     c.   net profit and loss
     d.   cross-sectional

_____ 17.   The current ratio, the acid-test ratio, and net working capital are the major _____ ratios.

     a.   liquidity
     b.   profitability
     c.   debt
     d.   activity

_____ 18.   Which of the following ratios would measure the return owners receive on their investment?

     a.   acid-test
     b.   debt-to-equity
     c.   return on equity
     d.   interest coverage

_____ 19.   If a firm has current assets totaling $97,000 and current liabilities totaling $54,000, the current ratio would be

     a.   ($97,000 divided by $54,000), 1.8 to 1
     b.   ($54,000 divided by $97,000), 0.6 to 1
     c.   ($97,000 plus $54,000, divided by 2), 75.5 to 1
     d.   0.97 to 1

_____ 20.   An acid-test ratio of at least _____ is preferred.

     a.   0.25
     b.   0.50
     c.   0.75
     d.   1.0

MATCHING QUESTIONS: SECTION A

a.	accounting	i.	long-term liabilities
b.	common-size statements	j.	current liabilities
c.	bookkeeping	k.	net working capital
d.	current assets	l.	annual report
e.	current ratio	m.	accounting equation
f.	debt ratios	n.	selling expenses
g.	net profit margin	o.	double-entry bookkeeping
h.	net profit	p.	financial reports

MATCHING DEFINITIONS. *Directions: Match the terms above with the definitions below.*

_____ 1. Ratio of net profit to net sales.

_____ 2. Liabilities that come due more than one year from the date of the balance sheet.

_____ 3. Calculated by subtracting all expenses from all revenues.

_____ 4. Measure the degree and effect of the firm's use of borrowed funds to finance its operations.

_____ 5. Expenses related to marketing and distribution of the company's products.

_____ 6. Every transaction recorded as two entries.

_____ 7. Total current assets less total current liabilities.

_____ 8. Express each item as a percentage of some given base, such as sales.

_____ 9. The process of collecting, recording, classifying, summarizing, reporting, and analyzing the financial activities of firms.

_____ 10. Liabilities due within a year of the date of the balance sheet.

_____ 11. The ratio of total current assets to total current liabilities.

_____ 12. Assets which can be converted into cash within 12 months.

_____ 13. The relationship among assets, liabilities, and owners' equity.

_____ 14. A yearly document that describes the firm's financial status.

_____ 15. The system used to record a firm's financial transactions.

_____ 16. Balance sheets and income statements.

MATCHING QUESTIONS: SECTION B

a.	fixed assets	i.	general and administrative expenses
b.	balance sheet	j.	gross profit (gross margin)
c.	ratio analysis	k.	income statement
d.	auditing	l.	inventory turnover rate
e.	liabilities	m.	acid-test (quick) ratio
f.	gross sales	n.	managerial accounting
g.	net loss	o.	financial accounting
h.	cost of goods sold	p.	GAAP

MATCHING DEFINITIONS.   *Directions: Match the terms above with the definitions below.*

_____ 1.   Summarizes a firm's position at a specific point in time.

_____ 2.   Total amount of sales.

_____ 3.   Calculated by subtracting all expenses from all revenues.

_____ 4.   The speed at which inventory moves through the firm and is turned into sales.

_____ 5.   Long-term assets used by the firm for more than a year.

_____ 6.   Provides financial information that can be used to evaluate and make decisions about operations.

_____ 7.   The process of reviewing the records used to prepare financial statements.

_____ 8.   Focuses on preparing the financial reports used by managers and outsiders to track the firm's performance and compare it with other firms.

_____ 9.   Summarizes a firm's revenues and expenses over some period.

_____ 10. Calculating and interpreting financial ratios to assess a firm's performance and condition.

_____ 11. Difference between net sales and cost of goods.

_____ 12. Expenses that cannot be linked to either cost of goods sold or sales.

_____ 13. Rules agreed on by accountants, defined by the Financial Accounting Standards Board.

_____ 14. Current ratio, excluding inventory as a current asset.

_____ 15. What a firm owes to its creditors.

_____ 16. Total expense of buying or producing the firm's goods or services.

MATCHING QUESTIONS: SECTION C

a.	net sales	i.	intangible assets
b.	owners' equity	j.	statement of cash flows
c.	private accountants	k.	profitability ratios
d.	retained earnings	l.	liquidity ratios
e.	revenues	m.	public accountants
f.	trial balance	n.	operating expenses
g.	expenses	o.	debt-to-equity ratio
h.	depreciation	p.	accounts payable

MATCHING DEFINITIONS. *Directions:* *Match the terms above with the definitions below.*

_____ 1. Amounts owed for things bought on credit.

_____ 2. The relationship between the amount of debt financing and the amount of equity financing.

_____ 3. Measure of how well the firm is using its resources to generate profit.

_____ 4. Measure of the firm's ability to pay its short-term debts as they come due.

_____ 5. The costs of generating revenues.

_____ 6. Accountant employed within organizations.

_____ 7. Assignment/allocation of the original cost of an asset over the years which it is expected to produce revenues.

_____ 8. Interim summary of ledger account totals.

_____ 9. Gross sales less discounts, returns, and allowances.

_____ 10. The amounts left over from profitable operations.

_____ 11. Long-term assets with no physical existence.

_____ 12. Dollar amount of sales plus other income received.

_____ 13. Independent accountants who serve organizations or individuals for a fee.

_____ 14. A summary of the money flowing into and out of the firm.

_____ 15. Expenses of running the business not directly related to producing or buying its products.

_____ 16. The total investment in the business.

CHAPTER REVIEW

1. What is the difference between financial and managerial accounting?

2. Owners' equity is also called net worth. What does that mean?

3. What are some examples of assets and liabilities that might appear on a balance sheet?

4. Would the following be classified as selling expenses or as cost of goods sold? Explain.

   advertising expenses

   delivery charges

5. What ratio(s) can be used to measure a firm's ability to pay its short-term debts?

6. When we have income statements with the detailing of revenues and expenses, why is a statement of cash flows needed?

EXPERIENCING BUSINESS 19-1

FINANCIAL STATEMENTS

To do this exercise:

1. Indicate to the left of each of the following items whether it belongs on the balance sheet (B) or the income statement (I).

2. Then construct a simple balance sheet and income statement from the information.

3. What is the owners' equity for this company?

4. Did the company make a profit or incur a loss?

_____	Accounts payable	$35,000
_____	Office supplies	2,300
_____	Inventory, January 1	30,000
_____	Accrued expenses	4,750
_____	Interest	3,300
_____	Cash	16,500
_____	Gross sales	320,000
_____	Long-term liabilities	12,000
_____	Rent	13,000
_____	Purchases	98,000
_____	Marketable securities	3,800
_____	Administrative salaries	23,700
_____	Accounts receivable	32,500
_____	Fixed assets	45,000
_____	Inventory, December 31	23,000
_____	Depreciation	3,400
_____	Sales discounts	3,400
_____	Notes payable	7,750
_____	Retained earnings	40,000
_____	Operating expenses	72,000
_____	Insurance	3,000
_____	Owners' equity	???

(Answers to this exercise are provided at the end of the chapter.)

EXPERIENCING BUSINESS 19-2   RATIO ANALYSIS

To do this exercise:

Calculate the following from the information provided.

      Current ratio:

      Quick ratio:

      Net working capital:

      Net profit margin:

      Return on equity:

      Inventory turnover:

      Debt-to-equity:

<u>Data from financial statements</u>

Current assets	$565,000
Current liabilities	158,000
Beginning inventory	320,000
Ending inventory	400,000
Net profit	61,000
Net sales	800,000
Owners' equity	1,035,000
Cost of goods sold	445,000
Total liabilities	308,000

(Answers to this exercise are provided at the end of the chapter.)

ANSWER KEY (CHAPTER 19)

TRUE-FALSE

1.			2.			3.		
	a.	F		a.	T		a.	T
	b.	T		b.	F		b.	T
	c.	T		c.	F		c.	T
	d.	F		d.	F		d.	T
	e.	F		e.	F		e.	F
	f.	F		f.	T			

4.	a.	T		5.	a.	F		6.	a.	F
	b.	F			b.	F			b.	T
	c.	T			c.	T			c.	F
	d.	T			d.	T		7.	a.	T
	e.	T			e.	F			b.	T
	f.	F			f.	F			c.	T
	g.	T			g.	T			d.	T
									e.	F
									f.	F

MULTIPLE-CHOICE

1.	a		11.	d
2.	d		12.	b
3.	c		13.	c
4.	c		14.	a
5.	b		15.	a
6.	d		16.	d
7.	c		17.	a
8.	a		18.	c
9.	c		19.	a
10.	b		20.	d

MATCHING QUESTIONS:

SECTION A

1.	g		9.	a
2.	i		10.	j
3.	h		11.	e
4.	f		12.	d
5.	n		13.	m
6.	o		14.	l
7.	k		15.	c
8.	b		16.	p

SECTION B

1.	b		9.	k
2.	f		10.	c
3.	g		11.	j
4.	l		12.	i
5.	a		13.	p
6.	n		14.	m
7.	d		15.	e
8.	o		16.	h

SECTION C

1.	p		9.	a
2.	o		10.	d
3.	k		11.	i
4.	l		12.	e
5.	g		13.	m
6.	c		14.	j
7.	h		15.	n
8.	f		16.	b

CHAPTER REVIEW

1. The focus of financial accounting is the summary and presentation of the firm's performance as a basis for comparison with other firms. One important use is for external investors. The accounting practices are highly regimented.

   The focus of managerial accounting is the internal use of information by management to evaluate operations. The firm has latitude here to summarize data as it finds useful.

2. The word "net" indicates the amount remaining after certain deductions have been made. Net worth, then, refers to the total investment in the business, including not only the initial investment but also the retained earnings over time, "net of" (after subtraction of) all liabilities incurred.

3. Assets: plant equipment, buildings, inventory, raw materials

   Liabilities: accounts payable, notes payable, income taxes payable

4. As selling expenses, since both directly relate to the cost of marketing and distribution.

5. The current ratio or the acid-test (quick) ratio. The latter is more "strict" than the former because it excludes inventory. A firm must first sell the inventory and collect cash before it has the ability to pay.

6. Revenues may lead to net profit, but the ability to pay bills depends on cash. For example, a firm may be "profitable" but have significant receivables (money owed by customers). Delays in collection would affect the firm's cash flow.

EXPERIENCING BUSINESS 19-1

B	Accounts payable	$35,000
I	Office supplies	2,300
I	Inventory, January 1	30,000
B	Accrued expenses	4,750
I	Interest	3,300
B	Cash	16,500
I	Gross sales	320,000
B	Long-term liabilities	12,000
I	Rent	13,000
I	Purchases	98,000
B	Marketable securities	3,800
I	Administrative salaries	23,700
B	Accounts receivable	32,500
B	Fixed assets	45,000
B/I	Inventory, December 31	23,000
	(ending inventory appears on both statements)	
I	Depreciation	3,400
I	Sales discounts	3,400
B	Notes payable	7,750
B	Retained earnings	40,000
I	Selling expenses	72,000
I	Insurance	3,000
B	Owners' equity	???

Balance Sheet as of December 31, 1996

ASSETS
Current Assets:

Cash	$16,500	
Marketable securities	3,800	
Accounts receivable	32,500	
Inventory	23,000	
Total Current Assets		$75,800

Fixed Assets:

Fixed assets		45,000
Total Assets		$120,800

LIABILITIES AND OWNERS' EQUITY
Current Liabilities

Accounts payable	$35,000	
Notes payables	7,750	
Accrued expenses	4,750	
Total Current Liabilities		$47,500

Long-term Liabilities:

Long-term liabilities	12,000	

Total Liabilities

		$ 59,500

Owners' Equity:

Retained earnings	$40,000	
Owners' Equity	21,300	
Total Owners' Equity		61,300
Total Liabilities and Owners' Equity		$120,800

Income Statement for Year Ended December 31, 1996
Revenues:

Gross sales	$320,000	
Less Sales discounts	3,400	
Net Sales		$316,600

Cost of Goods Sold:

Inventory, January 1	30,000	
Purchases	98,000	
Goods available for sale	128,000	
Less Inventory, December 31	23,000	
Cost of Goods Sold		105,000

GROSS PROFIT $211,600

Operating expenses:

Selling expenses		$ 72,000

General and administrative expenses:

Administrative salaries	$23,700	
Office supplies	2,300	
Interest	3,300	
Rent	13,000	
Depreciation	3,400	
Insurance	3,000	
Total Gen. & Admin. Exp.	$ 48,700	
Total Operating Expenses		$120,700

Net Profit Before Taxes $ 90,900

EXPERIENCING BUSINESS 19-2

Current ratio:
 Current Assets ÷ Current Liabilities =
 565,000 ÷ 158,000 = 3.58

Quick ratio:
 (Current Assets − Inventory) ÷ Current Liabilities =
 (565,000 − 400,0000) ÷ 158,000 = 1.04

Net working capital:
 Current Assets − Current Liabilities =
 565,000 − 158,000 = 407,000

Net profit margin:
 Net Profit ÷ Net Sales =
 61,000 ÷ 800,000 = .08 = 8%

Return on equity:
 Net Profit ÷ Owners' Equity =
 61,000 ÷ 1,035,000 = .06 = 6%

Inventory turnover:
 Cost of Goods Sold ÷ Average Inventory
   Average Inventory =
   (Beginning Inventory + Ending Inventory) ÷ 2 =
   (320,000 + 400,000) ÷ 2 = 360,000

 Cost of Goods Sold ÷ Average Inventory =
 445,000 ÷ 360,000 = 1.24

Debt-to-equity:
 Total liabilities ÷ Owners' Equity =
 308,000 ÷ 1,035,000 = 30%

PART EIGHT

FINANCE

This part of the text provides insights into all of the major financial aspects of a firm and how it functions in the world of business. Chapter 20 explains what money is and financial institutions that deal with it primarily. Chapter 21 explains the role of finance in the firm and the basics of financial planning and investment decisions. Chapter 22 describes and explains securities—stocks and bonds—and the markets in which they are bought and sold. Understanding finance is central to the successful management and survival of any business organization.

FINANCIAL INSTITUTIONS

OUTLINE

LEARNING GOALS

After studying this chapter, you should be able to:

1. Define money and understand its three main functions.
2. Describe the makeup of the money supply and define M1, M2, and M3.

(continued)

259

3. Identify the key members of the U.S. financial system and explain financial intermediation.

4. Distinguish between depository and nondepository financial institutions, and list the key types of each.

5. Discuss the services offered by commercial banks.

6. List the main functions of the Federal Reserve and the tools it uses to manage the money supply.

7. Describe the role of the FDIC.

8. Understand the reasons for recent banking crises, and discuss the future of banking.

TESTING YOUR KNOWLEDGE

TRUE-FALSE

Directions: *Test your knowledge of each learning goal by answering the true-false questions following each goal.*

1.   Define money and understand its three main functions.

_____   a.   Money is anything generally accepted as a means of exchange.

_____   b.   Money serves as a standard of value.

_____   c.   Flowers would be a better form of money than clam shells on a tropical island.

2.   Describe the makeup of the money supply and define M1, M2, and M3.

_____   a.   Demand deposits are the single largest component of the money supply.

_____   b.   Credit cards are money.

_____   c.   Checks are the most popular form of payment in the United States.

_____   d.   Currency includes coins, paper money, money orders, and traveler's and cashier's checks.

_____   e.   The basic money supply is called M3.

3.   Identify the key members of the U.S. financial system and explain financial intermediation.

_____   a.   Almost all Americans take part in the U.S. financial system.

_____   b.   Households are not important participants in the U.S. financial system.

_____   c.   Financial institutions are the heart of the financial system.

_____   d.   Overall, businesses and governments borrow more money than they save.

4.   Distinguish between depository and nondepository financial institutions, and list the key types of each.

_____   a.   The main depository institutions are insurance companies, pension funds, brokerage firms, and finance companies.

_____   b.   Commercial banks are the largest group of depository financial institutions.

_____   c.   Thrifts do not include savings banks.

_____   d.   Savings banks are federally-chartered banks.

_____ e. Insurance companies are major funds suppliers.

_____ f. A pension fund invests only in the organization by which its members are employed.

5. Discuss the services offered by commercial banks.

_____ a. Commercial banks may be chartered by the state or federal government.

_____ b. About one third of all U.S. commercial banks are chartered by the state in which they are based.

_____ c. The ten largest U.S. commercial banks account for about 25 percent of banking industry deposits.

_____ d. When banks make loans, they create new money.

_____ e. The income from a bank's loans and investments supplies money with which the bank pays interest to depositors, expenses, and taxes.

_____ f. Electronic funds transfer systems (EFTS) use FAX machines to make financial transactions and transfers.

6. List the main functions of the Federal Reserve and the tools it uses to manage the money supply.

_____ a. The fourteen district banks of the Federal Reserve focus on regional policy issues.

_____ b. When the Fed sells bonds, it puts money into the economy.

_____ c. The Fed seldom uses its power to change consumer credit rules or margin requirements.

_____ d. The Fed mints coins and prints money and distributes them to banks.

_____ e. The Fed has set rules governing the time it takes for checks to clear.

_____ f. The Fed's three tools for managing the money supply are open market operations, reserve requirements, and the discount rate.

7. Describe the role of the FDIC.

_____ a. The FDIC is an independent, quasi-public corporation.

_____ b. The FDIC may cover deposits of over $100,000

_____ c. All member banks in the Federal Reserve System must be insured by the FDIC.

8. Understand the reasons for recent banking crises, and discuss the future of banking.

_____ a. To help thrifts improve their profits, Congress deregulated them.

_____ b. Risky real estate loans and high interest rates were key factors in most of the S&L losses.

_____ c. The banking industry has been immune to the ills that plagued S&Ls.

_____ d. U.S. banks have more regulations than many foreign banks, which makes it difficult for them to compete for international loans.

_____ e. Deregulation has greatly decreased the services that banks are allowed to offer.

_____ f. Merger activity among U.S. banks has been on the rise recently.

MULTIPLE-CHOICE

Directions: *Put the letter of the response that best completes each of the following statements in the blank at the left.*

_____   1.   Without money, goods and services must be exchanged directly. This is called

a.   full-bodied money exchange.
b.   a barter system.
c.   medium of exchange.
d.   store-of-value exchange.

_____   2.   As a _____, money is used to hold wealth.

a.   store of value
b.   medium of exchange
c.   unit of account
d.   all of the above

_____   3.   Money as a medium of exchange

a.   can be used instead of goods to help make transactions.
b.   serves as a yardstick.
c.   can be used to hold wealth.
d.   can be easily measured.

_____   4.   The desirable physical characteristics of money are

a.   durability, portability, and divisibility.
b.   divisibility, durability, and liquidity.
c.   portability, durability, and continuing stability.
d.   durability, divisibility, and stability.

_____   5.   Today, when currency wears out, it can be replaced with new coins and bills. This is the physical characteristic of

a.   portability.
b.   divisibility.
c.   liquidity.
d.   durability.

_____   6.   The broadest measure of the money supply is

a.   M1.
b.   M2.
c.   M3.
d.   M4.

_____   7.   Money moves from suppliers to demanders within the financial system through

a.   bank holding companies.
b.   monetary policy.
c.   financial intermediation.
d.   reserve requirements.

_____ 8. The financial institutions offering the widest range of financial services are

    a. commercial banks.
    b. credit unions.
    c. mutual savings banks.
    d. savings and loans.

_____ 9. Those in the economy with money to invest are called

    a. demanders of funds.
    b. suppliers of funds.
    c. financial intermediators.
    d. commercial banks.

_____ 10. Which of the following is tax exempt?

    a. credit union association
    b. commercial lending bank
    c. savings and loan association
    d. savings bank

_____ 11. About ____ percent of all S&Ls are chartered by the federal government.

    a. 10
    b. 20
    c. 30
    d. 40

_____ 12. Which of the following is basically a savings cooperative?

    a. mutual savings bank
    b. credit union
    c. pension fund
    d. life insurance company

_____ 13. In most countries, banks are chartered

    a. by neither national nor state government.
    b. only by the national government.
    c. by national government and state governments.
    d. half by national government and half by people.

_____ 14. Which of the following are chartered by state government agencies?

    a. state banks
    b. national banks
    c. Federal Reserve banks
    d. commercial banks

_____ 15. All national banks must

    a. belong to the Federal Reserve System.
    b. stay away from the Federal Reserve System.
    c. be chartered by the state government agencies.
    d. hold at least 40 percent of all banking deposits.

_____ 16. Deposits that can be drawn on without notice by means of checks, or by with-drawal of funds, are _____ deposits

     a.   savings
     b.   time
     c.   demand
     d.   bond

_____ 17. Canada has _____ large nationwide banks.

     a.   four
     b.   five
     c.   six
     d.   seven

_____ 18. National banks hold about _____ percent of all banking deposits.

     a.   20
     b.   40
     c.   60
     d.   80

_____ 19. Deposits that are kept on deposit for a specified period of time with a guaranteed interest rate are _____ deposits.

     a.   savings
     b.   bond
     c.   time
     d.   demand

_____ 20. The Federal Reserve System consists of _____ Federal Reserve banks.

     a.   8
     b.   12
     c.   16
     d.   20

MATCHING QUESTIONS SECTION A

a.	financial intermediation	g.	thrift institutions
b.	commercial banks	h.	credit unions
c.	savings banks	i.	pension funds
d.	brokerage firms	j.	money
e.	currency	k.	S&Ls
f.	M1	l.	finance companies

MATCHING DEFINITIONS. *Directions: Match the terms above with the definitions below.*

_____ 1. Anything that is acceptable as payment for goods and services.

_____ 2. Cash held in the form of coins and paper money.

_____ 3. The basic money supply—currency held by the public, demand deposits, and traveler's checks.

_____ 4. The process by which financial institutions ease the transfer of funds from suppliers to demanders.

_____ 5. Accept customer deposits and use them for consumer and business loans.

_____ 6. Offer savings and interest-bearing checking accounts.

_____ 7. Make about a third of the home mortgages in the U.S.

_____ 8. Nonprofit, member-owned financial cooperatives.

_____ 9. Operate much like S&Ls.

_____ 10. Pay retirement benefits to their employees or members.

_____ 11. Buy and sell securities.

_____ 12. Make short-term loans for which the borrower puts up security.

MATCHING QUESTIONS: SECTION B

a.	bank holding company	g.	national banks
b.	demand deposits	h.	money market accounts
c.	time deposits	i.	EFTS
d.	ATM	j.	POS machines
e.	NOW account	k.	CDs
f.	state banks		

MATCHING DEFINITIONS. *Directions: Match the terms above with the definitions below.*

_____ 1. Chartered by the Comptroller of the Currency.

_____ 2. Account for about 40 percent of total bank deposits.

_____ 3. A corporation that owns two or more banks.

_____ 4. A type of checking account that pays interest.

_____ 5. Funds that can be withdrawn at any time.

_____ 6. Savings accounts that pay interest, but cannot be withdrawn on demand.

_____ 7. Savings accounts that pay the market rate.

_____ 8. Pay a certain interest rate for money left on deposit for a certain period of time.

_____ 9. Financial transaction made with the telephone or a computer.

_____ 10. Lets customers make withdrawals 24 hours a day.

_____ 11. Lets customers use debit cards to pay for purchases.

Matching Questions: Section C

a.	discount rate	g.	reserve requirements
b.	federal funds rate	h.	margin requirements
c.	FDIC	i.	NCUA
d.	SAIF	j.	FSLIC
e.	selective credit controls	k.	float
f.	open market operations	l.	federal funds

Matching Definitions.   *Directions: Match the terms above with the definitions below.*

_____   1.   Purchase and sale of government bonds by the Fed.

_____   2.   Now range from 3 to 10 percent on different types of deposits.

_____   3.   The interest rate the Fed charges member banks.

_____   4.   Called interbank loans.

_____   5.   The rate charged on federal funds.

_____   6.   The minimum amount of cash an investor must put up for securities.

_____   7.   Includes consumer credit rules and margin requirements.

_____   8.   The time between when a check is written and when the funds are actually deducted from the account.

_____   9.   Insures the deposits of commercial banks.

_____ 10.   Protected S&Ls until 1988.

_____ 11.   Under the control of the FDIC, took over the role of insuring thrifts.

_____ 12.   Insures credit union deposits.

CHAPTER REVIEW

1.   What are the three main functions of money?

2.   Describe the three components of the money supply.

3. Identify the key players in the financial market.

4. Discuss the three major tools used by the Fed to manage the money supply.

5. What are some of the changes affecting the banking industry in the future?

6. What are the four main functions of the Federal Reserve?

7. Identify the role of the FDIC.

EXPERIENCING BUSINESS 20-1

DISAPPEARING LOCAL BANKS

Banks are merging because the long-standing restrictions on interstate banking have been eased. What has that meant for the so-called local or home-town bank?

To do this exercise:

Check the major banks in your community.

1. Are any locally owned?

2. If the banks are regional or interstate, who owns the bank (what is the parent corporation)?

3. In general, do you think the trend to regional banking has helped or hurt the communities?

EXPERIENCING BUSINESS 20-2

CHECKING ACCOUNTS

The increased competition for customer deposits, especially demand deposits (checking) has led to many "special accounts." These are package deals wherein a depositor gets some incentives for depositing with that institution. Typically, these accounts have some minimum requirements such as an associated time deposit or minimum balance. Perhaps the requirement is "marketing oriented," such as accounts for senior citizens.

To do this exercise:

Check with at least one bank and one thrift institution in your area.

1. What special or premium accounts do they offer?

2. What are the qualifying or minimum requirements?

3. What incentives or bonus services do they offer?

4. Would you personally be interested in such an account?

ANSWER KEY (CHAPTER 20)

TRUE-FALSE

1.	a.	T		d.	F	7.	a.	T
	b.	T		e.	T		b.	T
	c.	F		f.	F		c.	T
2.	a.	F	5.	a.	T	8.	a.	T
	b.	F		b.	F		b.	T
	c.	T		c.	T		c.	F
	d.	T		d.	T		d.	T
	e.	F		e.	T		e.	F
3.	a.	T		f.	F		f.	T
	b.	F	6.	a.	F			
	c.	T		b.	F			
	d.	T		c.	T			
4.	a.	F		d.	F			
	b.	T		e.	T			
	c.	F		f.	T			

MULTIPLE-CHOICE

1.	b	11.	c
2.	a	12.	b
3.	a	13.	b
4.	a	14.	a
5.	d	15.	a
6.	c	16.	c
7.	c	17.	c
8.	a	18.	c
9.	b	19.	c
10.	a	20.	b

MATCHING QUESTIONS: SECTION A

1.	j	7.	k
2.	e	8.	h
3.	f	9.	c
4.	a	10.	i
5.	b	11.	d
6.	g	12.	l

MATCHING QUESTIONS: SECTION B

1.	g	7.	h
2.	f	8.	k
3.	a	9.	i
4.	e	10.	d
5.	b	11.	j
6.	c		

MATCHING QUESTIONS: SECTION C

1.	f	7.	e
2.	g	8.	k
3.	a	9.	c
4.	l	10.	j
5.	b	11.	d
6.	h	12.	i

CHAPTER REVIEW

1. Money's three main functions are as a medium of exchange to make transactions easier, as a unit of account to measure the value of goods and services, and as a store of value to hold wealth.

2. The three components of the money supply are currency (coin and paper money), demand deposits (checking accounts), and time deposits (interest earning deposits that can't be withdrawn on demand). The basic money supply—currency in circulation, demand deposits, and traveler's checks—is termed M1.

3. Households, businesses, and governments are the key players of the U.S. financial system.

4. The Fed has three tools: open market operations, reserve requirements, and the discount rate.

    When the Fed purchases government bonds, it puts money into the economy. The opposite occurs when the Fed sells bonds.

    When the Fed raises the amount that banks must hold in reserve, the banks have less money to lend, and the economy slows down. Lowering the reserve requirements makes more money available for loans, lowers interest rates, and stimulates the economy.

    If the Fed wants to stimulate the economy, it may lower the discount rate (the interest rate charged to member banks).

5. Important trends include a streamlining of operations, the internationalization of the financial markets, tailoring services to customers, and the continuing merger of financial institutions.

6. The Federal Reserve performs four main functions: carrying out monetary policy, setting rules on credit, distributing currency, and making check clearing easier.

7. The FDIC insures bank deposits against loss in the event of bank failure, sets banking policies and practices, and reviews banks annually to make sure they obey its regulations. The FDIC helps financially troubled banks by lending them money, arranging for a merger with a stronger bank, buying their loans, or providing more capital. When a bank fails, the FDIC tries to arrange a merger. If it can't, it sells the bank's assets and pays depositors directly.

FINANCIAL MANAGEMENT

OUTLINE

LEARNING GOALS

After studying this chapter, you should be able to:

1. Understand the role of finance and the financial manager.

2. Discuss the need for financial planning and the difference between forecasts and budgets.

3. Explain how a firm invests its money, and compare short-term and long-term expenses.

4. Describe the main sources of unsecured and secured short-term financing, and discuss their costs.

5. Distinguish between debt and equity as sources of long-term financing, and describe their relationship to leverage and the cost of capital.

6. Describe the main sources of long-term debt and equity financing, their key features, and their costs.

TESTING YOUR KNOWLEDGE

TRUE-FALSE

*Directions: Test your knowledge of each learning goal by answering the true-false questions
following each goal.*

1.   Understand the role of finance and the financial manager.

_____   a.   Financial management is closely related to accounting.

_____   b.   Finance is a central activity in every firm.

_____   c.   The main goal of the financial manager is to maximize profit.

2.   Discuss the need for financial planning and the difference between forecasts and budgets.

_____   a.   Short-term forecasts are often referred to as strategic plans.

_____   b.   Operating plans typically cover two to ten years.

_____   c.   Most budgets cover a one-year period.

3.   Explain how a firm invests its money, and compare short-term and long-term expenses.

_____   a.   Long-term expenses are often called operating expenses.

_____   b.   The financial manager wants to keep as little cash as possible and invest the
rest.

_____   c.   For the average manufacturing firm, accounts receivable represent 35 to 40
percent of total assets.

_____   d.   In a typical manufacturing firm, inventory may be nearly 20 percent of total
assets.

_____   e.   The purchase of a building is a capital expenditure but the purchase of a
computer is not.

_____   f.   Capital budgeting assesses how much a proposed project will add to a firm's
value.

4.   Describe the main sources of unsecured and secured short-term financing, and discuss their costs.

_____   a.   Trade credit is a form of secured short-term financing.

_____   b.   A line of credit is a guaranteed loan.

_____   c.   Commercial paper is a popular form of financing for large corporations.

_____   d.   Factoring is a costly form of financing.

_____   e.   Lenders usually charge higher interest rates on secured loans than on
unsecured loans.

_____   f.   Interest rates on short-term loans are usually tied to the prime rate.

5.   Distinguish between debt and equity as sources of long-term financing, and describe their
relationship to leverage and the cost of capital.

_____   a.   For a corporation, stock dividends paid to owners are a tax-deductible expense.

_____   b.   Leverage magnifies losses as well as gains.

_____   c.   Company policies about the mix of debt and equity vary.

_____   d.   The cost of capital is the maximum rate of return a firm should earn on its
investments.

6. Describe the main sources of long-term debt and equity financing, their key features, and their costs.

_____ a. A term loan has a maturity of less than a year.

_____ b. The cost of long-term debt financing is generally lower than the cost of short-term financing.

_____ c. A company does not have to pay dividends to stockholders.

_____ d. The cost of preferred stock is higher than the cost of debt financing.

MULTIPLE-CHOICE

Directions: *Put the letter of the response that best completes each of the following statements in the blank at the left.*

_____ 1. Estimates of future revenues, expenses, and capital needs are included in the _____ plan.

   a. management
   b. capital
   c. investment
   d. financial

_____ 2. The projection of immediate and shortly upcoming sales revenues for approximately twelve months is called a _____ forecast.

   a. single-term
   b. long-term
   c. short-term
   d. capital-term

_____ 3. A projection that covers a period between two to ten years is called a _____ forecast.

   a. external
   b. internal
   c. short-term
   d. long-term

_____ 4. Blueprints for estimating future revenues and expenses are called

   a. budgets.
   b. internal strategy.
   c. forecasting.
   d. capital plans.

_____ 5. Management's decisions to expand or sell existing facilities would be based on a

   a. short-term forecast.
   b. capital budget.
   c. trade credit.
   d. leveraged buyout.

6. Which of the following incorporates the firm's revenues and expenses and projects its future cash needs?

    a. operating budget
    b. cash management budget
    c. capital budget
    d. cash budget

7. Which of the following are bills owed by customers?

    a. accounts receivable
    b. trade credit
    c. credit accounts
    d. underwriting costs

8. Which of the following is money invested in the business by the owners?

    a. equity capital
    b. debt capital
    c. accounts receivable
    d. leverage

9. Profits not distributed to shareholders as dividends but reinvested in the business are called

    a. external earnings.
    b. internal earnings.
    c. retained earnings.
    d. floating capital profit.

10. Raising new capital from outside the business is called ____ financing.

    a. long-term
    b. internal
    c. retained earnings
    d. external

11. A loan from the seller to the buyer of goods and services, as a major source of short-term funds, is called

    a. a line of credit.
    b. trade credit.
    c. revolving credit.
    d. commercial paper.

12. A loan that is repaid over an extended time period, often 5 to 20 years, is called

    a. long-term debt.
    b. short-term debt.
    c. term-year credit.
    d. extended credit.

13. When a borrower does not need to put up collateral as a condition for receiving a loan, it is called

    a.   an unsecured loan.
    b.   a secured loan.
    c.   internal financing.
    d.   external financing.

14. A guaranteed agreement made by a commercial bank to lend the borrower funds up to a stated maximum amount is called a

    a.   single payment credit.
    b.   revolving credit agreement.
    c.   line of credit.
    d.   trade credit.

15. A short-term corporate IOU sold in the money market by large corporations to raise short-term funds is called

    a.   a credit line.
    b.   a line of credit.
    c.   a single payment note.
    d.   commercial paper.

16. Borrowed capital is called _____ financing.

    a.   optimal
    b.   equity
    c.   debt
    d.   trade credit

17. Capital invested in a business by its owners—the stockholders—is called _____ capital.

    a.   optimal
    b.   trade credit
    c.   equity
    d.   debt

18. The base rate that banks charge their most favored and creditworthy customers is called the _____ rate.

    a.   prime
    b.   discount
    c.   floating
    d.   capital

19. Which of the following changes each time the prime rate of interest is adjusted upward or downward by leading banks?

    a.   variable interest rate
    b.   floating interest rate
    c.   lending interest rate
    d.   line of credit

_____ 20. Which of the following does a secured loan usually require?

      a. an agreement
      b. collateral
      c. a variable
      d. a pledge

MATCHING QUESTIONS: SECTION A

a.	risk-return tradeoff	i.	operating budgets
b.	long-term forecasts	j.	unsecured loans
c.	capital budgets	k.	cash budgets
d.	cash management	l.	capital expenditures
e.	accounts receivable	m.	internal financing
f.	cash flow	n.	trade credit
g.	capital budgeting	o.	budgets
h.	marketable securities	p.	short-term forecasts

MATCHING DEFINITIONS.   *Directions: Match the terms above with the definitions below.*

_____ 1. The inflows and outflows of cash.

_____ 2. Profits reinvested in the business.

_____ 3. The higher the risk, the greater the required return.

_____ 4. Projected one-year expenses and revenues.

_____ 5. Plans that cover two to ten years.

_____ 6. Formal written forecasts of revenues and expenses.

_____ 7. Forecast the firm's inflows and outflows of cash.

_____ 8. Forecast outlays for fixed assets.

_____ 9. Combines sales forecasts with estimates of production costs and operating expenses.

_____ 10. Making sure enough cash is on hand to pay bills.

_____ 11. Investments that can easily be converted into cash.

_____ 12. Sales that have not been collected.

_____ 13. Investment in land and buildings.

_____ 14. Selecting long-term expenses that offer the best returns.

_____ 15. Assets are not pledged as security.

_____ 16. Credit extended to the buyer by the seller.

MATCHING QUESTIONS: SECTION B

a. line of credit
b. secured loans
c. term loan
d. prime rate of interest
e. underwriting
f. mortgage loan
g. commercial paper

h. leverage
i. stock dividend
j. factoring
k. venture capital
l. revolving credit agreement
m. financial management
n. rights offering
o. single-payment note

MATCHING DEFINITIONS. *Directions:* *Match the terms above with the definitions below.*

_____ 1. A loan that is repaid in one lump sum.

_____ 2. An agreement between a bank and a business, allowing the business to borrow up to a certain amount if the bank has the funds to lend.

_____ 3. A guaranteed line of credit.

_____ 4. Unsecured short-term debt offered by large corporations.

_____ 5. Loans backed by specific assets.

_____ 6. Selling a firm's accounts receivable.

_____ 7. The lowest short-term interest rate.

_____ 8. The use of debt financing to magnify the firm's rate of return.

_____ 9. A business loan with a maturity of more than one year.

_____ 10. Uses real estate as collateral.

_____ 11. Selling a new issue of stock to an investment banker.

_____ 12. Direct sales of new issues to the firm's stockholders.

_____ 13. Payment in the form of stock.

_____ 14. Form of financing popular with high-tech companies.

_____ 15. The art and science of managing a firm's money.

CHAPTER REVIEW

1. List the key activities of the financial manager.

2. What is the difference between a financial forecast and a budget?

3. Differentiate between short-term and long-term expenses.

4. Identify the main sources of unsecured and secured short-term financing.

5. Explain the use of leverage by a firm.

EXPERIENCING BUSINESS 21-1   MANAGING FINANCES

Financial management is closely related to accounting, but the accountant's main function is to collect and present financial data. Financial managers use financial statements and other information to make financial decisions. This exercise provides the opportunity to apply some of the concepts from Chapter 19, Accounting, in analyzing finances.

To do this exercise:

Select two companies in the same business or industry and obtain an annual financial report for each. Your college or public library should have reports on hand. If the report is not the latest, it will not stop you from completing the exercise.

Answer the following:

1. Balance sheet:
    a. What is the debt-to-equity ratio of each company?
    b. Is there a difference in the leverage of the companies?
    c. What type(s) of debt does each company have?
    d. What conclusions can you make about the financing?

2. Statement of cash flows:
    a. What types of operating flows are involved?
    b. What types of investment flows are involved?
    c. What types of financing flows are involved?

EXPERIENCING BUSINESS 21-2

FINANCING GROWTH IN A SMALL BUSINESS

To do this exercise:

Interview one or more small business managers or owners.

1. What are some of their concerns in financial management?

2. How do they control costs?

3. What "tools" do they have? (Who does their accounting? Does the service provide analysis, etc.?)

4. Is financing growth an issue? (Has it been a limitation? If not, how did they finance it?)

ANSWER KEY (CHAPTER 21)

TRUE-FALSE

1.	a.	T		d.	T	5.	a.	F
	b.	T		e.	F		b.	T
	c.	F		f.	T		c.	T
2.	a.	F					d.	F
	b.	F	4.	a.	F	6.	a.	F
	c.	T		b.	F		b.	F
3.	a.	F		c.	T		c.	T
	b.	T		d.	T		d.	T
	c.	F		e.	T			
				f.	T			

MULTIPLE-CHOICE

1.	d	11.	b
2.	c	12.	a
3.	d	13.	a
4.	a	14.	b
5.	b	15.	d
6.	d	16.	c
7.	a	17.	c
8.	a	18.	a
9.	c	19.	b
10.	d	20.	b

MATCHING QUESTIONS: SECTION A

1.	f	9.	i
2.	m	10.	d
3.	a	11.	h
4.	p	12.	e
5.	b	13.	l
6.	o	14.	g
7.	k	15.	j
8.	c	16.	n

MATCHING QUESTIONS: SECTION B

1.	o	9.	c
2.	a	10.	f
3.	l	11.	e
4.	g	12.	n
5.	b	13.	i
6.	j	14.	k
7.	d	15.	m
8.	h		

CHAPTER REVIEW

1. The financial manager's key activities are (1) financial planning, (2) investment (spending money), and (3) financing (raising money).

2. A financial forecast is a projection of future developments within a firm. A budget is a formal written forecast of revenues and expenses that sets spending limits. Budgets are a way to control expenses and compare the actual performance to the forecast.

3. Short-term, or operating, expenses support current production and selling activities. Long-term, or capital, expenditures are funds used for such items as land, building, machinery, and equipment.

4. The main sources of unsecured short-term financing are trade credit, bank loans, and commercial paper. Pledging accounts receivable or inventory and factoring accounts receivable are major forms of secured short-term financing.

5. Leverage is the use of debt financing to magnify the firm's rate of return. The use of debt increases risk, but it also increases potential profits. If the earnings are greater than the interest payments on the debt, the firm will earn a higher rate of return than if equity financing had been used.

SECURITIES AND SECURITIES MARKETS

CHAPTER

22

OUTLINE

(continued)

LEARNING GOALS

After studying this chapter, you should be able to:

1. Compare common stocks, preferred stocks, bonds, mutual funds, futures contracts, and options.
2. Describe the U.S. securities markets.
3. Explain the key securities market laws and regulatory agencies.
4. Understand investors and their goals.
5. Outline the steps involved in opening a brokerage account and making securities transactions.
6. Identify the main sources of investment information.
7. Understand how to interpret stock, bond, and mutual fund quotations.
8. Discuss current issues facing the securities markets.

TESTING YOUR KNOWLEDGE

TRUE-FALSE

Directions: Test your knowledge of each goal by answering the true-false questions following each goal.

1. Compare common stocks, preferred stocks, bonds, mutual funds, futures contracts, and options.

   _____ a. The price of common stock generally does not change as much as the price of preferred stock.

   _____ b. Investors like common stock because of the steady dividend income.

   _____ c. Stockholders are the creditors of a corporation.

   _____ d. Mutual funds pool investors' funds to buy securities that meet stated investment goals.

   _____ e. Futures contracts pay interest or dividends.

   _____ f. Debentures are unsecured bonds.

   _____ g. To earn a profit in options, an investor must correctly guess future price movements.

   _____ h. With both futures and options, the price paid for the contract is the maximum amount that can be lost.

2. Describe the U.S. securities markets.

   _____ a. New securities may be bought and sold in the secondary market.

   _____ b. A membership on a securities exchange is known as a "chair."

   _____ c. The trading floor of the over-the-counter market is located in Chicago and is linked by Nasdaq with dealers and brokers throughout the country.

   _____ d. Securities prices rise in a bull market.

3. Explain the key securities market laws and regulatory agencies.

_____ a. The securities markets are regulated by both state and federal governments.

_____ b. The Securities Act of 1933 was passed by various individual states to regulate the sale of securities.

_____ c. The Securities Exchange Act of 1934 and its 1964 amendment gave the SEC power to control the organized and OTC exchanges.

4. Understand investors and their goals.

_____ a. Investment is a short-term strategy; speculation is a long-term strategy.

_____ b. Institutional investors are not a major force in the securities markets.

_____ c. Dividend yield is calculated by dividing the current annual dividend by market price.

_____ d. Risk and return are directly related.

_____ e. Diversification may be interesting for the investor but does not reduce investment risk.

5. Outline the steps involved in opening a brokerage account and making securities transactions.

_____ a. Both bonds and stock are traded with brokers.

_____ b. With a margin account, security purchases are paid for in full.

_____ c. A market order is used to limit an investor's loss if the stock market begins to crash.

6. Identify the main sources of investment information.

_____ a. Stockholders reports are a questionable source of information about a corporation.

_____ b. Very few investment newsletters give subscribers specific buy and sell recommendations.

7. Understand how to interpret stock, bond, and mutual fund quotations.

_____ a. The P/E ratio is calculated by dividing the earnings per share by the current market price.

_____ b. Quotes for preferred stocks are listed with common stock quotes.

_____ c. Price quotations for mutual funds differ from stock quotations.

_____ d. Bond prices are expressed as a percentage of the par value.

8. Discuss current issues facing the securities markets.

_____ a. The change from a bull to a bear market is usually slow.

_____ b. All trading by insiders is illegal.

_____ c. Many large investors are now handling trades without Wall Street services.

MULTIPLE-CHOICE

Directions: *Put the letter of the response that best completes each of the following statements in the blank at the left.*

_____ 1. The ownership interest in a corporation takes the form of

     a. bonds.
     b. stocks.
     c. options.
     d. futures contracts.

_____ 2. Which of the following are the two *major* types of stock?

     a. participating and common
     b. common and secured
     c. convertible and preferred
     d. common and preferred

_____ 3. Stockholders have a residual claim on the firm's

     a. management.
     b. assets and profits.
     c. management and profits.
     d. book value.

_____ 4. Securities whose owners receive preferential treatment in the payment of dividends is(are)

     a. bonds.
     b. common stock.
     c. preferred stock.
     d. option stock.

_____ 5. Which of the following have voting rights in a corporation?

     a. common stockholders
     b. preferred stockholders
     c. bondholders
     d. creditors

_____ 6. Profits that are reinvested in the firm and *not* paid out as dividends are called

     a. cash dividends.
     b. retained earnings.
     c. future earnings.
     d. commissions.

_____ 7. If a company experiences financial difficulties, it can

    a. omit payment of preferred stock dividends only.
    b. omit payment of both preferred and common stock dividends.
    c. omit payment of common stock dividends only.
    d. double its payments on preferred and common stock dividends.

_____ 8. Which of the following does *not* provide voting rights and has a dividend rate that is usually fixed?

    a. common stock
    b. preferred stock
    c. common bonds
    d. municipal bonds

_____ 9. A type of corporate bond secured by a specific asset of a company is called a ____ bond.

    a. debenture
    b. mortgage
    c. registered
    d. secured

_____ 10. A bond that is transferable to common stock at a specific rate is called a ____ bond.

    a. convertible
    b. preferred
    c. participating preferred
    d. cumulative preferred

_____ 11. An IOU that bears no interest but is sold at a discount and matures in less than one year is called a Treasury

    a. note.
    b. bond.
    c. bill.
    d. stock.

_____ 12. Financial services that pool the funds they raise from investors and then invest these resources in stocks, bonds, and other securities are called

    a. options.
    b. mutual funds.
    c. margins.
    d. futures contracts.

_____ 13. Which of the following allows its holders to buy or sell an amount of a specified commodity at a future date at an agreed-upon price?

    a.   futures contract
    b.   mutual fund
    c.   balanced contract
    d.   mutual contract

_____ 14. The largest U.S. stock exchange is the

    a.   OTC.
    b.   Regional.
    c.   AMEX.
    d.   NYSE.

_____ 15. The "Big Board" is another name for the

    a.   AMEX.
    b.   NYSE.
    c.   Regional.
    d.   OTC.

_____ 16. The _____ Stock Exchange is the world's second largest.

    a.   London
    b.   New York
    c.   Tokyo
    d.   Hong Kong

_____ 17. A debenture is

    a.   the legal document setting forth the provisions of the bond program.
    b.   a special type of preferred stock.
    c.   a type of bond backed solely by the reputation of the issuing firm.
    d.   a special type of bond issued by small, relatively unknown corporations.

_____ 18. The Dow Jones Industrial Average is comprised of _____ industrial stocks.

    a.   30
    b.   20
    c.   15
    d.   65

_____ 19. A stock quoted at 13 7/8 is selling for

    a. $13.875
    b. $130.87
    c. $13.78
    d. $137.80

_____ 20. On a securities exchange the number of shares in a round-lot is

    a. 10
    b. 50
    c. 100
    d. 500

MATCHING QUESTIONS: SECTION A

a.	dividends	h.	voting rights
b.	preferred stock	i.	principal
c.	bonds	j.	secured bonds
d.	junk bonds	k.	convertible bonds
e.	mortgage bonds	l.	interest
f.	common stock	m.	securities
g.	underwriting	n.	debentures

MATCHING DEFINITIONS. *Directions: Match the terms above with the definitions below.*

_____ 1. Investment certificates issued by corporations.

_____ 2. Represents ownership in a corporation.

_____ 3. Corporate profits distributed to stockholders.

_____ 4. Give common stockholders one vote for every share owned.

_____ 5. Its owners get their dividends before common stockholders.

_____ 6. Long-term debt obligations.

_____ 7. The coupon rate.

_____ 8. Par value.

_____ 9. High-risk bond.

_____ 10. Have specific assets pledged as collateral.

_____ 11. Secured by real estate or equipment.

_____ 12. Unsecured bonds.

_____ 13. Can be exchanged for common stock.

_____ 14. Buying securities from corporations and reselling them to the public.

MATCHING QUESTIONS: SECTION B

a.	mutual fund	g.	futures contracts
b.	organized stock exchanges	h.	primary market
c.	OTC	i.	Nasdaq
d.	bond ratings	j.	bear market
e.	bull market	k.	investment banker
f.	options	l.	secondary market

MATCHING DEFINITIONS.   *Directions: Match the terms above with the definitions below.*

_____ 1. Letter grades assigned to bond issues.

_____ 2. Pools its investors' funds to buy securities.

_____ 3. An agreement to buy commodities at a future date.

_____ 4. Entitle the holders to buy or sell stock during a specified time.

_____ 5. Where new securities are sold to the public.

_____ 6. Where "old" securities are sold.

_____ 7. Specializes in selling new securities.

_____ 8. Account for about three fourths of the total dollar amount of stock traded.

_____ 9. Not a specific institution with a trading floor.

_____ 10. The sophisticated system that links OTC dealers and brokers.

_____ 11. Securities prices rise.

_____ 12. Prices of securities go down.

MATCHING QUESTIONS: SECTION C

a.	diversification	i.	speculation
b.	investment	j.	odd lot
c.	round lot	k.	P/E ratio
d.	market indexes	l.	insider trading
e.	program trading	m.	DJIA
f.	dividend yield	n.	Standard & Poor's 500
g.	stockbroker	o.	circuit breakers
h.	market averages	p.	fourth market

MATCHING DEFINITIONS.   *Directions: Match the terms above with the definitions below.*

_____ 1. A long-term strategy.

_____ 2. The purchase and sale of high-risk securities.

_____ 3. A popular way to assess the dividends paid on common stock.

_____ 4. Combining securities with different patterns and amounts of returns.

_____ 5. One who is licensed to buy and sell securities.

_____ 6. Less than 100 shares of stock.

_____ 7. Stock bought in blocks of 100 shares.

_____ 8. Calculated by dividing the current market price by earnings per share.

_____ 9. Measure current price behavior against an earlier base value.

_____ 10. Measures the stock prices of a group of 30 large well-known corporations.

_____ 11. Is broader than the DJIA.

_____ 12. Using computers to automatically buy and sell securities.

_____ 13. They stop trading for a short cooling-off period.

_____ 14. The use of information not available to the public.

_____ 15. Lets traders make transactions directly without using brokers.

_____ 16. Track average price behavior of a group of securities.

CHAPTER REVIEW

1. Why would someone buy common stock rather than preferred stock? Why would someone buy preferred stock rather than common stock?

2. Identify and describe the three major types of debt securities sold by the U.S. Treasury.

3. What is the difference between an organized exchange and the over-the-counter market?

4. Outline the key points of the major federal laws that regulate the securities market.

5. Describe the three major investment goals.

6. List the major sources of investment information.

7. Differentiate between the DJIA and the Standard & Poor's 500 stock index.

8. What has been done to avoid a repeat of "Black Monday"?

EXPERIENCING BUSINESS 22-1

MARKET INFORMATION

To do this exercise:

Using the financial information provided in a recent edition of *The Wall Street Journal,* answer the following:

1. *Stock Exchange Quotation.* What information do the following provide?

    Div.

    Yld

    P-E Ratio

    Close

2. *Bond Quotation.* What information do the following provide?

    Cur Yld

    Close

3. *Mutual Fund Quotation.* What information do the following provide?

    NAV

    Offer Price

EXPERIENCING BUSINESS 22-2

DISCOUNT BROKERS

As an individual, to purchase a company's stock in the market (the stock market, actually a secondary market dealing in "used" stock), you must deal through a broker.

To do this exercise:

If you look in the telephone listings (yellow pages) under something like Stock and Bond Brokers, you will find many brokers listed.

1. Some advertise "full service"; others advertise "discount." What do these terms mean? What is the difference between a full-service and a discount broker?

2. What type of individual might prefer a full-service broker?

3. What type of individual might prefer a discount broker?

ANSWER KEY (CHAPTER 22)

TRUE-FALSE

1.	a.	F	3.	a.	T	6.	a.	F
	b.	F		b.	F		b.	F
	c.	F		c.	T	7.	a.	F
	d.	T	4.	a.	F		b.	T
	e.	F		b.	F		c.	T
	f.	T		c.	T		d.	T
	g.	T		d.	T	8.	a.	T
	h.	F		e.	F		b.	F
2.	a.	F	5.	a.	T		c.	T
	b.	F		b.	F			
	c.	F		c.	F			
	d.	T						

MULTIPLE-CHOICE

1.	b	11.	c
2.	d	12.	b
3.	b	13.	a
4.	c	14.	d
5.	a	15.	b
6.	b	16.	c
7.	b	17.	c
8.	b	18.	a
9.	d	19.	a
10.	a	20.	c

MATCHING QUESTIONS: SECTION A

1.	m	8.	i
2.	f	9.	d
3.	a	10.	j
4.	h	11.	e
5.	b	12.	n
6.	c	13.	k
7.	l	14.	g

MATCHING QUESTIONS: SECTION B

1.	d	7.	k
2.	a	8.	b
3.	g	9.	c
4.	f	10.	i
5.	h	11.	e
6.	l	12.	j

MATCHING QUESTIONS: SECTION C

1.	b	9.	d
2.	i	10.	m
3.	f	11.	n
4.	a	12.	e
5.	g	13.	o
6.	j	14.	l
7.	c	15.	p
8.	k	16.	h

CHAPTER REVIEW

1. A major reason or advantage of owning common stock is the price appreciation, which is usually much greater than that of preferred stock. A second reason is the fact that you would have voting rights. This would be very important in the event of a hostile takeover.

   Preferred stockholders, on the other hand, have the advantage of a steady dividend income.

2. The U.S. Treasury sells Treasury bills, Treasury notes, and Treasury bonds. Treasury bills mature in less than a year and are issued with a minimum par value of $10,000. Treasury notes have maturities of ten years or less, and Treasury bonds have maturities as long as twenty-five years or more. Both notes and bonds are sold in denominations of $1,000 and $5,000.

3. Organized exchanges are those like the New York Stock Exchange and the American Stock Exchange, and the various regional and foreign exchanges, places where securities are resold. The over-the-counter market is a telecommunications network linking dealers throughout the United States.

4. The Securities Act of 1933 protects investors by requiring disclosure of important information regarding new securities issues. The Securities Exchange Act of 1934 and its 1964 amendment created the Securities and Exchange Commission and granted it broad powers to regulate the organized security exchanges and the over-the-counter market. In 1970 the Securities Investor Protection Corporation (SIPC) was established to protect consumers in the event of financial failure of a brokerage firm.

5. Investors wishing to supplement their income will choose securities that provide a steady reliable source of *income* from stock dividends, bond interest, or both. Another important investment goal is *growth*, or increasing the value of the investment. *Safety*—protecting one's invested funds—is yet another investment goal.

6. Major sources of investment information are *The Wall Street Journal, Barron's, Business Week, Fortune,* and *Money*. Other sources are subscription services and investment newsletters, stockholders' reports, brokerage firm research reports, and security price quotations.

7. The most widely used market index is the Dow Jones Industrial Average (DJIA). It measures the stock prices of a group of 30 large, well-known NYSE corporations. The S&P 500 is broader. It includes 400 industrial stocks, 20 transportation stocks, 40 public utility stocks, and 40 financial stocks.

8. One action was to create circuit breakers. Under certain conditions, they stop trading for a short cooling-off period. The NYSE computer system was also upgraded to handle a greater volume of shares.

PART NINE

FURTHER DIMENSIONS AND OPPORTUNITIES

Part Nine rounds out the study of business. It focuses on the legal and tax environment surrounding the firm (Chapter 23) and on issues of risk and insurance for the firm and its employees (Chapter 24).

THE LEGAL AND TAX ENVIRONMENT

OUTLINE

LEARNING GOALS

After studying this chapter, you should be able to:

1. Describe the sources of law, the U.S. court system, business law and the Uniform Commercial Code, and nonjudicial methods of settling disputes.

2. Describe the elements of legally enforceable contracts, and explain how breaches of contract are settled.

3. Understand the key concepts of property law.

4. Discuss other key types of business law: agency law, tort law, product-liability law, and bankruptcy law.

5. Understand the government's role in regulating businesses, and discuss the impact of deregulation.

6. Explain the taxation of business income, and list four other types of taxes affecting business.

TESTING YOUR KNOWLEDGE

TRUE-FALSE

Directions: *Test your knowledge of each learning goal by answering the true-false questions following each goal.*

1. Describe the sources of law, the U.S. court system, business law and the Uniform Commercial Code, and nonjudicial methods of settling legal disputes.

    _____ a. Common (case) law is the body of law that has evolved out of court decisions rather than by legislatures.

    _____ b. Even today, cases settled by the courts become precedents for settling similar cases in the future.

    _____ c. Statutory law is written law enacted by legislatures at all levels.

    _____ d. Common law is the chief source of new law in the United States.

    _____ e. Administrative law consists of the rules, regulations, and orders passed by boards, commissions, and agencies of governments.

    _____ f. Business law is the body of law that governs commercial dealings.

    _____ g. All business law is grouped together under the Uniform Commercial Code.

    _____ h. The Uniform Commercial Code sets forth the rules that apply to commercial transactions between businesses and between individuals and businesses.

    _____ i. The Uniform Commercial Code has been adopted by all states.

    _____ j. By standardizing laws, the Uniform Commercial Code simplifies doing business across state lines.

    _____ k. The level above the trial court in the judicial system is the appellate court.

    _____ l. The losing party in a case in a trial court may appeal directly to the U.S. Supreme Court.

    _____ m. With arbitration, the parties present their case to an impartial third party and agree to accept the third party's decision.

    _____ n. Arbitration is a more flexible approach than mediation.

2. Describe the elements of legally enforceable contracts, and explain how breaches of contract are settled.

    _____ a. An express contract can be based on written or spoken words.

    _____ b. An implied contract creates a legal obligation.

    _____ c. Mutual assent, capacity, consideration, legal purpose, and legal form are the essential requirements for a valid contract.

    _____ d. "Offer" and "acceptance" are essential parts of the requirement "consideration."

    _____ e. Breach of contract occurs when one party fails (without legal excuse) to fulfill the terms of the agreement.

    _____ f. The only legal remedy for breach of contract is payment of damages.

    _____ g. Specific performance is the most common method of settling a breach of contract.

3. Understand the key concepts of property law.

    _____ a. The rights and duties of owning, using, and selling property are covered by property law.

    _____ b. Real property is land and everything permanently attached to it.

    _____ c. Personal property is property that is movable.

    _____ d. Property can include something that has no physical substance.

    _____ e. Patents, copyrights, and trademarks are examples of intellectual property.

    _____ f. Patents, copyrights, and trademarks are examples of intangible personal property.

4. Discuss other key types of business law: agency law, tort law, product-liability law, and bankruptcy law.

    _____ a. Agency law covers the administrative powers of boards, commissions, and agencies of the different levels of government.

    _____ b. Agency is a legal relationship in which one person or business authorizes another person or business to act for them.

    _____ c. A tort is a civil, or private, act that harms other people or their property.

    _____ d. A tort can be a breach of contract.

    _____ e. Torts are public wrongs and are settled in criminal courts.

    _____ f. Product liability refers to manufacturers' and sellers' responsibility for defects in the products they make and sell.

    _____ g. Under "strict liability" the manufacturer is relieved of responsibility if all possible care is taken to prevent defects.

    _____ h. Bankruptcy is a legal procedure by which individuals or businesses are relieved of their debts.

    _____ i. Most bankruptcies are in the category of liquidation.

5. Understand the government's role in regulating businesses, and discuss the impact of deregulation.

    _____ a. Antitrust regulations are laws that seek to keep the marketplace free from influences that would restrict competition.

    _____ b. Offering a customer discounts that are not offered to all other purchasers buying on similar terms is price discrimination.

    _____ c. Over the last decade the U.S. government has been actively promoting deregulation.

    _____ d. Deregulation has drastically changed some once-regulated industries.

    _____ e. Consumers seldom benefit from deregulation.

6. Explain the taxation of business income and list four other types of taxes affecting business.

    _____ a. Corporations, partnerships, and sole proprietorships pay incomes taxes as businesses.

    _____ b. Property taxes are assessed on real and personal property.

    _____ c. Payroll taxes include unemployment taxes for states only; there are no federal unemployment taxes.

    _____ d. Sales taxes are levied on all goods.

    _____ e. Excise taxes are placed on specific items by federal, state, or local governments.

MULTIPLE-CHOICE

Directions: Put the letter of the response that best completes each of the following statements in the blank at the left.

_____   1.   The legislative branches of government develop and enact

      a.   natural laws.
      b.   common laws.
      c.   statutory laws.
      d.   torts.

_____   2.   A type of law that consists of orders, rules, and regulations of government agencies is ____ law.

      a.   statutory
      b.   common
      c.   natural
      d.   administrative

_____   3.   Property that can be seen, touched, and physically relocated is ____ property.

      a.   tangible personal
      b.   intangible personal
      c.   personal
      d.   real

_____   4.   Which of the following is a representation made regarding the quality and performance of goods?

      a.   guarantee
      b.   warranty
      c.   contract
      d.   consumer license

_____   5.   Real property is also known as

      a.   a personal possession.
      b.   tangible property.
      c.   personal property.
      d.   real estate.

_____   6.   An instrument by which title to property is transferred from one owner to another is a

      a.   deed.
      b.   title.
      c.   bill of sale.
      d.   sales contract.

7. Which of the following is *not* a remedy for breach of contract?

    a. payment of damages
    b. apology
    c. restitution
    d. specific performance

8. A _____ gives the inventor exclusive rights to manufacture, use, and sell an invention.

    a. trademark
    b. patent
    c. copyright
    d. natural law

9. Which of the following is an exclusive right given to a writer, artist, composer, or playwright to use, produce, and sell his or her creation?

    a. trademark
    b. servicemark
    c. copyright
    d. patent

10. Which of the following is an identifying symbol, work, or design for a product?

    a. copyright
    b. trademark
    c. servicemark
    d. warranty

11. A copyright is issued to the creator of a work for

    a. the life of the creator.
    b. the life of the creator plus 50 years.
    c. 17 years.
    d. 21 years.

12. Which of the following is the legal relationship in which one person authorizes, expressly or by implication, another person to represent him or her?

    a. labor agreement
    b. contract
    c. agency
    d. binder

13. Which of the following occurs when a person fails to exercise due care in his or her actions?

    a. crime
    b. negligence
    c. tort
    d. deliberate intent

_____ 14. When a creditor of a business files a bankruptcy petition, it is known as

    a. involuntary bankruptcy.
    b. voluntary bankruptcy.
    c. negligence.
    d. tort.

_____ 15. Which of the following provides for the quick and efficient resolution of bankruptcy cases?

    a. Bankruptcy Reform Act
    b. Uniform Commercial Code
    c. Sherman Antitrust Act
    d. Clayton Act

_____ 16. Which of the following has been a focal point of controversy regarding business?

    a. property taxes
    b. management
    c. government regulation
    d. income tax rate

_____ 17. The _____ Act was passed in 1890 in order to curb monopoly powers of large companies that undermined the existence of smaller companies and reduced competition.

    a. Sherman Antitrust
    b. National Environmental Protection
    c. Clayton
    d. Celler-Kefauver

_____ 18. A capital gain occurs when a firm sells assets or security investments for

    a. less than original value.
    b. more than original value.
    c. less than book value.
    d. more than depreciated value.

_____ 19. Which of the following must be paid on wages, salaries, and commissions that are paid to the employees of a business?

    a. property taxes
    b. sales taxes
    c. income taxes
    d. payroll taxes

_____ 20. The United States has which of the following systems of income tax rates as they apply to businesses?

    a. dual
    b. combined
    c. regressive
    d. singular

Matching Questions: Section A

a.	agency	i.	antitrust regulation
b.	bankruptcy	j.	administrative law
c.	common law	k.	appellate courts
d.	damages	l.	intangible personal property
e.	contract	m.	express contract
f.	arbitration	n.	restitution
g.	lobby	o.	product liability
h.	property	p.	breach of contract

Matching Definitions.   *Directions: Match the terms above with the definitions below.*

_____ 1. The manufacturers' and sellers' responsibility for defects in the products they make and sell.

_____ 2. Specifies the terms of the agreement in either written or spoken form.

_____ 3. Body of unwritten law that has evolved out of court decisions.

_____ 4. The legal relationship in which a principal authorizes an agent to act for or represent him or her.

_____ 5. Rules, regulations, and orders passed by boards, commissions, and agencies of government.

_____ 6. An organization that tries to convince legislators to support the interest of the group which the organization represents.

_____ 7. The rights and interests in any object that can be owned.

_____ 8. When one party to a contract fails to fulfill the terms of the agreement.

_____ 9. Methods of settling disputes whereby the parties agree to present their case to an impartial third party and agree to accept the third party's decision.

_____ 10. Something that has no physical substance but can be owned.

_____ 11. Courts at the level above trial courts.

_____ 12. Laws that keep companies from entering into agreements to control trade through a monopoly.

_____ 13. An agreement that sets forth the relationship between parties regarding the performance of a specified action.

_____ 14. Money awarded to a party harmed by a breach of contract.

_____ 15. A legal procedure by which individuals or businesses that cannot meet their financial obligations are relieved of their debts.

_____ 16. Canceling a contract and returning to the situation that existed before the contract.

Matching Questions: Section B

a.	property law	i.	statutory law
b.	business law	j.	Uniform Commercial Code (UCC)
c.	real property	k.	specific performance
d.	capacity	l.	price discrimination
e.	sales contracts	m.	trial courts
f.	tort	n.	personal property
g.	consideration	o.	mediation
h.	implied contract	p.	mutual assent

Matching Definitions.   *Directions: Match the terms above with the definitions below.*

_____ 1. Land and everything permanently attached to it.

_____ 2. The body of law that governs commercial dealings.

_____ 3. A court order requiring the breaching party to perform the duties under the terms of the contract.

_____ 4. Covers the rights and duties of owning, using, and selling property.

_____ 5. Sets forth rules that apply to commercial transactions; adopted by forty-nine states to simplify doing business across state lines.

_____ 6. Property that is movable.

_____ 7. Written law enacted by legislatures at all levels.

_____ 8. Legal ability of a party to enter into contracts.

_____ 9. Methods of settling disputes whereby the parties present their case to a neutral third party who helps the parties negotiate a settlement.

_____ 10. Courts of general jurisdiction.

_____ 11. To offer a customer price discounts that are not offered to all other purchasers buying on similar terms.

_____ 12. Voluntary agreement by both parties to the terms of the contract.

_____ 13. A civil, or private, act that harms other people or their property.

_____ 14. Depends on the acts and conduct of the parties to show agreement.

_____ 15. Contracts for the transfer of goods from a seller to a buyer for a specified price.

_____ 16. Exchange of some value or benefit between the parties.

CHAPTER REVIEW

1. Why is the concept of "precedents" so important in our American legal system?

2. A purely gratuitous promise is generally not enforceable as a contract. One of the essential requirements is for "consideration," an exchange of some legal value or benefit. In some transactions, however, we see statements such as "for the sum of one dollar and other valuable consideration." What does that mean?

3. What does the concept of "strict liability" mean in product-liability law? What are some implications for business?

4. The text provides examples of federal government regulation such as regulation of competition, marketing activities, and consumer rights. What are some examples of significant local government regulation?

5. Sales taxes are important revenues sources for state and local governments. Is such a system really justified when the burden of collecting is placed on the merchant, often a very small business?

EXPERIENCING BUSINESS 23-1 — THE COURT SYSTEMS AND JURISDICTION

The United States has a highly developed court system which includes both federal and state courts. Jurisdiction is the authority to hear a dispute; no court has authority to hear every sort of dispute.

To do this exercise:

You will have to consult sources beyond the information available in the textbook. A business law text would be a readily available source. Another would be to talk to an attorney.

Consider the following:

1. With fifty-one legal systems—that is, a federal court system and fifty different state court systems—how is jurisdiction determined?

2. When a corporation is incorporated in one state (for example, Ohio) but a dispute arises while doing business in another state (for example, Indiana), what possible state or federal jurisdictions can be involved?

3. How does globalization, the internationalization of business, affect jurisdiction?

EXPERIENCING BUSINESS 23-2 — ADMINISTRATIVE LAW

Administrative law—the rules, regulations, or orders passed by boards, commissions, and agencies of federal, state, and local governments—can be very significant for businesses. Many businesses have regular contact with federal, state, or local administrative agencies even though they have no contact with the court system. These agencies decide a variety of issues.

To do this exercise:

Select one or more examples from each of the following categories, and identify how the federal/state/local agency could significantly affect a business.

Federal:
  Securities and Exchange Commission
  National Labor Relations Board
  Federal Trade Commission
  Occupational Safety and Health Administration
  Federal Drug Administration
  Internal Revenue Service
  U.S. Department of Justice (Immigration and Naturalization)

State:
  public utility commission
  licensing boards
  environmental protection agency
  civil rights commission
  tax authority

Local:
  zoning boards
  planning commissions
  health department
  tax authority

ANSWER KEY (CHAPTER 23)

TRUE-FALSE

1.	a.	F		c.	T		f.	T
	b.	T		d.	F		g.	F
	c.	T		e.	T		h.	T
	d.	F		f.	F		i.	T
	e.	T		g.	T	5.	a.	T
	f.	T	3.	a.	T		b.	T
	g.	F		b.	T		c.	T
	h.	T		c.	T		d.	T
	i.	F		d.	T		e.	F
	j.	T		e.	T	6.	a.	F
	k.	T		f.	T		b.	T
	l.	F	4.	a.	F		c.	F
	m.	T		b.	T		d.	F
	n.	F		c.	T		e.	T
2.	a.	T		d.	F			
	b.	T		e.	F			

MULTIPLE-CHOICE

1.	c	11.	b
2.	d	12.	c
3.	a	13.	b
4.	b	14.	a
5.	d	15.	a
6.	a	16.	c
7.	b	17.	a
8.	b	18.	b
9.	c	19.	d
10.	b	20.	a

MATCHING QUESTIONS: SECTION A

1.	o	9.	f
2.	m	10.	l
3.	c	11.	k
4.	a	12.	i
5.	j	13.	e
6.	g	14.	d
7.	h	15.	b
8.	p	16.	n

MATCHING QUESTIONS: SECTION B

1.	c	9.	o
2.	b	10.	m
3.	k	11.	l
4.	a	12.	p
5.	j	13.	f
6.	n	14.	h
7.	i	15.	e
8.	d	16.	g

CHAPTER REVIEW

1. Precedents are important for two reasons:

   (1) The system of common law is based on court decisions and the precedents of the prior determinations.

   (2) Even with a pertinent statute the court cannot always find a clear answer. Often the law was enacted with broad language and general terms because the legislators could not foresee all the possible situations that could arise. Here the courts' interpretations set precedents for future cases.

2. Essentially, it meets the legal test for consideration yet permits considerable ambiguity as to the specific terms.

3. Strict liability means that a manufacturer or seller is liable for any personal injury or property damage caused by defective products and packaging, even if all possible care has been taken to prevent such defects.

   The increasing number of product-liability cases and the large awards that result are seen by some as a threat to America's competitiveness by discouraging new product development.

4. Answers will vary. Should consider areas such as zoning, building code, public safety and inspection, operating licensing, etc.

5. Answers will vary. Essentially, there is no good alternative if the intent is a consumption tax. Historically, much of the burden of tax collection has been placed on the business—look at the complexity in computing, collecting, and remitting payroll taxes, for example.

RISK AND INSURANCE

OUTLINE

LEARNING GOALS

After studying this chapter, you should be able to:

1. Define risk, and explain why individuals and businesses buy insurance.

2. Discuss the four ways of managing risk, and tell what makes a risk insurable.

3. Distinguish between public and private insurance companies.

4. Understand the problems facing insurance companies.

5. Explain the difference between property and liability insurance, and describe the main types of coverage.

6. Understand what health insurance covers and where it can be obtained.

7. Define life insurance, and identify the forms it may take.

TESTING YOUR KNOWLEDGE

TRUE-FALSE

Directions: Test your knowledge of each learning goal by answering the true-false questions following each goal.

1.   Define risk, and explain why individuals and businesses buy insurance.

   _____   a.   Risk management plays a vital role in the overall management of a business.
   _____   b.   Some risks are not insurable.

2.   Discuss the four ways of managing risk, and tell what makes a risk insurable.

   _____   a.   Risk is a part of life.
   _____   b.   Some risks can be avoided.
   _____   c.   Risk assumption is the willingness to bear a risk without insurance.
   _____   d.   Safety measures that reduce or eliminate the possibility of financial loss are examples of self-insurance.
   _____   e.   To be insurable, the loss from a risk must be accidental.

3.   Distinguish between public and private insurance companies.

   _____   a.   Only half of the states have an unemployment insurance program.
   _____   b.   Medicaid is available for those over the age of 65.
   _____   c.   Mutual insurance companies are profit-oriented companies owned by stockholders.

4.   Understand the problems facing insurance companies.

   _____   a.   Profit margins for insurance companies have remained relatively high.
   _____   b.   Some insurance companies are ceasing to insure individual homes and automobiles.
   _____   c.   State insurance regulators recently raised capital requirements to strengthen the industry.

5.   Explain the difference between property and liability insurance, and describe the main types of coverage.

   _____   a.   Property insurance covers damage to one's own property as well as to property of others.
   _____   b.   Property insurance policies usually include a coinsurance clause.
   _____   c.   Under no-fault automobile insurance each party pays for his or her damages in the event of an accident.
   _____   d.   Inland marine insurance covers loss or damage to goods being shipped by rail or airplane.
   _____   e.   A surety bond protects employers from dishonest employees.

6.   Understand what health insurance covers and where it can be obtained.

   _____   a.   About 85 percent of all Americans are covered by some form of health insurance.

_____ b. Medicare is a welfare program, funded by federal and state governments, that pays the medical bills of the poor.

_____ c. HMOs are one of the fastest-growing types of health care.

_____ d. Many large companies are turning to PPOs to control their health care costs.

7. Define life insurance, and identify the forms it may take.

_____ a. Most group life insurance plans are whole life policies.

_____ b. Whole life has no cash value.

_____ c. Term life insurance is also called straight life insurance.

_____ d. Universal life insurance was developed to help insurance companies compete for investment funds.

MULTIPLE-CHOICE

Directions: *Put the letter of the response that best completes each of the following statements in the blank at the left.*

_____ 1. The process of evaluating a firm's total exposure to perils and then formulating strategies to minimize losses is done by

    a. speculative risk.
    b. risk management.
    c. risk avoidance.
    d. risk assumption.

_____ 2. One method of dealing with risk is keeping away from situations that can lead to loss, or

    a. transference.
    b. assumption.
    c. avoidance.
    d. prevention.

_____ 3. Four ways of handling risk are

    a. transference, avoidance, prevention, and training.
    b. assumption, transference, prevention, and exposure.
    c. prevention, assumption, avoidance, and distribution.
    d. avoidance, assumption, prevention, and transference.

_____ 4. A company that does not insure its inventories, buildings, and fixtures since its stores are spread out over the entire country has chosen

    a. associative risk.
    b. distributive risk.
    c. risk assumption.
    d. loss prevention and reduction.

_____ 5. Which of the following is *not* a way of handling risk?

    a. avoidance
    b. transference
    c. propulsion
    d. assumption

_____ 6. Financial loss due to fire, theft, auto accident, injury, or illness is an example of

    a. no-fault insurance.
    b. insurable risks.
    c. uninsurable risks.
    d. accidental risk.

_____ 7. The primary reason individuals and businesses buy insurance is to

    a. invest their money safely.
    b. provide total compensation in the event of a loss.
    c. prevent various types of risk.
    d. provide protection against the economic effects of various types of risk.

_____ 8. Airlines that maintain their aircraft and thoroughly train their pilots and flight attendants are using what method to reduce their loss?

    a. risk avoidance
    b. risk assumption
    c. risk transference
    d. risk reduction

_____ 9. The surgeon who pays an insurance company to bear some or all of his or her malpractice risk is using

    a. risk transference.
    b. risk assumption.
    c. risk avoidance.
    d. speculative risk.

_____ 10. The sustained activity calculated either to reduce the chance that a loss will occur or to reduce the loss itself is referred to as

    a. risk assumption.
    b. risk reduction.
    c. risk avoidance.
    d. associative loss.

_____ 11. The contract between the person or business that is being covered by insurance and the company that issues the policy is the

    a. sales contract.
    b. risk deed.
    c. insurance policy.
    d. detail policy.

_____ 12.   Installing sprinklers in a building is handling risk by

        a.   avoidance.
        b.   assumption.
        c.   risk reduction.
        d.   transference.

_____ 13.   Which of the following is *not* a basic type of insurance?

        a.   health
        b.   social
        c.   life
        d.   property and liability

_____ 14.   Owned collectively by its policyholders, an insurance cooperative is basically a(n) _____ insurance company

        a.   national.
        b.   mutual.
        c.   co-op.
        d.   international.

_____ 15.   _____ insurance covers financial losses from injuries to others and damage to others' property.

        a.   Property
        b.   Umbrella
        c.   Liability
        d.   Group

_____ 16.   The major difference between a mutual insurance company and a stockholder insurance company is

        a.   ownership rights.
        b.   types of insurance offered.
        c.   strength of sales price.
        d.   attractiveness of advertising.

_____ 17.   Which of the following requires the property owner to buy an amount of insurance coverage equal to a specified percentage of the value of property?

        a.   real value insurance
        b.   insurance
        c.   property insurance
        d.   coinsurance

_____ 18.   Malpractice-type lawsuits against lawyers, accountants, doctors, and college professors can be covered by

        a.   Blue Cross/Blue Shield.
        b.   no-fault insurance.
        c.   professional liability insurance.
        d.   liability insurance.

_____ 19. The benefits provided to employees who are injured at work or who contract employment-related illnesses is _____ insurance.

    a. health
    b. unemployment
    c. workmen's compensation
    d. professional liability

_____ 20. Insurance covering the insured's life for a specific number of years is _____ life insurance.

    a. whole
    b. endowment
    c. credit
    d. term

MATCHING QUESTIONS: SECTION A

a. risk avoidance	h. deductibles
b. self-insurance	i. speculative risk
c. insurance policy	j. insurable interest
d. risk	k. risk transference
e. underwriting	l. law of large numbers
f. risk reduction	m. risk management
g. insurable risk	

MATCHING DEFINITIONS. *Directions: Match the terms above with the definitions below.*

_____ 1. Analyzing the firm's operation and figuring out how to minimize losses.

_____ 2. The chance of financial loss due to a peril.

_____ 3. The chance of either loss or gain.

_____ 4. Staying away from situations that can lead to loss.

_____ 5. The willingness to bear a risk without insurance.

_____ 6. Loss prevention.

_____ 7. Paying someone to assume the risk.

_____ 8. Written agreement that specifies what is covered by insurance.

_____ 9. The process that determines the level of insurance coverage.

_____ 10. The chance of suffering a loss if a particular peril occurs.

_____ 11. One that an insurance company will cover.

_____ 12. Predicts the likelihood that the peril will occur.

_____ 13. Amounts that the insured must pay before benefits begin.

MATCHING QUESTIONS: SECTION B

a. worker's compensation
b. mutual insurance companies
c. business interruption insurance
d. property insurance
e. contingent business interruption insurance
f. home and building insurance
g. surety bond

h. professional liability insurance
i. liability insurance
j. product-liability insurance
k. unemployment insurance
l. health insurance
m. coinsurance
n. Social Security

MATCHING DEFINITIONS.   *Directions: Match the terms above with the definitions below.*

_____   1. Program that pays laid-off workers weekly benefits.

_____   2. Covers the expenses of job-related injuries.

_____   3. Old-Age, Survivors, Disability, and Health Insurance

_____   4. Agreement to reimburse for nonperformance of a contract.

_____   5. Owned by their policyholders.

_____   6. Covers damage to the insured's assets.

_____   7. Covers financial losses to others.

_____   8. Protects property owners from financial losses.

_____   9. Requires the property owner to buy insurance equal to a percentage of the property value.

_____ 10. Covers losses due to a closed business.

_____ 11. Covers losses to major suppliers or customers.

_____ 12. Covers losses from malpractice.

_____ 13. Covers claim of injury from the use of a product.

_____ 14. Covers losses resulting from illness or injury.

MATCHING QUESTIONS: SECTION C

a. managed care programs

b. HMOs

c. term insurance

d. cash value

e. PPO

f. whole life insurance

g. variable life insurance

h. Blue Cross/Blue Shield

i. universal life insurance

j. national health insurance

k. credit life insurance

l. group insurance

m. key person life insurance

MATCHING DEFINITIONS. *Directions: Match the terms above with the definitions below.*

_____ 1. A group of not-for-profit health insurance plans.

_____ 2. Available to employees of a firm or members of a trade association.

_____ 3. Require authorization before nonemergency hospitalization.

_____ 4. Prepaid medical expense plans.

_____ 5. A cross between an HMO and a traditional insurance plan.

_____ 6. A federally sponsored health insurance program.

_____ 7. Has no cash value.

_____ 8. Also called straight life.

_____ 9. Combines term insurance and a savings plan.

_____ 10. Surrender value.

_____ 11. Allows the policyholder to decide how the premium should be invested.

_____ 12. Guarantees repayment of a loan.

_____ 13. Insures the lives of key employees.

CHAPTER REVIEW

1. Identify the four ways of managing risk.

2. What are the six criteria for insurable risks?

3. How are mutual insurance companies different from stock insurance companies?

4. What are some of the problems facing the insurance industry?

5. In what ways do property and liability insurances differ?

6. Identify the main types of life insurance and their major features.

7. Describe briefly the six basic types of health insurance.

EXPERIENCING BUSINESS 24-1   RISK MANAGEMENT

Risk management—analyzing the firm's operations, evaluating the potential risks, and figuring out how to minimize the losses—can be extremely involved for any "large" business. However, many small businesses are also very much in need of this analysis and a managed or explicit approach to risk management.

To do this exercise:

Consider the following types of small business; identify the areas of risk; and suggest an approach(es) to risk management: avoidance, assumption, reduction, or transference.

(One example is provided; what could be another area/approach for that situation?)

	Areas of concern	*Approach(es)*
1. Retail merchant operating out of storefront location	a. personal injury to customer, e.g. a fall	transference (insurance policy)
	b. (another?)	
2. Retail merchant dealing exclusively through catalog with mail/telephone orders		
3. Service provider operating out of fixed location such as "drop off" day care, automobile repair, etc.		
4. On-site service provider such as lawn service, home repair, etc.		

EXPERIENCING BUSINESS 24-2

HEALTH INSURANCE

A major concern for many employees is the availability of health care benefits through their employer. This can be a determining factor in employment for many individuals, and that makes health care benefits a major consideration in recruiting and retaining "good" employees. However, the cost of providing health care benefits has become a "burden" for employers. Part of the response has been a variety of options and alternatives to attempt to balance the perceived benefits with the costs. For an individual employee, this can present a complicated, almost bewildering set of choices as to what program and what options they elect.

To do this exercise:

Look into a particular employer's health care benefit program.

Suggested sources:

- your employer
- spouse's, relative's, or friend's employer
- a business or governmental agency that you may be interested in working for (contact the human-resources department)
- the college (contact the human-resources department)

1. What options are available to employees?

2. Has the employer changed to (or considered) a managed care approach?

ANSWER KEY (CHAPTER 24)

TRUE-FALSE

1.	a.	T		4.	a.	F		6.	a.	T
	b.	T			b.	T			b.	F
2.	a.	T			c.	T			c.	T
	b.	T		5.	a.	F			d.	T
	c.	T			b.	T		7.	a.	F
	d.	F			c.	T			b.	F
	e.	T			d.	T			c.	F
3.	a.	F			e.	F			d.	T
	b.	F								
	c.	F								

MULTIPLE-CHOICE

1.	b	11.	c
2.	c	12.	c
3.	d	13.	b
4.	c	14.	b
5.	c	15.	c
6.	b	16.	a
7.	d	17.	d
8.	d	18.	c
9.	a	19.	c
10.	b	20.	d

MATCHING QUESTIONS: SECTION A

1.	m	8.	c
2.	d	9.	e
3.	i	10.	j
4.	a	11.	g
5.	b	12.	l
6.	f	13.	h
7.	k		

MATCHING QUESTIONS: SECTION B

1.	k	8.	f
2.	a	9.	m
3.	n	10.	c
4.	g	11.	e
5.	b	12.	h
6.	d	13.	j
7.	i	14.	l

MATCHING QUESTIONS: SECTION C

1.	h	8.	f
2.	l	9.	i
3.	a	10.	d
4.	b	11.	g
5.	e	12.	k
6.	j	13.	m
7.	c		

CHAPTER REVIEW

1. Risk can be managed (1) by avoiding situations known to be risky, (2) by assuming the responsibility for losses due to certain types of risks, (3) by reducing it through safety measures, and (4) by transferring risk to an insurance company.

2. (1) The loss must be accidental;

   (2) there must be a large number of similar exposures to a particular peril;

   (3) the loss must be financially measurable;

   (4) the chances of the perils striking all the insured parties at once must be very small;

   (5) the amount of loss must be significant; and

   (6) the insurance company must be able to set the criteria under which it will issue coverage.

3. Stock insurance companies are profit-oriented companies owned by stockholders. The stockholders do not have to be policyholders, and the policyholders do not have to be stockholders. Their profits come from insurance premiums in excess of claims payments and operating expenses and from investments in securities and real estate.

   Mutual insurance companies are owned by their policyholders. They are not-for-profit organizations and chartered by each state. Any excess income is returned to the policyholder-owners as dividends, used to reduce premiums, or retained to finance future operations. The policyholders elect the board of directors who manage the company.

4. The price of property and liability policies and the huge growth in liability lawsuits and catastrophic claims have strained the resources of the insurance industry. Liability claims from pollution damage are also a problem. To compete for funds with other financial institutions, life insurance companies offered policies that earned a high rate of return; as interest rates rose, profits decreased. Insurance companies, like S&Ls, also invested in real estate and junk bonds, which dropped in value.

5. Property insurance covers losses arising from damage to property owned by the insured person or business. Liability insurance covers losses due to injuries to others and damage to their property determined to be caused by the insured.

6. *Term life* gives protection only and has no cash value. *Whole life* covers the insured's life and has a cash value. *Universal life* combines term life with a tax-deferred savings plan and lets the insured party decide how much of the premium goes to insurance and how much gets invested in the cash account. *Variable life* combines insurance with a savings plan and lets the insured party decide how much of the premium goes to insurance and how much gets invested in the cash account. *Credit life* guarantees repayment of a loan on the death of the insured. *Key person life insurance* insures the lives of key employees.

7. Regular medical expense insurance pays all or part of the doctor's fees and other medical services. *Hospitalization insurance* covers hospital charges. *Surgical insurance* covers surgical fees. *Major medical insurance* covers losses that exceed the limits on hospitalization and surgical insurance. *Dental insurance* pays for a percentage of dental expenses. *Disability insurance* provides monthly payments to those unable to work as a result of an accident or illness.